D0618527

SCOTTISH FIRSTS

To Michael, my Scottish first

Scottish Firsts

A Celebration of Innovation and Achievement

Elspeth Wills

MAINSTREAM
PUBLISHING

EDINBURGH AND LONDON

First published in Great Britain in 2002 by
MAINSTREAM PUBLISHING COMPANY (EDINBURGH) LTD
7 Albany Street
Edinburgh EH1 3UG

ISBN 1 84018 611 9

Reprinted 2003

A catalogue record for this book is available from the British Library

Typeset in Allise and Van Dijck

Printed in Great Britain by
Bookmarque Ltd, Croydon, Surrey

Contents

Introduction

It comes as no surprise that the Scots claim to have invented penicillin, the steam engine, television and the telephone, but what about aspirin, Bovril, the cotton reel, Dolly, ecology, the 'f' word, the grand piano, hypnosis, interferon, jellied marmalade, the kangaroo, the letter copier, the Mac, nude mice, orange shrub, the pregnancy scanner, the *Queen Mary*, road surfacing, the syringe, Tower Bridge, unshrinkable underwear, the video recorder, the World Cup, X-rays, the Yuletide card and absolute zero? Scots have helped to shape every letter of this alphabet and many more, enough to fill a bookshelf of achievement. This is perhaps to be expected from a country that produced the first editors of the *Encyclopaedia Britannica* and the *Oxford English Dictionary*. As dreamers, inventors, thinkers, word coiners, explorers and adopters, the Scots have been first in the most unexpected areas of life.

Scottish Firsts embraces both thinkers, like Patrick Geddes, pioneer of town planning, and doers, like the Stevensons, whose lighthouses made the seas safe for shipping. Most Scots combined thinking and doing. Lord Kelvin was not only the giant of nineteenth-century physics, but also helped to make the Atlantic telegraph work. Some Scots died long before the world delivered their dream or recognised their achievement, whether C.M.'s vision of the telegraph or Bennie's of railways in the air. Like the world's first cyclist some Scots stayed close to home, while others explored the world's wild places or settled the globe from Edinburg, Texas to Dunedin, New Zealand.

Why did such a small country produce so many who sought to put first against their name? Geography had a hand in it. As a nation bounded on three sides by the sea, trade had been vital to Scotland's survival from earliest times. In the Middle Ages, Scots looked east to Scandinavia and the Baltic: from the seventeenth century they looked west to the newly discovered wealth of the Americas: by the late nineteenth century they looked to the entire world. With trade came the exchange of culture and new ideas, a fertile interaction which shaped the Scots' cosmopolitan outlook. From the seventeenth century, Scottish students drank with their counterparts in Paris and Leiden, and American medics frequented Edinburgh's howffs. Scottish explorers and colonial administrators had a reputation for 'going native', by absorbing the cultures in which they found themselves.

The poverty of much of the land forced Scots to head for the bright lights of the big cities or go west to seek new opportunities. With them they took their curiosity and openness to ideas. Others discovered the richness that lay literally under their feet, fuelling the Industrial Revolution and making Glasgow the 'workshop to the world'. The new industries of cotton, iron, steel and shipbuilding created new challenges that Scottish engineers were well placed to meet. Innovation developed its own momentum – how to make things ever faster, smaller, more powerful and more efficient. Where else did the Tsar go when he wanted a circular yacht, or an Indian Maharajah when he yearned for a summer palace of iron? Glaswegians could deliver dreams.

With its emphasis on hard work and just rewards, the Presbyterian ethic helped to create the enterprising outlook of the engineer and the probity of the banker. Its stern precepts lay behind the drive of the missionary-explorers and the fervour of the social reformers. The emphasis on the individual, and their right to have a say in government, influenced the democratic outlook of the world's new nations and the American dream of the self-made man. Even chafing at the bit against religion had a positive outcome: by one calculation, an eighth of the great Scottish scientists were sons of the manse. These sons, from David Brewster to John Logie Baird, took very different paths in order to escape parental pressure to head up the stairs and into the pulpit.

Education provides the strongest clue as to why the scale of Scottish achievement is disproportionate to the number of Scots. The people of this small country have always valued learning. Even before the Reformation, Scotland was the first nation in Europe to introduce an element of compulsory education, in the same year as Christopher Columbus discovered America. The change to the Presbyterian religion provided a new impetus: everyone had to learn to read in order to study the Bible, and ministers had to be suitably educated in order to write their sermons. By 1600, Scotland had twice as many universities as the rest of Britain.

While Oxbridge offered a finishing school for young aristocrats and a training college for clerics, Scottish universities were welcoming young men from all walks of life and were exploring new subjects of direct relevance to the changing world around them. They established the world's first Chairs in anatomy, engineering, naval architecture and even, albeit briefly, technology, The remarkable outpouring of ideas, and the urge to rethink the world that marked the eighteenth-century Scottish Enlightenment, encouraged practicality, ingenuity and a love of learning for its own sake: its impact was revolutionary.

Where are the great inventors of today? Wha's like us and are they a' deid? If a recent survey showing that most Scottish school children who had heard of James Watt thought that he had invented the light bulb is to be believed, we have even buried our 'deid'. There are many more inventions today and many more nations competing in the race to be first. In the twenty-first century's multinational culture, it is much more difficult to identify the individual than in the days of Messrs Boulton and Watt. In many ways, the days of the individual inventor are over, with discoveries made by teams of specialists and patents taken out in the name of companies. In the time of Watt and Black, ideas were a free commodity to be exchanged and explored by anyone with a contribution to make, regardless of their knowledge of the subject. Today, few are confident enough to stray from their chosen field.

Only the passage of time will tell whether a big idea is a long-term winner and will distinguish the leap in the dark from the glitter of novelty. Scots still have that unique blend of idealism, tempered with practicality, that has characterised their achievements of the past 300 years. They still value education, their country producing more graduates per head of population than any other in Western Europe. Today the Kerr cell and Bell's photophone are finding their place in opto-electronics and telecommuncations. It was only when Dolly bleated, that the world's media grabbed their atlases to discover where on earth Roslin was. Dolly was a world first and one of the most significant discoveries of the late twentieth century.

Scots can be confident that out there somewhere, someone is creating a new Scottish first: a hard disk that can fit in the palm of your hand, fat-free carrot cake, a cash machine that can recognise you by your eye, the world's most energy-efficient freezer, 'intelligent' potatoes that glow when they need water. If this book is rewritten in a hundred years time, will any of these recent Scottish firsts be included? Only time will tell.

1

Napoleon and Dolly: Exploring the Body

From antiseptic surgery to the first adult mammal clone, it is in the life sciences that Scotland has had the greatest influence on the world. The roots of Scottish medicine go as far back as the end of the fifteenth century with the UK's first Chair in Medicine at Aberdeen University being followed by the foundation of the UK's first medical school at Edinburgh. As early as 1597, Master Peter Lowe, founder of the Glasgow Faculty of Physicians and Surgeons, helped to take surgery out of the hands of the barbers when he published the first textbook on the subject in the English language. Gradually the view gained ground that the body was subject to the laws of physics and chemistry, rather than the will of divine providence. At the start of the seventeenth century, however, most Scots still had to go abroad for medical training, notably to the University of Leiden in the Netherlands: by the end of the century Leiden was offering professorships to people like Dr Archibald Pitcairne, a founder of the Edinburgh Medical School.

In a remarkably short space of time, Edinburgh became a world centre of medical education. Between 1751 and 1800, 87 per cent of British qualified doctors were trained in Scotland and most American doctors proudly hung a certificate from Edinburgh on the walls of their consulting room. The only qualified doctor among the founders of Harvard Medical School was an Edinburgh graduate. Scottish-born and trained doctors made their mark around the world, the fate of nations resting in their hands. Throughout the eighteenth century, Scots doctors were frequent residents at the Russian court, Dr John Rogerson's most celebrated patient being Catherine the Great. As the Tsar's medical attendant, Dr James Wylie was the only outsider present at the historic meeting of

Alexander I and Napoleon at Tilsit, and Dr Archibald Arnott witnessed Napoleon's death throes on St Helena. In childbirth and on her deathbed, Queen Victoria recognised the worth of a Scottish physician.

The first tasks in tackling disease are to understand how the body works and diagnose what may be going wrong. Until the early twentieth century, when X-rays allowed doctors to see inside the body for the first time, the only options open to the medical investigator were the naked eye and the surgeon's knife applied to the patient, or more often the corpse. In the days before specialisation, a doctor was often a Jack of all trades – surgeon, physician, anatomist and obstetrician. Two sons of an East Kilbride farmer, William (1718–83) and John Hunter (1728–93) were among the finest all-rounders, advancing the frontiers of medical knowledge on several fronts. Both believed in the view later immortalised by Dr Johnson that 'the noblest prospect a Scotchman ever sees is the high road that leads him to England'.

THE HUNTERS' KNIFE

Elder brother William was the leading anatomist and obstetrician of his day, helping to put the latter on a scientific footing. Although an early promoter of the need for close links between anatomy and surgery, by 1748 he had abandoned both in favour of a more lucrative practice in obstetrics. In 1768, the year that he became the first Professor of Anatomy at the Royal Academy, he opened a medical school at his London home where he assembled a collection of anatomical and pathological specimens to support his teaching. As his practice grew to include the royal family – he delivered Queen Charlotte's first child, the future George IV – so did his wealth, allowing him to extend his collection to paintings, books, manuscripts and curiosities. He bequeathed his collection to Glasgow University where it formed the basis of the Hunterian Museum.

One of the greatest surgeons of the eighteenth century, William's younger brother, John, has gone down in history as the father of scientific surgery. The youngest of a family of ten with little time for formal education, in 1748 he set off on horseback to

London to join his brother William, his first job being to prepare dissected anatomical specimens for him. John's skill with the scalpel was such that he was performing operations a year later. Thereafter, he combined a post as a teaching surgeon at St George's Hospital with his interest in anatomy, resorting to body-snatchers when legitimate supplies of corpses ran out. After contracting tuberculosis in 1761, he served as an army surgeon in France and Portugal to benefit from the warmer climate. On his return to London in 1764, he ran his own anatomy school and private surgical practice, although the latter proved slow to take off. In 1776, he was appointed physician extraordinary to George III, a remarkable achievement for a self-taught surgeon.

Hunter's army experience led him to revolutionise the attitude of a surgeon to his patients. Amputation had previously been the almost universal solution to injury or disease. Hunter showed that with careful post-operative treatment many wounds healed without this drastic remedy. He questioned the surgical need to enlarge gunshot wounds, disproving the belief that gunpowder was poisonous. His reputation rests on more than his surgical skills. His many original discoveries included the first suggestion that blood is a living substance, the function of the lymph glands and the function and structure of the placenta. He made innovative advances in the treatment of digestive complaints, dentistry, transplantation, inflammation and the management of shock. He pioneered tissue grafting, following a bizarre experiment when he grafted a human tooth on to a cock's comb. He developed what is still the standard treatment for the repair of a torn tendon, operating on himself after he damaged his Achilles tendon while dancing.

Hunter's importance lies not only in his discoveries, but also in his use of experiment to test his theories. A typical example was performed on a deer at Richmond Park. When he tied the artery supplying blood to one of the deer's antlers, which were in velvet, it became cold. Far from dying, however, within a few days the antler had regained its blood supply through the enlargement of connecting arteries above and below the ligature. Hunter was then able to apply the treatment successfully to aneurysms in human beings. He also carried out the first attempts at artificial insemination, when consulted in the late 1770s by a London cloth merchant who suffered from hypospadia, a birth defect of the penis. Hunter suggested that the merchant should collect his sperm and inject it into his wife's vagina with a warm syringe: a child was born the same year.

John Hunter was a difficult character. Never easy, relations with his brother William broke down completely in 1780 due to a dispute over which brother had made various gynaecological discoveries. His insatiable curiosity led to him keeping a menagerie at his country house in Berkshire, and to keeping tabs on the movements of an Irish giant whose cadaver he coveted. His powers of concentration were legendary: a contemporary described him as 'standing for hours, motionless as a statue, except that with a pair of forceps in each hand he was picking asunder the connecting fibres of some object that he was studying'. Fulfilling his own prophecy, John Hunter died from an angina attack brought on by a fit of rage.

Hunter removed surgery from its bloody associations with the barber and the butcher and raised it to its present professional status. Through his teaching, he was responsible for the establishment of surgery as an acceptable branch of professional medicine in Britain, Europe and North America. His approach helped surgeons to anticipate what they might find when speed, skill and accuracy meant the difference between life and death. One of the greatest surgeons to follow in Hunter's footsteps was James Syme (1799–1870) whose career spanned the introduction of anaesthesia.

THE NAPOLEON OF MEDICINE

Syme, a lawyer's son, was born within sight of Edinburgh Castle in the city which he made his lifetime home. It was at a meeting of the club, which Syme and a group of fellow students set up to conduct chemical experiments, that he discovered the effective solvent for India rubber that Charles Macintosh used in making waterproof cloth. While still a student, he became the assistant to the great surgeon–anatomist Robert Liston, whose splint is still used today, taking over his teaching duties when Liston resigned in 1823. He quickly established himself as a surgeon, pioneering amputation of tubercular joints. At first, in line with normal practice, Syme operated largely in his patients' homes, with the kitchen table doubling up as the operating table. The demand for his skills, however, coupled with his growing concern about the risks of operations in unhygienic surroundings, led him to open his own surgical hospital in 1829.

Despite being the most successful surgeon of his day, Syme still found time for research and writing. In 1831, he published his *Principles of Surgery* and a *Treatise on the Excision of Diseased Joints* which set out to raise the techniques of amputation from those of the butcher's shop. His clinical research included the demonstration of the ability of periosteum, the outer membrane that surrounds bone, to form new bone. In 1833, after a sharp contest with his old supervisor Liston, Syme was appointed to the Chair of Clinical Surgery at Edinburgh University. He immediately set out to reform clinical teaching, introducing the modern practice of students being present at patient consultations to develop their diagnostic skills. Admired by contemporaries as the 'Napoleon of Medicine', Syme continued to extend his surgical repertoire, developing an effective operation to correct aneurysm, the bulging of an artery wall, and the operation for the amputation of the ankle joint which still bears his name.

Stubborn and hot-headed, Syme delayed using anaesthesia as a result of a quarrel with its discoverer James Young Simpson. When Simpson, in Syme's eyes a mere obstetrician, ventured to suggest that Syme adopt his technique of acupressure to control bleeding in surgery, Syme did not simply reject his advice. While operating in front of a class of students, he called for a knife, cut Simpson's pamphlet on the subject into shreds, ground them into the sawdust with his foot and roared, 'There, gentlemen, is what acupressure is worth.' Syme, in time, was proved correct: Simpson's idea of using needles rather than ligatures to tie arteries did not prove a success. Aware of the risks of infection, Syme developed one of the earliest successful preventative techniques: leaving wounds completely open until the oozing of blood had ceased. His successor at Edinburgh University and English-born son-in-law, Joseph Lister (1827–1912), tackled the root of the problem in pioneering antiseptic surgery.

LET US SPRAY

Unlike his father-in-law, Lister was an enthusiastic believer in anaesthesia as it allowed the surgeon more time and the chance to go deeper. What, however, was the point if one in every two patients died a few days later from infected wounds? He was far from reassured by the knowledge that his ward in Glasgow's Royal Infirmary had been built on a graveyard where paupers and cholera victims were buried. Bodies were piled on top of each other to within inches of the top of the common grave, separated from the wards only by a 4 ft basement.

After learning in 1865 of Louis Pasteur's research into the micro-organisms that cause infection, it occurred to Lister to try to kill germs by treating wounds with chemicals. After one failure, on 12 August 1865, he successfully operated on 11-year-old James Greenlees for a compound fracture of the left shin. Six weeks later, James walked out of the hospital, his leg completely healed. Lister used carbolic acid and the death rate in his wards dropped dramatically. He covered everything in the operating theatre – wounds, dressings and instruments – with carbolic acid. The death rate fell again. He devised a spray which sent a fine mist of carbolic acid into the air above the patient to an enthusiastic chorus from theatre staff of 'let us spray!' The death rate continued to fall. Lister was now able to undertake more ambitious operations involving deeper incisions than were previously possible. The concept of antiseptic surgery was born.

Lister did not stop at the operating table in his war against germs. He was the first person to use dressings sterilised by heat, to introduce absorbent gauze dressings and to experiment with the use of tincture of iodine to sterilise the patient's skin. He discovered that sterile catgut was absorbed by the patient's tissues, avoiding the source of irritation and infection of the traditional silk surgical thread. He experimented by tying the carotid artery of a calf with catgut: when the calf was killed and opened up a month later, the catgut had disappeared, being replaced by a circle of living tissue. As far as his peers were concerned, Lister was a prophet crying in the wilderness. Although German surgeons were quick to adopt his new ideas, their British and American peers remained unconvinced, claiming to have tried his methods without success. One of

America's greatest surgeons, J.M.T. Finney, revealed the reason why. Despite Lister's insistence that all items in the operating theatre must be kept free of infection, surgeons still operated in frock coats; the older and filthier the frock coat, the higher status the surgeon. Instruments had wooden handles, which were, at best, given a perfunctory wipe with carbolic solution, and the sponges for swabbing wounds were used over and over again.

When invited, in 1876, to take up a post at King's College London, Lister felt it his duty to accept as he considered standards of surgery there to be very poor. He caused a furore by insisting on bringing his staff with him and on having his wards kept separate from those of other surgeons with less sanitary practices. It took a new generation of US surgeons to adopt the Listerian message in its entirety and their example at last convinced the British medical profession. Despite Lister's troubles with his colleagues, society at large recognised his gifts. As early as 1871, he was trusted to lance an abscess in Queen Victoria's left armpit. He was created a peer in 1883, succeeded Lord Kelvin as President of the Royal Society and became the first medical man to sit in the House of Lords. More recently, *Life* magazine recognised his lasting legacy by including him as one of the 100 people to have 'made the Millennium'. A fellow Scottish surgeon was to take advantage of antisepsis in pioneering the new techniques of deep surgery.

BONES AND BRAINS

The son of a Rothesay merchant who worked on Lister's wards as a dresser during his student days, William McEwen (1848–1924) built on his teacher's advances which had made long and complex operations possible. He evolved many of the techniques of brain surgery, laying the foundations of neurosurgery. He introduced the operation for mastoid, an ear disease, and devised an effective operation for the correction of knock-knees. He performed the first operation for the excision of a lung: until McEwen's time it was believed that the opening of the chest would result in the collapse of the lungs.

In 1880, McEwen demonstrated that periosteum was not the only source of new bone. His patient was a boy whose upper arm had been almost entirely destroyed by the disease osteomyelitis. Acting on his knowledge, gained through experimentation with animals, McEwen removed a series of bony wedges from the boy's shin bone and embedded them in a row in the muscles of his arm. The bones knitted together to give the boy a functioning arm again. This was the first effective bone graft operation.

McEwen took Lister's antiseptic procedures into the new realms of aseptic surgery. He boiled gauze for dressings and banished instruments with wooden or bone handles from the operating theatre rather than simply spraying them with carbolic. He used catgut that had been hardened in chromic acid, which rendered it aseptic, and extended the period of absorption by the patient's tissues. Realising the importance of nursing in post-surgical cases, working with the Matron of the Royal Infirmary of Glasgow, he devised the first systematic surgical training course for nursing staff. His concept of patient care was total. Although honours were heaped on him and he was invited to become Head of Surgery in Baltimore, Pennsylvania, he preferred to remain in Glasgow, the city to which he had devoted his career.

The advent of X-rays from 1895 was to revolutionise surgery by allowing doctors to see inside the body for the first time. Previously, the only option was to cut open the patient and have a look. One of the early pioneers of the application of X-rays to medicine was Dr John MacIntyre, who was lecturing on the 'New Photography' to the Royal Philosophical Society of Glasgow as early as 1896. He developed techniques for imaging the heart, lungs, spine and the inside of the skull, and his X-ray department at Glasgow Royal Infirmary was one of the earliest in the world. MacIntyre loved hosting dinner parties and entertained celebrity guests, including Sir Harry Lauder, by taking X-rays of their hands.

Once X-rays provided the means of studying tissues and the skeleton, doctors inevitably wanted to see deeper and more clearly and to avoid, where possible, the damaging effects of radiation. New technologies had to be developed and Scotland's traditional strengths in medicine and engineering combined to find some of the answers.

THE FIRST SNAP FOR THE FAMILY ALBUM

Nowadays the scan is a routine date in the calendar of pregnant women throughout the world, providing reassurance that all is well or alerting obstetricians to possible problems. The gift of that reassurance is due to the ingenuity of a Glasgow Professor of Midwifery, Ian Donald (1910–87).

In 1954, Ian Donald arrived in Glasgow to take up the Regius Chair of Midwifery with 'an elementary knowledge of radar from my days in the RAF and a continuing childish interest in machines, electronic or otherwise, or what my wife would refer to as my toys'. He was intrigued by the technology of ultrasonics as a diagnostic technique. Such techniques had been pioneered in the United States, but with the drawback that the only way that doctors could get results was by immersing the patient in a tank of water. Approaching the problem from a different angle, Donald realised the answer might lie in techniques used in the detection of flaws in metals, where probes coated with oil were applied directly to the material under test. He contacted engineers at the Clydeside plant of Babcock and Wilcox who were building boilers for nuclear power stations. Using their ultrasonic metal detecting devices, he experimented to see if he could trace any difference in various forms of pelvic tumour. In 1955, he took a memorable trip to the factory with various specimens to test and a lump of steak to use as a control: the screens revealed the differences.

Donald immediately set to work building a prototype, his early improvisations including a contraceptive sheath. A medical friend on a visit from South Africa volunteered to purchase a packet as he was not known in Glasgow: when, however, the shop assistant asked him what type he wanted, he panicked and replied that he would need to go over to the car to find out. Once the technical problems were overcome, Donald had to tackle the scepticism of his colleagues. He won them over by saving a patient whose case had previously been diagnosed as terminal, using his scanner to correct what turned out to be a misdiagnosis. In 1957, Donald turned his attention to the use of the scanner in pregnancy. With the help of a Glasgow engineering firm, Kelvin Hughes, he developed a two-dimensional scanner and, in 1958, went public with his results. Further developments, such as the use of Polaroid photography to provide detailed results at the patient's bedside followed rapidly, culminating in the unveiling of an automatic scanner in 1960.

Donald opened up the way for the course of pregnancy to be monitored, leading to the increased health and wellbeing of both mother and baby-to-be: in 1970, a colleague used the scanner to identify a case of quintuplets at nine weeks. Professor Stuart Campbell of St George's Hospital, London, who trained with Donald on graduating from Glasgow University, is one of the pioneers of the new generation of scanners using 3D imaging to identify foetal abnormalities even earlier in pregnancy. In honour of his friend, Professor Asim Kurjak founded the Ian Donald Inter-University School of Medical Ultrasound in Croatia in 1981. It is one of the world's largest schools of medical ultrasound and the World Health Organisation's Collaborating Centre for Diagnostic Ultrasound.

SCANNING THE WHOLE BODY

Professor John Mallard of Aberdeen University pioneered a technology to look at the body in a different way. Professor Mallard's scanner was based on magnetic resonance imaging (MRI), which permits the presence of water inside the body to be detected and images of its distribution produced. This makes it possible to differentiate diseased from healthy tissue by detecting variations in the content and function of water in cells.

Professor Mallard arrived in Aberdeen in 1965 to take up Scotland's first Chair of Medical Physics, bringing with him a primitive 'radioactive scanner', which he had previously built in London. At Aberdeen, a radiologist saw the machine's diagnostic potential and used it to detect brain tumours, laying the foundation for nuclear medicine. The challenge was to build a machine capable of creating, processing and analysing images of the body. Unlike other research groups exploring the potential of MRI, the team chose to build a whole body scanner. After 12 years in development, they built the first MRI machine, which, in 1980, successfully scanned its first patient. Between 1981 and 1983 almost 1,000 patients were examined, and the world's first MRI images of various parts of the human body and examples of diseased tissue were produced. The first machine was so busy imaging Aberdeen patients that a second had to be built to allow development work on the scanner to continue.

Professor Mallard set up the company M & D Technology to capitalise on his invention. Given a very positive reaction from the medical profession, by early 1982 the company had orders for three machines, the success of the venture being recognised later that year when it won first prize in the British Technology Group Enterprise Award. Success, however, was short-lived. It proved impossible to raise more finance for development work, giving larger and better resourced international competitors the chance to steal the lead. By 1986, the bold experiment was over. According to Mallard, 'medical history books now say it was all done in America. It is as if they have never heard of Aberdeen.' The Granite City spawned a billion-dollar industry with scanners now found in major hospitals throughout the developed world producing images with undreamed of clarity. The team went on to build the Aberdeen Section Scanner – the first digital computer tomography (CT) scanner which images slices across the body – and are now working on a MRI scanner sufficiently compact to be used in a GP's surgery. Their work won the Queen's Anniversary Prize 2000.

Skeletons, organs, cells and DNA: each century has brought us closer to the very heart of life. As scientists start to understand the complex meanings of the language of our genes, it is easy to forget that less than two centuries ago our understanding of the cell was in its infancy. A Montrose botanist was one of the first to shed some light on what lay within.

THE LITTLE NUT

The son of an Episcopalian clergyman, Robert Brown (1773–1858) spent his early career as an army doctor and his spare time pursuing his hobby of botany. This brought him to the attention of the distinguished naturalist and explorer, Sir Joseph Banks, through whose influence Brown was appointed naturalist on the Flinders expedition to chart the coast of the still largely unexplored Australian continent. Brown returned with a collection of over 4,000 specimens, larger than that of all previous expeditions to

Australia put together and containing 1,700 previously unknown specimens.

On his return, 'nothing was allowed to divert his eye from his microscope and his books'. He became Banks' librarian and on his death in 1820 inherited his house, library and botanical collections. On the transfer of the last two to the British Museum, Brown was appointed the first Keeper of the Museum's Botanical Department. Here he set about arranging and classifying collections from around the world, grouping plants by habitat, characteristics and anatomy, the basis of his reputation as Britain's greatest nineteenth-century botanist. In 1825, he distinguished gymnosperms, plants such as conifers with naked seeds, from the other major group of seed plants, the angiosperms, whose seeds are surrounded by an ovary wall. Brown was influential, even in the timing of his death. He had been due to lecture to the learned Linnean Society: the vacant slot in the programme was taken up by Charles Darwin and Alfred Wallace's paper announcing the theory of evolution by natural selection.

Brown's lasting reputation rests on two major discoveries. He was the first person to recognise that the small body that could sometimes be seen inside plant cells was a regular feature of cells generally. In 1831, he named this body the 'nucleus', from the Latin 'little nut', the name it has borne ever since. The Fife anatomist John Goodsir (1814–67) continued Brown's exploration of the cell, recognising it as the starting point for all plant and animal life and the centre of nutrition, and postulating that it was divided into a number of different functions. The German pathologist Rudolf Virchow dedicated the first edition of his classic work on cell theory to Goodsir, describing him as 'one of the earliest and most acute observers of cell life'.

The discovery that bears Brown's name – Brownian motion – arose from a routine investigation of plant pollen in 1827. One day, as Brown was viewing a suspension of pollen under a microscope, he noted that the individual grains were moving about in an irregular fashion. At first he attributed this to hidden 'life' within the pollen, but when he repeated the same experiments with grains of dyestuff, he found the same effect. This was the first evidence for the existence of atoms based on observation rather than deduction, a discovery that was to have major repercussions in fields very different from botany: James Clerk Maxwell in his kinetic theory of gases, Thomas Graham in his work on colloids and William Ramsay in his explanation of the energy that caused Brownian motion, all of which helped to unravel the mystery of the atom.

Over a century later, a Scottish chemist provided some of the clues as to what went on inside Brown's nucleus.

LORD TODD ALMIGHTY

Sir Alexander Robertus Todd (1907–97), whose father worked for the Glasgow subway, graduated from his local university before studying at Frankfurt and Oxford. His lifetime interest was in the chemistry of natural products of biological importance. On his return to Scotland as a chemistry lecturer at Edinburgh, he began his ground-breaking investigation of thiamine (Vitamin B1), working out its structure and how to make it. He later worked out the structure of Vitamin E, as well as isolating the active principle in cannabis resin.

In 1944, he became Professor of Organic Chemistry at Cambridge, where he developed his interest in the chemistry of the nucleic acids, DNA and RNA. He put together all their naturally occurring nucleotide components, proving experimentally that they produced compounds that were identical with those obtained from nucleic acids. He also was the first person to synthesise the biochemical compounds adenosine diphosphate (ADP) and adenosine triphosphate (ATP), of crucial significance in how the cell handles energy. His work provided a key building block that allowed Watson and Crick to put forward the double helix as the structure of DNA. When on the brink of publishing their findings, they were told to check their chemistry with Todd.

It was during his time at Edinburgh that Todd met and married Alison, the daughter of Nobel Prize winner Henry Dale. He won his own Nobel Prize for Chemistry in 1957, the first time the prize had been awarded for work relating to the structure of nucleic acids: five years later he was created Baron Todd of Trumpington. This allowed his staff, 'the Toddlers' – among whom he inspired great affection – to call him 'Lord Todd Almighty': previously he had been known as 'Todd Almighty' because of his great height.

HELLO DOLLY

In February 1997, a small agricultural research laboratory outside Edinburgh rather belatedly announced the birth of a lamb. It made world headlines. Dolly was no ordinary sheep. She was the first animal cloned from a cell taken from an adult mammal, the result of collaboration between the Roslin Institute and PPL Therapeutics Ltd. Until Dolly, almost all biologists believed that the cells in our bodies were fixed in their roles. Dolly, derived from an udder cell of a six-year-old sheep, proved them wrong. The fact that Dolly was cloned from a cell taken from an adult ewe showed that even differentiated cells can be 'reprogrammed' into all the cell types that make up an animal.

Dolly was cloned using the technique known as nuclear transfer. Cells from a Finn Dorset ewe were cultured in the laboratory, individual cells were then fused with unfertilised eggs from which the genetic material had been removed. Some 277 of these 'reconstructed eggs' were cultured for six days in temporary recipients. Of the eggs that appeared to have developed normally, 29 were implanted into 13 surrogate Scottish Blackface ewes. One gave birth to Dolly 148 days later.

Dolly came from a long line of successful Roslin 'ancestors'. First of all there was Tracy, a transgenic sheep that secreted 35g of the human protein, alpha-1-antitrypsin, a protein which protects the lungs, in each litre of her milk. In 1995, along came Megan and Morag, representing a significant breakthrough, as they were derived by nuclear transfer from cells from early embryos that had been cultured for several months in the laboratory. In July 1997, Polly joined this remarkable flock, the first transgenic lamb produced by nuclear transfer. The donor cell was modified with the gene coding for human blood clotting factor IX, absence of which gives rise to haemophilia.

Dolly took cloning from the realms of science fiction to the centre of public debate. The race to clone is on. Research groups around the world have successfully cloned mice, cattle, goats and pigs, but have failed as yet to clone rabbits, rats, monkeys, cats, dogs or humans. What is clearly emerging is that the success rate of cloning is very low and that cloned animals may experience premature ageing and other health problems. Extinct animals are likely to remain in *Jurassic Park*. The aim of the Roslin Institute, and other responsible research groups, is to apply cloning techniques to benefit human health by using animals to produce transplant organs, human proteins and perhaps one day to 'reprogramme' malfunctioning human cells.

What is the news of the twentieth century's most famous Scot? In the early hours of Easter Monday, 1998, Dolly had a little lamb, Bonnie, conceived in the way that sheep know best. Five healthy lambs later, Dolly now suffers from arthritis in her left hind hip and knee: at 5½ years old she is quite young to suffer this condition, which is being treated with anti-inflammatory drugs. Clippings from her coat have been knitted into a jersey for the Science Museum in London and the Museum of Scotland has promised to make Dolly the most famous stuffed Scot ever when she eventually dies.

UNRAVELLING THE MYSTERIES OF LIFE

★ **The proof that mammals can lay eggs:** William Hay Caldwell. On winning the first Balfour Studentship at Cambridge University in 1883, Caldwell used the money to travel to Australia and settle the controversial question of whether monotremes, like the duck-billed platypus, really laid eggs. After four months' hunting in the bush he killed a platypus, with an unlaid egg inside her. He telegraphed triumphantly, 'Monotremes oviparous, ovum meroblastic'. One of the most succinct announcements of a scientific discovery ever made, these four words ended an 85-year-old mystery – monotremes do lay eggs; those eggs contain large amounts of yolk; the yolk is not divided into cells. A large-yolked, undivided egg is what birds lay: the monotreme egg is, therefore, just like a bird's egg.

★ **The first demonstration that DNA in a chromosome is an uninterrupted single molecule:** Harold Callan (1917–93), Professor of Natural History at St Andrews University. DNA was previously believed to exist in packets along the chromosome.

★ **The existence of life in the deep oceans:** the Challenger Expedition

(1872–6). The first systematic study of the deep oceans was a peculiarly Scottish affair, with Edinburgh graduate and future Professor of Natural Philosophy, Charles Wyville-Thompson, as scientific leader and Canadian-born John Murray as naturalist. Murray became Director of the Challenger office in Edinburgh and was largely responsible for the 23-year task of compiling the 50-volume report of the expedition's findings. The expedition answered three apparently simple questions: how deep are the oceans; what is the bottom of the deep ocean made of; and does life exist there? It succeeded for the first time ever in systematically sampling the deep seafloor, plotting the ocean's currents and temperatures, mapping the bottom deposits and outlining the contours of the ocean basins, including the discovery of the mid-Atlantic Ridge and what was named the Challenger Deep. The finding of 715 new genera and 4,717 new species of ocean life disproved once and for all that the deep oceans were barren and lifeless.

★ **Programmed cell death:** first discovered by Sir Alastair Currie, John Kerr and Andrew Wylie at Aberdeen University. In 1972, they announced that cells could 'commit suicide', a process of immense significance in understanding many diseases from cancer to Alzheimer's. They coined the name 'apoptosis' to describe the process from the ancient Greek meaning the 'falling of leaves': it was later discovered that Hippocrates, the father of Western medicine had used the same word as a medical term in describing gangrene.

★ **Lysozyme:** the natural antiseptic protein found in tears was first identified by Sir Alexander Fleming (1881–1955).

★ **Feline leukaemia virus:** the cause of one of the commonest diseases in cats was discovered by Professor Jarrett of Glasgow University Veterinary School in 1964. The discovery led to an effective vaccine being developed.

★ **The nude mouse:** Norman Grist discovered and bred a hairless mouse in the Virus Laboratory of Ruchill Hospital, Glasgow, in 1962. It turned out that this mouse not only lacked hair due to a genetic mutation, but also a properly developed thymus, providing the first animal model of a severe immunodeficiency disorder. The 'test tube with a tail' has proved of immense value in medical research as, lacking the T cells of the immune system, it does not reject transplants. Human cancers can be transplanted on to the mouse and their growth studied to shed new light on the development of this killer disease.

★ **Paleobiology, the study of ancient life:** pioneered by William Nicol (1768–1851). A lecturer in natural philosophy at Edinburgh University, around 1815 he cemented pieces of fossil wood and minerals on to a glass plate using Canadian balsam. He ground down the sample into slices so fine that one could see through them with a microscope. This allowed him to use cell patterns to suggest what kind of plant the sample might have been.

★ **The first effective mouse model for the study of the cystic fibrosis gene:** Professor David Porteous, MRC Human Genetics Unit, Edinburgh, 1992.

★ **The theory of evolution by means of natural selection:** proposed independently by Alfred Russell Wallace (1823–1913). His father was Scots and claimed to trace his family tree back to William Wallace. Wallace sent his paper to Charles Darwin who arranged for joint publication. Wallace's paper also prompted Darwin to publish an outline of the large volume of research he had accumulated in support of his theory – *The Origin of Species*.

DISCOVERING THE HUMAN BODY

★ **The first scientific classification of diseases of the stomach including ulcers:** the anatomist Matthew Baillie (1761–1823). A nephew of the Hunter brothers, Baillie also illustrated the lesions associated with strokes 30 years before the French pathologist Jean Cruveilhier.

★ **Discovery that the brain has distinct areas corresponding to different functions:** Sir Charles Bell (1774–1842). Educated at Edinburgh High School and University, while a student Bell published with his brother John, a distinguished surgeon, a book on anatomy illustrated with his own drawings. The success of subsequent volumes and the popularity of his private anatomy lessons aroused the jealousy of the Medical Faculty, who succeeded in banning him from the Infirmary, forcing him to move to London, where he combined anatomy teaching with operating on the wounded of the Napoleonic wars. As well as his ground-breaking discoveries, he published the first guide to anatomy for artists.

★ The disease, Bell's palsy, which results in spasms in the facial muscles: Sir Charles Bell (1774–1842).

★ The discovery that the nerves entering the front of the spine are responsible for movement while those entering the back are responsible for feeling: Sir Charles Bell (1774–1842). Bell proposed what later became known as the Bell–Magendie Law, which French physiologist Francois Magendie confirmed experimentally.

★ First description of leukaemia: John Hughes Bennett (1812–75). A Professor at Edinburgh University, he described the disease six weeks before the German pathologist Rudolf Virchow. He pioneered the use of microscopes in pathology and introduced physiology and pathology into the medical curriculum. A modernist, he opposed the practice of bloodletting and supported the admission of women to medicine. A laboratory at Edinburgh University is named after him, funded by a donation from his daughter, Mrs Harriet Cox, wife of Robert Cox, the Edinburgh gelatine manufacturer.

★ The connection between vertigo and the inner ear: Alexander Crum Brown (1838–1922).

★ Identification of the cause of brucellosis and sleeping sickness: Sir David Bruce (1855–1931). Bruce was born in Australia where his Scottish parents briefly went to try their luck in the Gold Rush. After training at Edinburgh, he pursued an adventurous career as an army doctor and researcher in Malta and Africa, accompanied by his wife, a skilled microscopist and nurse, whom he credited with an equal share in his discoveries. He died four days after her while her funeral was taking place.

★ Cheyne-Stokes respiration, a common form of irregular breathing associated with hydrocephalus and terminal disease: John Cheyne (1777–1836). The son of an Edinburgh surgeon, he spent most of his career in Ireland. Ironically, he is regarded by some as the 'Father of Irish Medicine', despite having served as an assistant surgeon in a British artillery corps that helped to defeat them at the Battle of Vinegar Hill during the Irish Rebellion of 1798.

★ First description of pernicious anaemia: James Scarth Combe (1796–1883). Although Combe, an Edinburgh GP, described a case in 1822, the disease was for many years known as Addison's disease after Sir Thomas Addison, whose description in 1849 was better known.

★ **Description of Crohn's Disease:** Sir Thomas Kennedy Dalziel (1862–1924). Having carried out investigative autopsies on 13 of his patients with intestinal disorders, in 1913 the Glasgow surgeon gave a highly accurate description of the condition 20 years before US physician Burrill Crohn, after whom the bowel disorder is named.

★ **First description of the anatomy of the peritoneum:** James Douglas (1675–1742). Douglas was a landowner outside Edinburgh who became the personal physician to Queen Caroline, wife of George II. As well as describing the peritoneum, the thin membrane that lines the abdominal and pelvic cavities and covers most abdominal organs, several features of the human body are named after him, notably the pouch of Douglas.

★ **The first doctor to describe scarlet fever:** William Douglass (1691–1752) emigrated to Boston from where he also introduced variolation as a means of inoculation to America.

★ **Identification of the relationship of parts of the brain to the movement of different limbs and the operation of particular senses:** Sir David Ferrier (1843–1928). Using electrical stimulation of brain areas in animals, he mapped the position of many brain functions including the centres for smell and hearing.

★ **Puerperal fever:** Dr Alexander Gordon (1752–99). He identified that the fever which killed many women following childbirth was similar to if not the same disease as erysipelas and that it was carried between patients by doctors and midwives. He admitted, 'It is a disagreeable declaration for me to mention that I was myself the means of carrying the infection to a great number of women.' Half a century later, the Viennese doctor Ignaz Semmelweis's insistence on hygiene in the wards made dramatic inroads on the maternal death rate. Another Aberdonian, Alexander Ogston, made the actual link between puerperal fever and erysipelas: both diseases were due to the Staphylococcus bacterium.

★ **The cause of 'the bends':** the painful condition suffered by divers who ascend too quickly due to nitrogen bubbles forming in their joints was first identified by John Scott Haldane (1860–1936).

★ **The Haldane Table governing safe diving depths and procedures:** drawn up by John Scott Haldane (1860–1936). An Edinburgh graduate in medicine, Haldane worked as a demonstrator at University College, Dundee. He was fascinated by foul smells, going round the Dundee slums in search of evidence of the relationship between clean air and health. He travelled the London Underground collecting air samples in a jar that he hung out of the window. His proof that the level of carbon monoxide was unacceptably high led to the electrification of the Tube lines. Approached by the Admiralty in 1905 to investigate diver exhaustion, he experimented with goats in the Firth of Clyde. He proved that the adverse effects of breathing CO_2 in deep water were significantly greater than on the surface and compiled the tables published by the Royal Navy in 1908 still used in computer form today. As well as being a distinguished population biologist and populariser of science, his son, J.B.S. Haldane worked out how to survive at great depths, advised the navy on safer submarine escape routes and perfected the mixing of oxygen and helium that makes diving to great depths possible.

★ **Identification of the parasite involved in the disabling disease leishmania which affects 18 million people largely in the developing world:** Sir William Boog Leishman (1865–1926). The disease was originally called dum-dum fever after the military hill station outside Calcutta where the Glaswegian first identified the parasite in a diagnostic stain taken from a soldier's spleen.

★ **Identification of the clinical symptoms of hypothermia:** James Lind (1716–94). Lind observed that seamen often died after having been rescued from the sea and described the danger signs of the condition.

★ **The systematic treatment of heart disease:** Sir James MacKenzie (1853–1925). Perthshire-born and Edinburgh-trained, while working in a busy Lancashire GP practice, MacKenzie made many important discoveries in cardiology, including the benign nature of some irregular heartbeats, which previously resulted in patients being treated as invalids. He moved to London as a consultant in 1907, becoming the world authority of his day on heart disease. In 1917, he moved to St Andrews to set up an

Institute of General Practice, pioneering the specialist training of GPs.

★ **The lifecycle of the malaria parasite:** Sir Patrick Manson (1844–1922). Born in Old Meldrum, Aberdeenshire, Manson studied medicine at Aberdeen before pursuing a career as a medical officer in Taiwan and Hong Kong. In 1877, he identified the parasite responsible for elephantiasis, the disease which results in severe swelling of the limbs. He linked it to a mosquito, going on to establish the full life cycle and mode of action of the parasite. On his return to the UK in 1889, he became the driving force behind the formation of the London School of Tropical Medicine. His proof that diseases could be carried by insects led him to discover the cause of other diseases, including sleeping sickness and bilharzia. In 1894 Manson suggested to his student, Sir Ronald Ross (1857–1932), born in India of Scots ancestry, that mosquitoes might carry malaria, guiding him through the research which led to the identification of the carrier. Manson even allowed his experimental mosquitoes to feed on his son Patrick, a medical student at Guy's Hospital, London. Within 15 days, Patrick developed malaria. It was Ross alone, however, who won the Nobel Prize in 1902.

★ **The foramen of Monro, the opening connecting the two lateral ventricles or cavities of the brain within the centre of the brain:** Alexander Monro (1733–1817). He was Secundus of a remarkable trio, known as Primus, Secundus and Tertius, as grandfather, father and son were all called Alexander. Together they held the Professorship of Anatomy at Edinburgh University for 126 years.

★ **The discovery and naming of the staphylococcus bacterium as the organism responsible for wound infection:** Sir Alexander Ogston (1844–1929). Regius Professor of Surgery at Aberdeen University, he named it staphylococcus because he thought that its appearance resembled a bunch of grapes.

★ **The significance of putrefaction in spreading disease:** Sir John Pringle (1707–82). He listed contaminated marsh water, excrement remaining exposed in hot weather, crowded military hospitals and rotting bedding straw as the sources for putrefaction, the main killer of armies. A baronet's son from the Borders, Pringle's first career was as a moral philosopher. In 1743, he gave up the

Chair at Edinburgh University to become physician to the Earl of Stair, then a military commander in Flanders. This was the start of his second career and the one which earned him the title of 'Father of military medicine', his *Observations on the Diseases of the Army* revolutionising the subject. He was with the victorious Duke of Cumberland after Culloden and ended his days as physician to George III.

★ **The identification of the various forms of dysentery as a single disease:** Sir John Pringle (1707–82). Pringle also identified jail fever and hospital fever as typhus, leading to better ventilation in public places.

★ **The Argyll Robertson pupil:** named after Douglas Argyll Robertson (1837–1909), the Edinburgh ophthalmologist who first observed the phenomenon in 1869. It is a common symptom of neurosyphilis, where the pupil of the eye is small and responds slowly, if at all, to light while retaining normal reaction to accommodation and convergence.

★ **The effect of the adrenal gland on blood pressure:** the Englishman, Sir Edward Sharpey-Schäfer, who held the Chair of Physiology in the University of Edinburgh from 1899–1933. This was the first example of a chemical produced in one place influencing the behaviour of a distant part of the body, leading rapidly to the discovery of hormones. He also devised the Schäfer method of artificial respiration, adopted by the Royal Life Saving Society as the standard life-saving procedure.

★ **First clinical description of tuberculous meningitis:** Aberdeenshire doctor Robert Whytt (1714–66). Whytt also identified the seat of reflex action. He conducted the first animal experiments on reflex actions and showed that they were controlled from the spinal cord.

THE SCOTS MEDICAL DICTIONARY

Words that have come into widespread use include:

★ **Acupressure:** used by James Young Simpson (1811–70) to describe his method of controlling bleeding in surgery. The word he coined has remained in the language for holistic healing by finger pressure.

★ **Hypnotism:** Fife-born James Braid (1795–1860), who studied medicine at Edinburgh, called hypnotism after the Greek god of sleep: the trance-like state was also known as 'Braidism'.

★ Influenza: coined by Sir John Pringle (1707–82).

★ Nervous energy: first used by William Cullen (1710–90).

★ Neuroses: first used by William Cullen (1710–90).

★ Nucleus: first used of the heart of the cell by Robert Brown (1773–1858).

★ Stimulus and response (reflexes): Robert Whytt (1714–66).

★ Molars, incisors, bicuspids and cuspids: John Hunter (1728–93) first named in his *Natural History of Human Teeth*, published in 1771.

OPERATIONS BY SCOTS SURGEONS

★ The Caesarean section: transformed by Glaswegian Professor Murdoch Cameron from a rarely used and normally fatal procedure to a routine operation. His first patient, Cathy Colquhoun, aged 27, was delivered on 10 April 1888, her son – Caesar Cameron Colquhoun – weighing in at 6 lb 12 oz. When the patient was sick four days later, she rejected an offer of champagne, asking instead for 'guid soor dook' (buttermilk). Cameron's third patient was an unmarried mother. Cameron arranged for her to hold her wedding to her partner John at the Glasgow Royal Maternity Hospital, his first two patients acting as maids of honour.

★ Keyhole surgery: pioneered in the UK by Maltese-born Professor Alfred Cuschieri (1938–) of Ninewells Hospital, Dundee. He is responsible for many instruments and techniques that have turned major operations into routine procedures, making them safer by replacing the surgeon's scalpel with the endoscope.

★ The first successful operation using hypnosis: James Esdaile (1808–59). A Perth doctor working in Calcutta, Esdaile performed 2,000 operations under hypnosis without pain, reducing the death rate from 50 per cent to 5 per cent. He also discovered the level of hypnosis at which natural anaesthesia occurs – known as the Esdaile state in his honour.

★ Europe's first lung transplant: performed by Andrew Logan at Edinburgh Royal Infirmary in 1968.

★ The first operation in the UK using ether: William Scott. In December

1846, the Cunarder *Acadia* brought the news of the successful use of ether as an anaesthetic by dentist William Morton, from Boston to Britain. The ship's surgeon, James Fraser, took with him a supply of ether when he returned to his home in Dumfries. There he presented it to local doctor, William Scott, who used it successfully on 29 December, to perform an operation, probably an amputation. It was the first operation using anaesthesia in Britain, although Scott did not publicise his achievement until much later. A letter describing the technique was sent to London and on the same day ether was used for a dental procedure. It was, however, the first public operation on a patient under general anaesthesia by another Scots surgeon, Robert Liston, two days later which hit the headlines, Liston remarking after the operation, 'This Yankee dodge certainly beats hypnotism.'

★ Operations for the removal of a number of joints, including that still known as Syme's disarticulation amputation for the ankle joint, and the first operations aimed at reconstructing damaged tissue paving the way for plastic surgery: James Syme (1799–1870).

★ The first successful kidney transplant in the UK: performed by Sir Michael Woodruff in Edinburgh Royal Infirmary on 30 October 1960. The patient was a 49-year-old with a healthy twin brother. The donor resumed work three weeks after the operation; the patient returned to work after 15 weeks. Pioneer kidney transplants faced the risk of rejection until the development of Imuran, still widely used after transplant surgery. Half of the first batch of the drug was used in Boston and the second half in Edinburgh, the Edinburgh patient becoming the second transplant patient in the world to be treated with the drug. It was a highly successful transplant, the kidney lasting for more than 20 years.

2

The Father of Limeys and the Poison Arrow Men: Finding the Cure

Since the first cave-dwellers discovered the benefits of roots and berries to ease their aches and pains, plants have played a major part in treating disease, for centuries being virtually the only source of drugs. Edinburgh's Royal Botanic Garden traces its roots to the Edinburgh Physick Garden of the seventeenth century, where herbs and plants were grown to supply the growing medical profession. In 1776, the *Materia Medica Catalogue*, the first modern pharmacopoeia listing drugs, their make-up, uses and recommended doses, was published in the capital. The compilers of the *Catalogue* would still recognise a few of the ingredients used in today's multi-million-pound drug industry.

The prevention and treatment of disease demands more than the surgeon's knife or the physician's prescription. Scottish medical schools and hospitals have played a disproportionate part, not only in the development of modern medical science and in the training of doctors, but also in developing innovative ways of promoting health, whether that of mother and baby, soldier or sailor, or the family of a patient diagnosed with TB. Some of their solutions have been disarmingly simple, such as the use of lemon juice in preventing scurvy.

THE WORLD'S FIRST CLINICAL TRIAL

Born and brought up in Edinburgh, James Lind (1716–94) went to sea as a surgeon's mate in the British Navy, patrolling the Channel during the War of the Austrian Succession. In these expansionist and belligerent times, command of the seas was the key to supremacy: yet scurvy, the disease caused by Vitamin C deficiency in the diet, could wipe out a third of a ship's crew on a long journey.

Lind studied the incidence of scurvy, finding that it occurred in towns under siege, long expeditions and sea voyages, in short, wherever the diet was limited and monotonous. In 1747, on board the HMS *Salisbury*, he carried out the world's first controlled clinical trial. Lind selected 12 sailors suffering from scurvy, grouped them in pairs and added different ingredients to the diet of each pair, including elixir of vitriol and half a pint of sea-water a day. He found that a diet which included lemon or lime juice was the most effective in reducing the symptoms, followed by one which included drinking draughts of cider. He worked out a way of preserving lemon juice, essentially by boiling it into fruit syrup so that 'the virtues of 12 dozens of lemons or oranges may be put into a quart bottle and preserved for several years'.

Lind devoted the rest of his life to campaigning for better conditions on board. While completing his degree on his return to Edinburgh, he published *A Treatise of the Scurvy* in 1754 and three years later, *An Essay on the Most Effectual Means of Preserving the Health of Seamen in the Royal Navy*, which exposed the appalling living conditions and diet aboard ship. After he was appointed to take charge of the naval hospital at Hasler in Hampshire, he made many recommendations as to improving health and hygiene, including hospital ships and separate sick bays. He showed that by exposing distilled water to air it lost its unpleasant taste, previously disguised by additives as bizarre as ground bones, soap and powdered chalk. Lind's last work was his *Handbook of Tropical Medicine*, the first authoritative work on the subject.

Lind could not persuade the authorities to adopt lemon juice as a cure for scurvy as long as sailors' lives were cheap, thanks to the enforced recruitment of seamen by the press-gangs. When Captain Cook adopted Lind's treatment, losing only one man in three years from scurvy, the authorities remained unimpressed. Even when Lind became personal physician to George III in 1783, he still could not carry the point. It was only in 1795, a year after Lind's death, that the navy, under pressure from the war against France, adopted Lind's remedy of giving citrus fruits to sailors. Fellow Scot Sir Gilbert Blane (1749–1834), who carried on Lind's work in putting the navy on a healthy footing, adopted the cheaper lime juice, thereby bestowing on British seamen the nickname of 'limeys'.

What Lind did for scurvy and the sea, another Scot did for tuberculosis and the city. At the turn of the twentieth century, TB accounted for one in eight deaths in Scotland, thriving in the cramped, unsanitary conditions of inner cities like Edinburgh's Old Town. One Scot set out to tackle the scourge of the closes.

THE WHITE PLAGUE

After graduating from Edinburgh University, Robert Philip (1857–1939), a son of the manse, studied in Vienna under Robert Koch, discoverer of the tubercule bacillus which caused TB. On his return to Edinburgh, Philip continued his investigations despite opposition by the medical establishment who were sceptical of diseases that could only be identified under the microscope. Appreciating the infectious nature of the disease, Philip was the first person to realise TB was a community problem and how to tackle its control. In 1887, he set up the Edinburgh Dispensary which not only provided diagnostic and treatment facilities, but also acted as the focus for his Edinburgh Anti-Tuberculosis Scheme, which promoted preventive measures such as the safe disposal of sputum and tracing family contacts. He supervised the design of Edinburgh's first sanatorium, the Royal Victoria Hospital for Consumption, ensuring that the allocated land was sufficient to create gardens in which patients could benefit from fresh air.

Despite Philip's conviction that the needs of the whole family of a TB patient must be addressed, including poor housing and diet, persuading the authorities to act proved an uphill struggle. He campaigned in support of the BCG vaccination and of making TB a notifiable disease, succeeding in the latter when in 1907 Edinburgh became the first city in the UK to make notification compulsory. This had the effect of almost doubling the number of cases reported each year. Philip ran education campaigns for schools and in 1923 his Tuberculosis Trust opened Gracemount Dairy Farm, one of the first to produce certified milk from a tuberculin-tested herd. As the world's first Professor of Tuberculosis from 1917, he passed on his vision to generations of students. A later holder of the Chair, Sir

John Crofton, initiated the practice of giving patients a powerful cocktail of drugs which cured more than 90 per cent of TB cases. He has taken up Philip's cudgels in the battle against the worldwide resurgence of the 'white plague'.

Philip did not live long enough to see the fruits of his campaign. His Edinburgh System for managing the disease was adopted worldwide, while new drugs, made possible by Sir Alexander Fleming's discovery of penicillin, slashed the death rates. The greatest achievement of all in eradicating the disease was the introduction of mass X-ray campaigns to identify carriers. In 1954, Edinburgh launched the UK's first community X-ray campaign in the Pilton housing estate with 300 volunteers trained to recruit their neighbours in advance of a week-long visit from the X-ray van. Attendance trebled and the approach was adopted in communities throughout Britain. With the unenviable title of the UK's TB capital, Glasgow went all out to break the world's X-ray record with a citywide advertising campaign, prize draws and an X-ray van on almost every corner. With over three-quarters of the population checked within five weeks, Glasgow's approach became a model for other UK cities.

Scots are renowned for their dogged tenacity. Another long battle with the military authorities ensued before William Boog Leishman (1865–1926), son of the Professor of Medicine at Glasgow University, managed to persuade them to adopt the anti-typhoid vaccine made from killed typhoid bacilli that he had helped Alroth Wright to develop in the 1890s. Leishman carried out meticulous statistical trials of the vaccine among troops in India and during the Boer War to help persuade the powers that be. It was largely due to his persistence and his perfection of the vaccine itself in 1913 that there was no major outbreak of typhoid during the First World War. An earlier tenacious Scot had to face opposition from a different quarter.

THE DRUG SNIFFER

The seventh son of a Bathgate baker, James Young Simpson (1811–70), entered Edinburgh University aged only 14, describing himself as 'a very poor, a very solitary, a very young and an almost friendless student'. Although his experience of watching Robert Liston operate nearly decided Simpson to be a law clerk instead, he persevered, proving to be an outstanding student. A growing New Town medical practice was combined from 1840 with the Chair of Midwifery at Edinburgh where his popularity with students led to his packed classes becoming the largest in the university.

Simpson hated pain, whether due to the agony of childbirth or the surgeon's knife. With the patient fully conscious throughout, speed was of the essence. Given the risks of shock and infection, amputation was often the only solution open to the surgeon and even then the odds against surviving infection were not good. Simpson showed that nearly one in two patients died shortly after amputation. George Wilson, a fellow doctor and holder of the world's first Chair of Technology at Edinburgh University, wrote to Simpson of the experience of having his leg amputated:

> Of the agony it occasioned I will say nothing. Suffering so great as I underwent cannot be expressed in words and thus fortunately cannot be recalled. I still recall with unwelcome vividness the spreading out of the instruments, the twisting of the tourniquet, the first incision, the fingering of the sawed bone, the sponge pressed on the flap, the tying of the blood vessels, the stitching of the skin, and the bloody dismembered limb lying on the floor.

In 1846, Simpson learned of the newly discovered use of ether as an anaesthetic by the US dentist of Scots descent, William Morton. Simpson invited a group of medical friends to his home in Queen Street to experiment by inhaling various 'noxious vapours'. After several 'happy' evenings, on 4 November 1847, after sniffing chloroform, the group simultaneously fell insensibly below the table to the alarm of the ladies present. When he came round Simpson realised that he had found the answer: 'This is far stronger and better than ether.' Four days later, Simpson became the first person to use anaesthesia in childbirth and chloroform in clinical practice when he delivered Wilhelmina Carstairs, a doctor's daughter.

Although one grateful mother was so delighted by Simpson's

painless delivery that she named her child 'Anaesthesia', at first Simpson's ideas aroused much controversy, being denounced as dangerous to health, morals and religion. Ministers fulminated from the pulpit that God had decreed the pain of childbirth as part of the curse of Eve and was now being deprived of the deep, earnest cries of women in childbirth. Simpson countered by pointing out that when God created Eve from Adam's rib, he first put Adam into a 'deep sleep'. Simpson's views were finally vindicated when he was appointed physician to Queen Victoria and chloroform was used to deliver her eighth child, Prince Leopold. Despite much criticism of the decision in the press, chloroform started to become fashionable, being known as 'anaesthesia a la reine'. Eventually, its use became universal, finding its way into village chemists' shops. It was, however, so zealously guarded that when Simpson once tried to purchase chloroform for his son's toothache, the shopkeeper refused him on the grounds that 'we dinna sell chloroform to folk that ken naething aboot it'.

Simpson was also a noted obstetrician making major advances in the operation to remove a woman's ovaries, the use of obstetric forceps and the introduction of silver wire sutures. He even had a prophetic streak, predicting the medical use of X-rays: 'by electrical and other lights we may render the body sufficiently diaphanous for the inspection of the practised eye of the physician or surgeon'. Respecting his wishes to lie with his forebears, on his death his family declined the honour of burial in Westminster Abbey. His American co-pioneers of anaesthesia met a less glorious fate. After 20 years of litigation with other claimants over who was the first person to use ether in an operation, William Morton died penniless. On seeing Morton's tomb crediting him as the founder of modern anaesthesia, another claimant went insane. Another experimenter with chloroform became addicted, throwing acid on a prostitute's clothes while under the influence and later committing suicide in jail.

But for Simpson, another Scot might have achieved more prominence in the alleviation of pain. James Esdaile (1808–59) from Perth achieved the first successful operation using the technique of hypnosis while working as a surgeon in Calcutta. The development was not followed up because of the success of ether and chloroform.

Even in the twentieth century, however, the effects of an anaesthetic could be as debilitating as the operation itself until scientists at Strathclyde University came up with the muscle relaxant drug, atracurium.

THE POISON ARROW DRUG

Before the development of such drugs, the anaesthetic itself had to act as a muscle relaxant, the high doses required resulting in a deep and dangerous depression of the patient's central nervous system. With atracurium, only enough anaesthetic is needed to ensure that the patient remains unconscious during the operation, making the surgeon's job easier and the operation safer.

The starting point for atracurium was curare, the blackish brown resinous substance from *Strychnos toxifera* and other deadly plants with which South American Indians tipped their arrows. When introduced into the bloodstream, it literally paralysed the victim. Surgical muscle relaxants, like atracurium, essentially work in the same way, the paralysis of the patient's diaphragm being counteracted by artificial respiration.

In the 1960s, a team of chemists and pharmaceutical scientists at Glasgow and Strathclyde universities took on the challenge of discovering a drug which did not persist in the body after the operation and allowed the patient to return to the ward breathing normally. Over more than a decade they unpicked the way in which the active compound in curare works, built a new structure that mimics these active ingredients and developed atracurium, one of the few drugs to have been designed and synthesised within a university environment. Code-named BW33A during the research phase, atracurium was introduced to the market as Tracrium and licensed in the late 1970s to Glaxo-Wellcome. Since its launch, world sales have exceeded £1bn. Ironically, the main competitor to the drug, Vecuranium, was developed at the same time by the Scottish research and development arm of the Dutch multinational, Organon.

Scots have helped to take the pain out of more than operations. The company that supplied James Young Simpson's experiments in anaesthesia was Duncan Flockhart and Co., one of three Edinburgh chemists who benefited from the discoveries of yet another member of the remarkable Gregory clan.

THE DROWSY DRUG

William Gregory (1803–58), Professor of Chemistry at Edinburgh University, played a significant part in the evolution of the pharmaceuticals industry from plant-based remedies to the mass production of chemically synthesised drugs, as well as laying the scientific foundations for Edinburgh's pre-eminence as a centre of pharmaceuticals manufacturing.

Gregory, a born experimenter, was dogged throughout his life by ill health, attributed to breathing in noxious chemical fumes from an early age. Fascinated by the challenge of unravelling the chemical make-up of matter, he was occasionally sent samples of unknown substances to analyse. On receiving a piece of Persian naphtha, he managed to extract paraffin, but having solved the puzzle, he laid the substance aside. It was left to others to found the Middle East oil industry and to fellow Scot James Young to earn the title 'Father of the oil industry'.

Gregory's contribution to chemistry was the production of pure hydrochloric acid, and to the emerging science of pharmaceuticals, the perfection and preparation of a number of compounds including chloroform and morphia. In 1831, he prepared morphine hydrochloride in pure crystalline form for the first time, opening up its true potential as a pain-relieving drug. An Edinburgh surgeon apothecary, John Fletcher Macfarlan, whose flourishing business did a large trade in laudanum, was so impressed by Gregory's work that by 1833 he was manufacturing morphine hydrochloride on a large scale. Fellow Edinburgh dispensing chemists, T. and H. Smith and Duncan Flockhart and Co., also entered the market.

Gregory helped these emerging pharmaceuticals businesses to manufacture chloroform for anaesthesia on a large scale. In 1863, David Rennie Brown, a partner of MacFarlan's, made the important discovery of how to prevent chloroform's tendency to decompose and yield the poison gas, phosgene, by adding a small amount of ethyl alcohol. Today, MacFarlan Smith, the company which emerged from these early manufacturing chemists, is the world's leading producer of opiate alkaloids, still retaining its headquarters in the city.

An earlier member of the Gregory clan put the family name in the nursery medicine cabinet. A nineteenth-century music hall ballad celebrates his invention: Gregory's Mixture:

> If in doubt lead with trumps is counsel so old
> As never to fail with the game in a fixture
> And medical men in their doubt I am told
> Are safe when they lead with Gregory's mixture.

In its innocent-looking paper packet, Gregory's mixture – *Pulvis Rhea Composita* – was the dynamite of the Victorian nursery, ready for action at the merest hint of stomach-ache, constipation or disobedience. A compound of rhubarb, magnesium carbonate and ginger it was, in its day, the most widely prescribed remedy in the pharmacopoeia.

James Gregory (1753–1821), Professor at Edinburgh University by the time he was 23, was a real character. A physician of the 'vigorous' school, he believed that disease should be attacked by a combination of 'free bloodletting, the cold effusion, frequent purging and blistering and the use of tartar emetic'. As a Latin scholar and translator of verse, Gregory also moved in Edinburgh literary society. His directness of approach to poetry criticism, as well as to medicine, led Robert Burns to comment, 'I believe in the iron justice of Dr Gregory, but like the devil, I believe and tremble.' Gregory's verbal attacks on medical colleagues – perpetrated in pamphlets of up to 700 pages long – led to his suspension from the Royal College of Surgeons. Having at one point come to blows in the street with the Professor of Midwifery and subsequently been sued for £100, Gregory remarked that he would have been happy to pay double the amount for another opportunity.

Another eccentric Scots doctor, now long forgotten, but in his day immensely influential, was John Brown (1735–88), founder of the Brunonian system of medicine.

A DOSE OF HIS OWN MEDICINE

The son of a Berwickshire labourer, Brown trained as a minister at Edinburgh University. For some reason, his nerve failed and he worked as a 'grinder' for a few years, writing essays on behalf of medical students for money and acting as a crammer for exams. This gave him a taste for medicine, which he studied under William Cullen, later falling out dramatically with the Professor over their differing approaches to the subject. Undeterred by his rejection by the medical establishment, Brown drew up his System, published in 1780 as *Elements of Medicine*.

At a time when the development of universal theories to explain and treat disease was very fashionable, Brown put forward the idea that life is a state of excitation produced by the normal action of external agents upon the body, disease being due to either an excess or a deficiency of excitation. Diseases were either 'sthenic' due to an excess of excitement, or to the opposite condition which he called 'asthenic'. They should be tackled by bloodletting and by stimulants or sedatives, depending on the degree of excitation. Brown believed in dosing himself with his own medicine – alcohol to stimulate the body and opiates to sedate it.

The source of his ideas may have been close to home; Brown being, according to one biographer, 'the only great drinker who ever exulted in that degrading vice, as justified by philosophical principles'. He kept bottles of whisky and laudanum on the table while lecturing, taking three or four doses from each during the course of his talk. A devout freemason, he founded the 'Roman Eagle' lodge where only Latin was allowed to be spoken. In 1786, he moved to London to try to make his fortune by lecturing on his System, dying of a fit of apoplexy brought on perhaps by a dose of his own medicine.

What is remarkable about the Brunonian System is that it gained such wide support. Brown's teaching caused riots between supporters and opponents of his System in Edinburgh and Göttingen in Germany. In America, his theories gained many adherents, in part because they admired his rise from humble origins. The Brunonian System, only finally abandoned well into the nineteenth century, was estimated to have been responsible for more deaths than the French Revolution and Napoleonic Wars together. Today, the wonder drug has replaced Universal Systems as the great white hope of treating disease. Two such drugs have won their Scottish discoverers the Nobel Prize, while a third has yet to deliver its promised potential. An Ayrshire farmer's son was responsible for what a fellow Nobel Prize winner, Peter Medawar, described as 'the most important discovery of the twentieth century'.

THE SECRET IN THE MOULD

The seventh of eight children, Alexander Fleming (1881–1955) was a country child who walked eight miles a day to primary school and, thereafter, became a weekly boarder at Kilmarnock High School. Aged fourteen, he joined his brothers in London working for five years as a shipping clerk before winning a scholarship to St Mary's Hospital Medical School. A brilliant student, from the start his main interest lay in bacteriology. He pioneered the introduction to Britain of salvarsan 606, the arsenic-based drug that killed the micro-organism responsible for syphilis and was one of the few physicians to administer it intravenously, the most effective, albeit the most difficult way. Such was the popularity of his clinic that he was nicknamed 'Private 606'. His experiences in a battlefield hospital laboratory in France during the First World War inspired him to search for a cure like salvarsan to tackle the infections to which many wounded soldiers all too quickly succumbed. His continued search after the war led to his discovery in 1922 of the protein, lysozyme – found in tears and skin. Although a natural antibiotic, it was not strong enough to tackle tougher breeds of bacteria.

It was while Fleming, by now Professor of Bacteriology at St Mary's, was working in his research laboratory that he 'accidentally' discovered penicillin. An untidy worker, he returned from a month's holiday in 1928 to discover that one of the culture plates that he had left in a dark corner in the laboratory displayed unusual characteristics. There were no bacterial colonies in the vicinity of the mould that had grown on the plate, which he used to grow staphylococcus bacteria. The bacteria had been killed by a substance in the mould, which Fleming called penicillin. As he laconically remarked, 'One sometimes finds what one is not looking for.'

Fleming quickly found that the mould was effective against a host of pathogens, his first patient being his assistant Stuart Craddock, whose infected sinus he treated by washing it out with a diluted penicillin broth. Fleming broke the news of his discovery in a paper to a meeting of the Medical Research Club in 1929. Audience reaction was nil. Although he struggled for some time to refine and grow his mould in quantity, Fleming was no chemist. It was only the impetus of the Second World War with the need for new treatments for wounded soldiers that drove pharmaceutical researchers, Howard Florey and Ernst Chain, to have another look at penicillin. They succeeded in isolating it and producing it in quantity. In 1941, mass production of the 'miracle drug' was switched to the USA to protect it from the risk of bombing.

In 1944, Fleming was awarded a knighthood for his work, and a year later the three developers shared the Nobel Prize for medicine. Fleming swore by a more traditionally Scottish remedy, however, for the common cold: 'A good gulp of whisky at bedtime – it's not very scientific but it helps.' Over 40 years later, another Scot stood on the same platform of the Stockholm Concert Hall to receive his Nobel Prize.

ICI 45,520

Until its launch in 1964, ICI 45,520 was the secret codename for Propranolol, the revolutionary drug invented by Sir James Black (1924–). A colliery manager's son from Fife, he followed in his brother's footsteps by studying medicine at St Andrews University, on graduating becoming a lecturer in the Physiology Department. It was here that he first became fascinated with the question which was to dominate his life: when and to what extent does local blood flow act as a metabolic throttle?

While helping to set up the new department of physiology at Glasgow University's Veterinary School, Black first developed the research interests which when later pursued in industry led to two remarkable drugs – finding ways of increasing oxygen supply to the heart in patients with narrowed coronary arteries and analysing the pharmacology of histamine-stimulated acid secretion. In his second interest there was a faint echo of the past as the medical thesis of his namesake, the physicist Joseph Black, nearly two centuries earlier was in stomach antacids. Over the intervening period, little had been done to address the problem effectively.

Propranolol, the first ever beta receptor antagonist, which rapidly entered popular language as the beta blocker, has revolutionised the treatment of heart disease, especially angina. It has delivered not only a longer but a better quality of life for millions of people with heart disease by helping the heart to beat steadily at a normal pace. In the late 1970s, Black studied the role of the hormone, histamine, which attaches to specific cells in the stomach lining, stimulating them to produce acid. He discovered cimetidine, a chemical that 'blocks' the histamine from attaching to these stomach cells. This was the active ingredient of Tagamet, the drug which relieves heartburn and stomach ulcers by reducing stomach acid for eight hours or longer. Knighted in 1981, Black was awarded the Nobel Prize for medicine seven years later.

A Scot may or may not have provided medicine with a future wonder drug. In the new century, the name of Alick Isaacs (1921–67) may win a place as one of the greatest alleviators of human disease, or his discovery may be overtaken by other developments. Only time will tell.

THE DRUG IN THE CARTOON

Alick Isaacs, the discoverer of interferon, was born in Glasgow where he graduated in medicine after winning all the major student prizes. Although involved with research very different from his subsequent work, his early years in the University's Department of Bacteriology convinced him that research, rather than medical practice or teaching, was his destiny. After winning a Rockefeller scholarship to join Sir Macfarlane Burnet's team at the University of Melbourne, which was carrying out exciting work on the influenza virus, he returned to the UK to take charge of the World Influenza Centre laboratory at the National Institute for Medical Research.

After years of painstaking research with a visiting Swiss researcher, Dr J. Lindemann, Isaacs published, in 1957, the original description of interferon. During an unconventional experiment with egg membranes and live viruses they observed that a live virus had failed to grow: something had 'interfered' with the process. They discovered for the first time that cells produce interferon as part of their response to attack by viruses. They produced interferon in human, monkey and calf cells and discovered that interferon from monkeys' kidneys successfully prevented the smallpox virus from multiplying in volunteers who had been inoculated with it. Only with the advent of new biotechnology techniques in the early 1980s, however, was it possible to produce interferon in any quantity.

Isaacs was not only a dedicated and brilliant researcher: he was a man of immense kindness and fun. He derived as much pleasure from the introduction of interferon into the *Flash Gordon* cartoon strip as from the many scientific tributes and honours. Tragically, he died at the early age of 45 while the full implications of his work were still being assessed. Today, three groups of interferons have been identified with the potential to treat a range of serious diseases from leukaemia to multiple sclerosis. Over 150 clinical trials are being conducted to test the potential of what may prove to be the twenty-first century's wonder drug. Sometimes, however, the simplest remedies prove to be the most effective.

A WOOLLY SOLUTION

One day Glasgow doctor Alexander Anderson (1794–1871) was called out because a child had fallen into a pot of boiling porridge. In her panic the mother, who worked from home as a cotton spinner, had wrapped her child in the first thing that came to hand, a wad of processed cotton waiting to be spun. From earliest times, raw cotton had been used as a way of staunching wounds. Its use, however, had been discredited by the medical profession on the grounds that the cotton contained bugs that caused more harm than the treatment helped. From the seventeenth century onwards rags were routinely used in Europe to bind wounds. Anderson observed, however, that his patient's scalds had already begun to heal, prompting him to conduct a series of trials using processed cotton-wool. In an article in the *Glasgow Medical Journal* of 1828, he advocated the use of cotton-wool in the treatment of burns. Observation and common sense always have a part to play in medical advance.

MEDICAL FIRSTS

★ The first antenatal and neonatal care clinics for mother and baby: John Ballantyne (1861–1923). As well as arguing for continuity of care, Ballantyne made the link between the health of the mother and of the unborn child, and the risks to both if the mother suffered from diseases like TB or syphilis.

★ The world's first woman doctor: James Stuart Miranda Barry (1795–1865). After training as a doctor at Edinburgh from 1809, Barry served in the army in places as far-flung as South Africa, the West Indies, Malta and St Helena, rising to the rank of Inspector General of Military Hospitals in Canada. Although a highly skilled and compassionate surgeon – in 1826, he carried out the first successful Caesarean section in Africa and possibly the English-speaking world – Barry was an outsider known for his temper, high-pitched voice and an ability to attract scandal. He provoked controversy with medical colleagues and the military authorities. No mean adversary herself, Florence Nightingale had a major contretemps with Barry during the Crimean War, describing him as 'the most hardened creature I ever met'. Only when laying out his corpse was it claimed that not only was Barry a woman, but that she had borne at least one child. Man, woman or, quite possibly, hermaphrodite, James Stuart Miranda Barry took his/her secret to the grave.

★ The Cochrane Collaboration: founded in 1993 in honour of Hawick-born Professor Archie Cochrane (1909–88) for his contribution to the development of epidemiology as a science. With 15 centres throughout the world, the Cochrane Collaboration aims to help people to make informed decisions about health care by systematically reviewing and making accessible the effects of health care interventions.

★ The first public asylum for the humane treatment of the mentally ill: Andrew Duncan (1744–1828). Born in St Andrews, Duncan, like his father, became a Professor of Medicine at Edinburgh University.

The death of his patient, the poet Robert Fergusson, in the appalling conditions of the city's Bedlam, inspired him to campaign for a new approach. His aim was to treat mental patients as being ill, rather than as little more than animals to be kept under lock and key. After a 15-year fundraising campaign, his hospital opened in 1807.

★ **The UK's first mother and child dispensary:** Sophia Jex-Blake (1840–1912). The pioneering Edinburgh GP established the Edinburgh Provident Dispensary for Women and Children in a poor district of the city in 1878. An early campaigner for the right of women to train in medicine, the high-spirited young Englishwoman chose to study at Edinburgh in 1869, the year that the university became the first in Britain to admit women. She survived student riots, university conservatism, refusal of the hospital authorities to allow her to train on the wards and challenges in the law courts to complete her degree, only to find that the university would not allow her to qualify. The University of Berne in Switzerland finally awarded her a medical degree.

★ **The founder of the future Royal Army Medical Corps:** Aberdonian Sir James McGrigor (1771–1858). He revolutionised army medicine, survived battle, typhoid and shipwreck, and became a close friend of and surgeon to the Duke of Wellington. His brother-in-law, Colquhoun Grant, Wellington's Head of Intelligence during the Napoleonic Wars, was 'the first respectable spy'.

★ **The first birth control clinic in the UK:** opened in London by the family planning pioneer, Marie Stopes (1880–1958), who was born and brought up in Edinburgh. Her Mother's Clinic, which opened in Holloway, north London, in 1920, pioneered a worldwide network of family planning clinics. In 1965, the distinguished Scottish obstetrician and pioneer of pregnancy termination, Sir Dugald Baird, started his campaign for 'freedom from the tyranny of excessive fertility' to become the fifth human right alongside freedom of speech and worship and freedom from want and fear.

★ **The Glasgow Coma Scale:** developed by G. Teasdale and B. Jennet in 1974 as a scoring system to quantify levels of consciousness after traumatic brain injury. It is the most widely adopted system of its kind in the world, used at the scene of accidents and in casualty and intensive care units. The Glasgow Outcomes Scale measures the longer-term likelihood and degree of rehabilitation after head injury.

★ **The world's first custom-built kidney transplant unit:** opened at the Western General Hospital, Edinburgh, in 1968. Designed to meet the requirements of transplant pioneer Sir Michael Woodruff, the Nuffield Transplantation Surgery Unit provided a germ-free environment for transplant patients and a model for kidney units worldwide.

THE TECHNOLOGY OF TREATMENT

★ **The first person in the world with a bionic arm:** Moffat hotelier Campbell Aird. A team of biomedical engineers at the Princess Margaret Rose Orthopaedic Hospital created the Edinburgh Modular Arm System in 1993 to replace his right arm which had been amputated a decade before. The bionic arm rotates at the shoulder, bends at the elbow, twists at the wrist and can grip using artificial fingers. An array of microsensors, attached to a cap worn on Aird's head, pick up electrical pulses sent by his brain to the absent arm muscles and uses them to control each movement of the bionic arm. He has since been fitted with a bionic hand designed by David Gow and his Edinburgh team.

★ **Pregnancy tests for birth defects:** Professor David Brock of Edinburgh University. In 1972, he announced his discovery that raised amniotic fluid alpha feto-protein was associated in pregnancy with open neural tube defects such as spina bifida in the child. Given that this protein is detectable in maternal serum, he pioneered the standard screening test for a number of diseases using the technique of amniocentesis. This involves the withdrawal, during the early stage of pregnancy, of a small sample of the fluid which bathes the embryo. From this fluid, cell cultures are grown in which foetal proteins can be detected. Professor Brock was one of the first scientists to apply markers to pre-natal screening. One of the markers he found was for cystic fibrosis, the most common inherited life-threatening condition.

★ **The UK's first iron lung:** designed by Robert Henderson (1903–2000), a young Aberdeen doctor. He saw a demonstration of the first practical iron lung, the so-called 'Drinker Respirator', on a visit to the USA. Excited at the new machine's possibilities, Henderson constructed one at his Aberdeen hospital in 1933. Within a month it had saved the life of a ten-year-old boy suffering from polio. Despite this success, Henderson was reprimanded by the authorities because he had secretly constructed it using hospital facilities. As a result, he abandoned the work.

★ Artificial insemination: first suggested by John Hunter (1728–93).

★ Surgical scissors with blunt points: Joseph Lister (1827–1912).

★ The sinus forceps: Joseph Lister (1827–1912). Lister invented a number of surgical instruments, some of which, like his sinus forceps, are still in use today and bear his name.

★ Catgut ligature for surgery: Joseph Lister (1827–1912). By experimenting on a calf, Lister showed that the catgut was absorbed by the body after a time and, therefore, could safely be left inside. This convinced him that animal experimentation was essential for medical advance. Although a Quaker, and strongly opposed to unnecessary cruelty, he defended the practice before the Royal Commission on Vivisection of 1875, despite being asked by Queen Victoria to condemn it publicly.

★ Bone-cutting forceps: Robert Liston (1794–1847). Liston bone forceps still appear in twenty-first-century catalogues of surgical instruments.

★ The Liston splint: a splint for the thigh still in use during the Second World War: Robert Liston (1794–1847).

★ The polygraph: Sir James MacKenzie (1853–1925). The instrument enabled two pulses to be recorded at the same time and compared. Used in the diagnosis of heart disease, the 'MacKenzie Ink Polygraph', the precursor of the electrocardiograph, allowed him to establish fundamental differences in different types of cardiac irregularity, a milestone in the history of cardiac disease.

★ The first inoculation for smallpox in Britain: Charles Maitland. In the eighteenth century, the 'monstrous speckles' killed 10 per cent of the population. Maitland, medical adviser to the British Ambassador to the Ottoman Empire, introduced to the UK the Turkish practice of variolation. A sample was taken from a patient who had suffered a mild dose of the disease and introduced into the person to be inoculated through the nose or skin. Maitland was granted a royal licence to try out variolation on six Newgate prisoners who were promised a full pardon if they submitted to the 'Royal Experiment'. The prisoners survived and were released. With the royal stamp of approval, the procedure was widely adopted. Edward Jenner, the Gloucestershire doctor who introduced the far safer and more effective agent of cowpox as protection against smallpox, previously practised variolation himself.

★ The 'long' obstetric forceps: William Smellie (1697–1753). Smellie ended the female monopoly of midwifery by introducing male physician midwives and putting midwifery on a firm medical basis. He laid down guidance on the use of forceps, arguing that they should only be used when absolutely necessary.

★ The hypodermic syringe: invented by Alexander Wood (1817–84), an Edinburgh physician and Secretary of the Royal College of Physicians in 1853. The syringe was first used to inject morphine as a painkiller.

THE SCOTTISH PRESCRIPTION

★ Dr Anderson's True Scots Pills: Dr Patrick Anderson, later to become physician to Charles I. One of the earliest patent medicines, the recipe for this compound of aloes and myrrh was brought back from Venice in 1603 by Anderson. The pills were still being manufactured in the twentieth century

★ The suggestion that the shape of a molecule determined how it acted as a drug: Alexander Crum Brown (1838–1922).

★ Efficacy of amyl nitrate in treatment of angina: Sir Thomas Brunton (1844–1916). He introduced the treatment when a house surgeon at Edinburgh Royal Infirmary.

★ Isolation of the active principle of hemlock: Robert Christison (1797–1882). Christison also wrote the ground-breaking *Treatise on Poisons*, the first textbook of toxicology in the English language. He led a charmed life as he often experimented on himself.

★ The discovery that quinine bark acted as a cure for malaria: George Cleghorn (1716–94). In 1761, Cleghorn, an Edinburgh-born and educated army surgeon, became the first Professor of Anatomy and Surgery at Trinity College, Dublin.

SCOTTISH FIRSTS

★ **Ranitidine:** developed by a team led by Sir David Jack, who was a student and lecturer in pharmacology at Glasgow University. Under the trade name Zantac, ranitidine became the world's best selling pharmaceutical, easing the symptoms of indigestion. Jack's career in the pharmaceuticals industry also included the development of Salbutomol, a treatment for asthma, Sumatriptan for migraine and Ondansetron for nausea.

★ **Apomorphine and ethylmorphine:** developed by the Edinburgh druggists J.F. Macfarlan, the first to produce commercial quantities of these painkillers. They also collaborated with Lord Lister to produce sterile dressings for aseptic surgery.

★ **Bitrex, the world's bitterest taste:** developed by the Edinburgh pharmaceuticals company Macfarlan Smith. The most widely available bitterer is added to products from drugs to domestic cleaners to stop people, especially young children, being poisoned.

★ **Aspirin:** developed by Dr Thomas John MacLagan, one-time Medical Superintendent at Dundee Royal Infirmary. He also ran a private practice in the Nethergate where, in 1876, he gave the world the ingredients of aspirin. He was the first person to recognise that the bitter-tasting extracts of willow bark containing salicin were a specific cure for rheumatic fever. This fuelled Felix Hoffman and his employer, the German chemicals company Bayer, to search for a more palatable derivative. They patented aspirin (acetylsalicilic acid) in 1899.

★ **The first artificial vaccine against viral hepatitis B:** Sir Kenneth Murray, Professor of Molecular Biology at the University of Edinburgh. The creation of the vaccine, which has saved countless lives worldwide, in 1978, was one of the first applications of genetic engineering. He also developed the first test to identify the presence of the disease.

★ **Physostigmine, the drug used to dilate the pupil:** isolated by Douglas Argyll Robertson (1837–1909), who discovered its presence in the calabar bean.

★ **The isolation of several drugs including aloin from aloes, santonin from artemisia and morphine from opium:** achieved by the Edinburgh pharmaceuticals firm T. & H. Smith in the mid-nineteenth century.

3

'Dafty' and the Wine Merchant's Son: Shedding the Light of Science

Few Scots today know the name of James Clerk Maxwell, much less what he did. Yet, arguably, 'Dafty' is Scotland's greatest scientist. Nobel Prize winner Richard Feynman ranked this shy, retiring Scot, who laid down the fundamentals behind electronics, as second only to Newton and Einstein in the history of physics, while Einstein himself said of the creation of Maxwell's equations, 'to few men in the world has such an experience been vouchsafed'. Einstein could only admire Scotland's scientific achievements, but Ernest Rutherford, who split the atom giving birth to nuclear physics, J.J. Thomson, who unravelled the mysteries of the electron, and Isaac Newton all claimed to have Scots blood in their veins. Scots can look closer to home for their contribution to scientific progress in areas as diverse as the theory of heat, the make-up of air and the origins of the earth.

Why did a small and relatively poor country produce so many great scientists? It is said that the Scots character combines the tenacity, idealism and canny good sense that foster scientific curiosity. The Scottish education system, with its emphasis on useful knowledge and breadth of subjects studied, produced rounded individuals with a strong practical bent. At his golden wedding, Sir James Dewar played the fiddle that he had made himself as a child. Dr James Gregory was the doyen of Edinburgh literary circles and was called upon whenever the civic authorities required the dignity of a Latin inscription. Although Charles Wilson invented the cloud chamber, usually Scots scientists kept their feet on the ground. Many appreciated the practical applications of their discoveries and sought to develop them, David

Brewster hoping to make his fortune from his kaleidoscope.

Especially in the eighteenth and early nineteenth centuries, the smallness and closeness of the Scottish scientific community allowed for a free flow of ideas and cross-fertilisation among different disciplines. Joseph Black's work on heat inspired James Watt to perfect the steam engine. When Watt moved to Birmingham, he joined the Lunar Society, a group of 14 scientists, four of whom were Scots, who met during the full moon to make travelling home easier. A fellow member was Erasmus Darwin, grandfather of Charles, who became a close friend of Scots geologist Charles Lyell. Lyell devoted much of his life to publicising the work of fellow geologist James Hutton. It was owing to Hutton's indisposition that the first part of his classic paper on the *Theory of the earth* was read to the Royal Society of Edinburgh by none other than Joseph Black. There are countless examples of the connectedness of the Scottish scientific community.

As science started to emerge from the dark realms of alchemy, one of Scotland's first practitioners was a laird whose castle is now a landmark within the campus of one of Scotland's newest universities. Until recently, when the calculator took the place of its seventeenth-century equivalent, every school pupil loved to hate John Napier (1550–1617), the inventor of logarithms.

PUTTING THE POINT IN THE DECIMAL

John Napier, the eighth Laird of Merchiston, lived in stirring times when Scotland was torn apart after the religious upheaval of the Reformation. A staunch Protestant, he directed his energies to designing instruments of war to meet the threat of a Spanish invasion following the execution of Mary Queen of Scots in 1587. His 'secret inventions' included: the forerunner of the armoured tank; a primitive submarine; a 'burning mirror' constructed with lenses to use as a fire-raising weapon; and artillery that could destroy life within a one-mile radius. Stories were legion that 'Marvellous Merchiston' had superhuman powers and that his pet black cock whispered the intimate secrets of his servants in his master's ear.

It is, however, for his mathematical, rather than his military, achievements that Napier has earned himself a place in history. In 1594, it occurred to him that all numbers could be expressed as fractional powers of a base number. Multiplication could then be carried out simply by adding the fractions and division by subtracting them. He devoted the next 20 years to calculating complex tables especially for use in astronomy. The process he devised of computing exponential expressions led him to call them proportionate numbers or logarithms. The notation he adopted included putting the point into the decimal fraction.

Although his motive in undertaking this mammoth task may have been to find the number of the Beast of the Apocalypse, when he finally published the fruits of his labours – *A Description of the Wonderful Law of Logarithms* – in 1614, his tables were immediately seized upon with delight by fellow mathematicians and astronomers. Towards the end of his life, Napier also invented a primitive computer. 'Napier's bones' consisting of ten rods made of bone, or ivory in the case of the upmarket models favoured by merchants, on which multiplication tables were printed: manipulating the rods allowed the user to perform sums quickly and accurately. Through his logs and bones, Napier relieved scientists and navigators of the drudgery of routine calculations, being said to have doubled the useful lifespan of the latter. The pockets of traders and bookkeepers throughout Europe soon rattled with his bones. The scale of the impact of Napier's inventions was similar to that of the pocket calculator of the twentieth century.

The seventeenth century saw the first of a name that was to be recorded in the annals of science for many generations.

'DAVIE DO A' THING' AND FAMILY

Spanning three centuries, the contribution of the Gregory family is remarkable for quantity as well as quality. From the marriage of Janet Anderson to John Gregorie, the minister of Drumoak parish on Deeside, ensued no less than 16 professors. In *Hereditary Genius*, Francis Galton, the nineteenth-century pioneer of the study of intelligence, cited the family as an example of the inheritance of scientific gifts. Nature did have a hand in shortening the odds, one early Gregory producing no fewer than 29 children. The Gregory genius probably stemmed from the maternal side of the family. Janet's father was nicknamed 'Davie do a' thing' because of his many practical skills; a relative was Professor of Mathematics at the University of Paris and Janet herself was an accomplished mathematician.

After being taught by his mother and spending several years in Italy, James Gregory (1638–75) took up the newly created Regius Chair of Mathematics at St Andrews University, not the most onerous of tasks as the duties consisted of two lectures a week and responsibility for answering any mathematical questions that might be put to the holder of the post. He left St Andrews in 1674 to take up the first Chair of Mathematics at Edinburgh University, having fallen out with his fellow professors because of his advanced views: Gregory was one of the first to embrace the new Newtonian physics. His time at Edinburgh was short. One evening while showing some students the satellites of Jupiter, he was struck blind and he died a few days later.

By the age of 24, Gregory had proposed the idea of the reflecting telescope, opening up the way for much more powerful instruments. He failed to find a glassmaker able to handle his complex design and so it was Isaac Newton rather than Gregory who produced the first practical reflecting telescope five years later. Gregory's design was undoubtedly the better of the two, Newton's telescope being difficult to use as the observer's head and the eyepiece blocked much of the incoming light. Gregory had solved this by adding a second concave mirror, which reflected the rays of light to the eyepiece. He was also the first person to observe the splitting of light by a diffraction grating, rather than a prism, using a seabird's feather as the grating. Out of deference to Newton, whom he knew to be working in the field, he did not pursue this line of enquiry. He also suggested the way of calculating the earth's distance from the sun, which was widely used until the nineteenth century. As a mathematician, Gregory and the German Leibnitz independently worked out the first ever infinite series for pi, Gregory introducing the term 'convergent series' into the language of algebra. He wrote the first textbook on calculus, anticipating Newton and Leibnitz in many aspects.

Edinburgh University was prepared to wait for another Gregory.

Eight years after his death they gave the vacant Chair to his nephew David (1659–1708) who, aged only 22, had yet to complete his degree. He followed in his uncle's footsteps, being the first person to propose the achromatic telescope lens, again long before it could be made in practice. He was one of the first to observe that inverting the curve made by a chain, fixed at both ends, creates a catenary arch, much used centuries later by the Spanish architect Antoni Gaudi. Gregory's real significance lies not as much in his original work, but in his influence, at Edinburgh and later Oxford, in popularising Newtonian physics. A close friend of the great man, he wrote the first textbook based on Newton's discoveries. Duncan, James, John and David – the Gregory Professors just kept on coming.

Scottish scientists have significantly influenced our understanding of heat, both hot and cold. Joseph Black (1728–99), the son of an Ulster-Scots wine merchant in Bordeaux, laid down some of the fundamental principles of the behaviour of heat, as well as being the first person to put forward the concept of a gas as distinct from air.

One of fifteen children, Joseph Black returned to Scotland to study arts until five years later his father insisted on him switching to medicine as being more useful: he later became a professor successively at both the universities of his student days, Glasgow and Edinburgh. His interest, as a student, in kidney stones led him to investigate other minerals with similar properties. His thesis for his medical degree proved to be a classic of chemistry recognising for the first time that magnesium is an element. In it he also showed that the compound calcium carbonate, could be converted to calcium oxide on being heated strongly, giving off a gas which could recombine with calcium oxide to form calcium carbonate again. What Black had discovered was carbon dioxide, although he called the gas 'fixed air' because it could be fixed into solid form again. Given that calcium oxide could be converted to calcium carbonate simply by exposure to air, it followed that carbon dioxide was a normal constituent of the atmosphere. To satisfy the medical examiners, he also pointed out the digestive benefits of white magnesium carbonate as an anti-acid.

While studying the behaviour of 'fixed air', Black observed that even after removing the carbon dioxide from a closed container in which a candle had burned, the remaining air would not support a flame. Black turned this problem over to his young assistant, Daniel Rutherford, the uncle of Sir Walter Scott. In 1772, Rutherford discovered nitrogen as an independent constituent of air and one which does not support combustion.

On becoming Professor of Medicine in Glasgow, Black encountered the young James Watt, at the time the university's instrument-maker, and through Watt became interested in heat. Black was the first person to recognise that the quantity of heat is not the same as its intensity or temperature. He was impatient for the Glasgow winter to arrive in order to confirm his theory that when ice was heated it slowly melted but did not change in temperature. Ice absorbs a quantity of what Black called 'latent heat' in melting, increasing the amount of heat it contained. Similarly, boiling water absorbed heat while remaining at the temperature of boiling point: this heat could be recovered when the resulting steam was recondensed. Black's discoveries provided Watt with the theory behind effective steam power. Black also showed that the amount of heat required to change the temperature of a substance by a given amount varied with the substance: different substance had different 'specific heats'. Although Black provided the clue that heat was a form of energy rather than, as was believed at the time, a weightless fluid, it was only when James Clerk Maxwell produced his kinetic theory of heat that Black's experiments were fully explained.

Like most scientists of the time, Black took a lively interest in practical problems, being one of the first to grasp the potential of using hydrogen in balloons. He introduced the manufacture of writing paper by the chemical bleaching of rags, rather than using unprinted linen, which slashed the price of paper. A lifelong bachelor and a vegetarian in his old age, he was a great frequenter of clubs, where his drinking companions included Adam Smith, David Hume and James Hutton. Throughout his life, Black continued to practise medicine: one of his patients was a nursemaid who was sacked as a result of his diagnosis of tuberculosis. Her young charge was the future Sir Walter Scott.

While Black explained the change of state from solid to liquid to gas, another Scot explored more complex relationships of matter.

GUNGE AND GOO

Fourteen-year-old Thomas Graham (1805–69) asked his professor at Glasgow University, 'Don't you think, Doctor, that when liquids absorb gases the gases themselves become liquids?' Although his father wanted him to become a minister, Thomas had other ideas, spending the next decade as a student at Glasgow and Edinburgh Universities and receiving his first payment for literary work. He spent the £6 on presents for his mother to whom he was devoted. At last, realising the necessity of earning a living, Graham taught chemistry to working men at the Glasgow Mechanics Institute before taking up the post of Professor of Chemistry at the Andersonian Institution in 1830. Although a brilliant experimenter in the lab, as a teacher he talked well above his students' heads and could not keep order. He moved to London in 1837 to take up the Chair of Chemistry at the recently founded University College and in 1855 became Master of the Royal Mint.

Graham's work in chemistry was original, fundamental and far in advance of his contemporaries. He proved that phosphoric acid forms several different compounds with water and demonstrated that alcohol is produced during bread-making by using it to ignite gunpowder. He even put forward the bold, if incorrect, theory that all elements may be no more than different forms of one primordial element. He was fascinated by the motion of atoms in gases and liquids, and in order to study their behaviour designed what became known as the Graham tube. He discovered the principle of atmolysis or the separation of gases by diffusion and in 1833 published his formula of how the rate of diffusion decreases as the density of the gas increases, still known as Graham's Law. In 1868, it was used to establish the chemical formula for ozone – O_3.

Although Graham's studies of the passage of gases through small openings and films greatly extended our knowledge of the motion of molecules, today he is best known as the 'Father of colloid science'. Colloids are gluey solutions in which the dispersed particles cannot be separated by filtration or gravity alone. Graham invented the process of dialysis using a membrane to separate substances in solution from colloids: one of the substances he succeeded in extracting was urea from urine. Graham's method is still in use in hospitals today to purify the blood of patients with kidney failure. He introduced several scientific terms into the English language including: atmolysis, dialysis, gel, sol as in aerosol and colloid. Graham was also active in public and professional life, serving on government committees on the efficacy of the ventilation of the new Houses of Parliament and on the purity of London's water supply. He was a founder member and the first President of the Chemical Society, the world's first national body in chemistry, and the first President of the Cavendish Society.

Another Scot finally laid to rest the idea that heat was a kind of fluid and his crowning achievement was even greater.

TELL ME HOW IT DOOS

How must the schoolmates of James Clerk Maxwell (1831–79) have rued the day that they nicknamed one of the world's greatest scientists 'Dafty', as later did Aberdeen and Edinburgh Universities in time regret turning him down as a professor.

Maxwell's father John, a prosperous advocate and landowner, took a keen interest in the scientific developments of his day, devising bellows for blast furnaces and an automatic feed for a printing press. He also designed his son's clothes, loose-fitting for health, but with little regard for appearance. James' early childhood was spent on the family estate at Glenlair in Galloway where his father encouraged his precocious curiosity about the world around him; he was never too busy to answer his small son's request to 'Tell me how it doos.' The results of James' constant experimenting was known in the family as 'Jamsie's durt'.

Strange clothes and a broad Galloway accent were of no help when ten-year-old James was sent to Edinburgh Academy. The school favoured the Classics and correct English, and James' modesty and country ways made him an easy target for the taunts of his fellow pupils. Yet, he had the toughness and independence of mind not only to survive the bullying, but to develop a life-long love of the Classics, as well as physics and maths. When he was 15, a paper he had written on a problem of geometry was read before the august Royal Society of Edinburgh.

In 1847, Maxwell went to Edinburgh University and from there to Cambridge, where his genius was quickly recognised, not only by academic prizes, but also by his election to the exclusive Apostles Club, whose membership was limited to the 12 brightest undergraduates. When he finished one examination in record time, he amused himself by translating the paper into Latin. From a Cambridge Fellowship, he was appointed Professor of Physics at Marischal College, Aberdeen, but on the college's merger with King's he was pipped at the post for the Chair of Physics at the new University of Aberdeen by the more politically astute 'Crafty' Thomson. He was then turned down by Edinburgh University, their chosen candidate being a better teacher. After five years as a Professor at King's College, London, Maxwell retired to continue his work in the attic of his Galloway home where he was at his happiest. He was eventually tempted back into academic life as the first holder of the Cavendish Chair of Physics at Cambridge University and the founding director of the Cavendish Laboratory.

How did this shy man, who only fully came to life when discussing a point of mathematics or philosophy, come to overthrow the existing model of the physical world? According to a Cambridge contemporary, 'it appears impossible for Maxwell to think incorrectly on physical subjects': he went on to prophesy that one day Maxwell 'would shine as a light in physical science'. This sums up the nature of Maxwell's genius, an uncanny instinct for the 'right' physical explanation combined with formidable mathematical ability. His insights were deep and far-reaching, opening up whole fields of science for the first time. His occasional tendency to slip up on details caused the German physicist Kirchoff, to comment: 'He is a genius, but one has to check his calculations.'

Maxwell had a lifelong interest in optics. He demonstrated that every colour can be matched by a combination of three suitably chosen colours of the spectrum and developed the theory of colour in relation to colour blindness. He took the world's first colour photograph, which he exhibited at a meeting of the Royal Institution in 1861. Its subject was a tartan ribbon bow taken against a black velvet background. He had the ribbon photographed three times using colour filters consisting of red, green and blue bottles of liquid which were placed between the camera and the subject. Glass positives from the collodion negatives were then projected on a screen by three separate lanterns, each fitted with a filter to correspond with its transparency.

In two areas, statistical mechanics and electromagnetism, he made the truly immense leap which laid the foundations for the development of twentieth-century electronics. At the time the theory that matter consisted of atoms was controversial. Despite plenty of supporting evidence from chemistry, many physicists regarded this theory as at best unnecessary and at worst dangerously misleading. By adopting a new statistical analysis of the motion of atoms in a gas, Maxwell not only accounted for many well-known properties, but predicted correctly, against intuition, that the viscosity or stickiness of a gas was independent of its pressure. He opened the way for the explanation of the properties of matter – first gases, then crystals, metals and liquids, and finally semiconductors – in terms of their atomic make-up.

Maxwell finally laid to rest the belief that heat was a kind of fluid. He redirected scientific thinking away from the determinism of classical physics towards the idea of probability that underpins modern physics. He founded the science of statistical mechanics with important advances in the kinetic theory of gases, and originated the concepts of cybernetics including that of feedback. Even more far-reaching was the definitive representation of electromagnetic fields in Maxwell's equations. Applying advanced mathematics to Michael Faraday's description of electricity and magnetism in terms of lines of force, he derived a system of equations that not only explained the known behaviour of electricity and magnetism, but predicted waves which moved through space at approximately the same speed as light. This led to a tempting hypothesis – light was an electromagnetic wave and there should, therefore, also be electromagnetic waves at other wavelengths. Maxwell set one of his students the task of detecting them, but his apparatus was far too insensitive. Eight years after Maxwell's death, Hertz fully verified his theory by detecting radio waves. From Maxwell's electromagnetic spectrum came the long and short waves of radio and radar, and the ultra-short waves of X-rays.

Several Scots were interested in the lower end of the temperature scale. In 1748, William Cullen, a doctor from Hamilton, was the first person to demonstrate artificial refrigeration, by letting ethyl ether boil into a partial vacuum. Using an air pump and a vessel of sulphuric acid to absorb vapour from the air, in 1810, Fifer Sir John Leslie succeeded in producing over 1 lb of ice in a single operation. The domestic fridge, however, had to wait for well over a century, as Cullen did not put his discovery to any practical use. In pursuit of the very cold, Sir James Dewar gave the world a means of keeping things hot, the vacuum flask.

PUTTING THE TEA IN THE FLASK

Sir James Dewar (1842–1923), an innkeeper's son from Kincardine-on-Forth, first experienced the effects of extreme cold when he fell through the ice. During his long convalescence from the resulting rheumatic fever, he learned how to make fiddles from the local joiner, acquiring the skill with his hands that he later used to such effect in designing scientific instruments. At Edinburgh University, he worked as a laboratory assistant to Professor J.D. Forbes, the first person to explain how glaciers flowed. In 1867, Dewar published his first scientific paper in which he described seven ways to represent the carbon compound, benzene. The paper brought him to the attention of the German chemist Kekule, later famous for determining the structure of benzene: the representation that Kekule used was one of Dewar's seven examples. Although Dewar held a Chair at Cambridge from 1875 until his death, he found that its conservative, academic atmosphere did not suit his temperament, very much that of the blunt, outspoken Scot and the practical, experimental scientist. He preferred to work in the laboratories of the Royal Institution in London where he held a second chair as Fullerian Professor.

It was while working on liquefying gases – Dewar was the first person to liquefy hydrogen and to solidify it – that he designed his vacuum flask in 1892, which made possible all subsequent developments in cryogenics, the physics of very cold temperatures. Needing a vessel which would keep his liquid gases cold and prevent frost forming, he came up with a double-lined vessel with a vacuum between the two layers. He later added a drop of mercury which condensed to form a mirror at liquid air temperatures. In 1904, he improved his design by adding a minute amount of charcoal in the vacuum to absorb any remaining gases, making it feasible to use a metal, rather than a glass, container as the outer layer of the flask. Although aware of the flask's ability to keep liquids hot as well as cold, Dewar showed no interest in his invention's wider possibilities. One of the glassmakers who produced Dewar's flask, the German Reinhold Burger, saw its potential and put the Thermos flask in the picnic basket.

Dewar's flask was essential to another Scot in exploring air. Boiling argon gave Sir William Ramsay the key to air's other rare ingredients.

THE KRYPTON FACTOR

Glaswegian Sir William Ramsay (1852–1916) was an all-rounder, enjoying music, languages and athletics, as well as maths and chemistry from childhood onwards: he even blew most of his own scientific glassware. After lecturing in Glasgow at the Andersonian College and the University, he became Professor of Chemistry at Bristol and then University College, London.

For some time scientists had puzzled over evidence suggesting that there might be a trace of some gas in air that was heavier than nitrogen and did not combine with oxygen. With Lord Rayleigh, Ramsay identified a new gas that made up about 1 per cent of the atmosphere and would not combine with any other element. They christened it argon, after the Greek word for 'inert'. Suspecting that argon was not unique but belonged to a family of gases sharing the same unusual characteristics, from 1895 Ramsay started a painstaking search for other rare gases. He discovered the first – helium – when searching the mineral kingdom for sources of argon. Then, after months spent in preparing 15 litres of argon by distilling it from liquid air, he liquefied it and allowed it to boil. The first fraction contained a new, light gas, which he called neon: the last fractions contained two heavy gases which he christened krypton and xenon, after the Greek for 'hidden' and 'stranger'.

When the German scientist, Friedrich Dorn, finally found the missing member of the rare gas family, radon, it was Ramsay who weighed a tiny quantity and determined its atomic weight. He was knighted in 1902, and received the Nobel Prize for Chemistry two years later. Ramsay's discovery of helium gave him an interest in radioactivity. He carried out his pioneering work on the chemistry of radium with a tiny sample given to him by Marie Curie. In 1903, working with Frederick Soddy, who was to win the Nobel Prize in 1921 for his discovery of isotopes while a lecturer at Glasgow University, Ramsay showed that helium was continually produced by naturally radioactive products. The explanation of their discovery – that the atom could in fact split – took physics into the hazardous nuclear waters of the twentieth century.

One Scot had his head in the clouds, but they were clouds of immense significance to nuclear physics.

SEEING THE SUBATOMIC WORLD

Charles Thomson Rees Wilson (1869–1959) was the son of a sheep farmer from Glencorse outside Edinburgh. His love of clouds, which he had inherited from the wide open landscapes of his earliest childhood, was to lead him in quite unexpected directions. While a researcher in a Cambridge laboratory, after a brilliant student career, Wilson tried to replicate the cloud effects he had watched on the top of Ben Nevis. He observed that the droplets that went to make up a cloud only formed in air containing dust particles. He reasoned that in the absence of dust, clouds must form by condensing about ions in the air: unlike neutral molecules, their electrical charge could act as a nucleus. On learning of the discovery of X-rays and radioactivity, Wilson was able to prove his theory by showing that ion formation, as a result of those radiations, could bring about more intensive cloud formation in the absence of dust.

Inspired by his discovery that X-rays, which charged the dust, greatly speeded up the process of forming water droplets, Wilson showed that charged subatomic particles travelling through supersaturated air left a track in the form of water droplets, in the chamber which he had designed for his experiments. By 1911, his cloud chamber allowed the human eye to see the events of the subatomic world for the first time. It is difficult to overestimate the stimulus to atomic physics of Wilson's elegant and simple cloud chamber: a picture which previously took researchers years to fit together, partially and laboriously, could now be seen in all its beauty and striking detail. Ernest Rutherford described the cloud chamber as 'the most original piece of apparatus in the whole history of science'.

Despite a host of international honours, including the Nobel Prize for Physics in 1927, Wilson remained a modest, unassuming individual, combining patience with intuitive creativity. He retained his fascination with the skies, becoming the first person to investigate cosmic radiation systematically and thus significantly increasing our understanding of thunderstorms. He never lost his love of his native Scotland, holidaying every year in the Highlands or on the island of Arran: some of his experiments were undertaken in a railway tunnel near Peebles. When he retired he came back to live in a small village outside Edinburgh where he roamed the hills and watched the clouds that had provided him with such inspiration.

The wild and immensely old landscape of their native land also inspired Scots to investigate what lay beneath.

CHALLENGING GOD'S TIME

Geology was the fourth career of James Hutton (1726–97). Brought up in the shadow of Arthur's Seat, the extinct volcano that frames much of the Edinburgh skyline, he trained as a doctor, but never practised. While still a student, Hutton and his friend, James Davie, experimented with producing sal ammoniac from Auld Reekie's soot, later basing a profitable chemical business on their discovery. Failing to find employment as a doctor in London, Hutton took up farming in Berwickshire for over a decade. Finally, in 1786, on the advice of his close friend Joseph Black, he sold his business interests, settled in Edinburgh and devoted the rest of his life to geology.

Before Hutton, geology did not really exist as a subject for study. Although sporadic discoveries had been made, no one had put forward a general theory of how the earth might have developed over what we now know to be its 4.5 billion-year history. Scientific enquiry was constrained by the prevailing religious view that God created the Universe about 4000 BC as laid down in the Book of Genesis. Continents emerged from the sea as the waters of the biblical flood retreated, other observable geological phenomena being the result of similar catastrophes. Hutton believed that the present was the key to the earth's past. He noticed that the soil in the fields he farmed was being eroded by weather, but not replaced: there had to be some way of replenishing the soil. His studies convinced him that the earth's surface had evolved over an immense period of time. Some rocks were laid down as sediment and compressed: others were formed of molten material thrust up from deep inside the earth by volcanic action: others were worn down by the action of wind and water.

What was revolutionary about Hutton's gradualist theory was the idea that the forces now slowly operating to effect change had been operating in the past at the same rate and in the same way: 'We find no vestige of a beginning, no prospect of an end.' He published his views in 1785 in *The Theory of the earth* in which he also put forward the modern theory of rainfall. The book received a hostile reception, especially in religious circles, although its impact was lessened by Hutton's dense, almost unreadable, prose style. Despite illness and the limitations of a quill pen, Hutton kept on writing – over 5,000 pages in all – not only on geology, but on the human mind and the philosophy of heat, light and fire. A bachelor cared for by his three sisters, he surrounded himself with like minds at the meetings of the weekly Oyster Club, which he founded with David Hume and Joseph Black.

Five years after his death, his friend John Playfair, Professor of Mathematics at Edinburgh University, published a clear and lucid summary of Hutton's theory, *Illustrations of the Huttonian Theory of the earth*. Now a classic of geological literature, at the time it helped to light the fuse that would rock the religious world. The widespread adoption of the concept of the restless rocks had to wait for the evangelising zeal of two other Scottish geologists.

MELTING ROCK

'To a geologist a rock is a page of the earth's autobiography with a story to unfold.' Sir James Hall (1761–1832), East Lothian laird, amateur geologist and briefly fellow student of Napoleon, decided to put Hutton's view to the test of fire. A visit to a glass factory, where he observed molten glass becoming opaque and crystalline when cooled very slowly, provided him with the inspiration. When he arranged for rock to be melted in a furnace, he discovered that if cooled quickly it would form a glassy solid, but if cooled slowly it would form a crystalline solid. He also demonstrated that if limestone was heated in a closed vessel, it would not decompose, but would melt and cool again to marble. Whereas time has christened Hutton the 'Father of geology', Hall is the 'Father of geochemistry'.

Hall proved Hutton's theory by exposing it to the rigour of laboratory techniques. Surprisingly, Hutton disapproved of the belief that one could not study vast planetary change through small laboratory experiments. Respecting his views, Hall did not publish his findings until after Hutton's death. Having proved the theory, all that remained was to win popular acceptance. Charles Lyell took on the challenge.

THE HAMMER OF THE SCOTS

Sir Charles Lyell (1797–1875) was brought up outside Kirriemuir in Angus, his father being both a botanist, after whom the family of mosses Lyellia is named, and a distinguished translator of Dante's poetry. It was while he was a law student at Oxford that Lyell developed an interest in geology. The landscapes he explored while travelling on the Continent made him think increasingly along the same gradualist lines as Hutton. When he encountered Hutton's *The Theory of the earth* he knew that geology was to be his life work.

In 1829, he published the first volume of his three-volume *Principles of Geology*, the work that finally established Huttonian theory as the basis of geology. Witty, well written and clearly argued, it went into 12 editions in Lyell's lifetime. He was the first person to discuss the age of metamorphic rocks and named the Eocene (dawn of recent), Miocene (less recent) and Pliocene (more recent) geological eras. Lyell's real achievement, however, was in putting the study of the earth on a scientific footing by tackling head on the more conventional scientists of his day and prevailing religious opinion. His success in walking the tightrope of controversy can be measured when in 1848 he was knighted at Balmoral by Queen Victoria.

One of Lyell's earliest converts was the young Charles Darwin, who became a close friend. According to Darwin, 'the greatest merit of the *Principles* was that it altered the whole tone of one's mind, and therefore that, when seeing a thing never seen by Lyell, one yet saw it through his eyes'. In turn, when Darwin first put forward his theory of evolution, Lyell was one of its earliest supporters, although in public he was not prepared to commit himself to the logical conclusion that humans were descended from animals, much to Darwin's disappointment. In *The Antiquity of Man*, published in 1863, Lyell pushed back the time frame for the evolution of man on the evidence of the fossil record, but acknowledged the possibility that humans were the product of a separate, divine creation, exempt from evolutionary theory. Lyell was buried in Westminster Abbey alongside his friend Darwin.

THE TESTIMONY OF THE ROCKS

While Lyell won over minds to geology, Hugh Miller (1802–56) captured the hearts of the people. The son of a sea captain, he preferred roaming the beaches round his home in Cromarty to attending school, his explorations giving him a lifelong passion for geology and fossils. Much of his working life was spent in Edinburgh, as stonemason, writer and editor of *The Witness*, the first newspaper supporting the newly formed Free Church of Scotland. Miller was a giant, both physically and intellectually. A self-taught geologist, he wrote about the history of the earth with such eloquence and imagination that he did much to arouse popular interest in the long distant past. He personified the battle between religion and geology, concluding that the Bible was not intended as a scientific textbook. Tragically, he committed suicide only three years before Darwin published *The Origin of Species* albeit the theory of evolution might have pushed Miller's faith too far.

DISCOVERED BY SCOTS
★ **Fluorescence**: Sir David Brewster (1781–1868). While using the fluorescent mineral fluorspar combined with solutions of quinine and chlorophyll, he discovered what he called 'internal

dispersion', reporting it to a meeting of the Royal Society of Edinburgh in 1833.

★ The universally adopted method of showing the structure of organic molecules with connecting lines indicating the chemical bonds: Alexander Crum Brown (1838–1922). A brilliant polymath with interests in pharmacology, physiology, phonetics, mathematics and crystallography, he was the first candidate to be awarded a Doctorate of Science from London University.

★ The carbon double bond in ethylene, which had important implications for the development of plastics: Alexander Crum Brown (1838–1922).

★ The structure of organic molecules: Archibald Scott Couper (1831–92). Couper developed the framework for understanding the structure by showing that a carbon atom can form chemical bonds with up to four other atoms, and that multiple carbon atoms can join together to create long chains. In 1858, while writing up his findings, he drew the first molecular diagrams in which the atoms were represented by their letter symbols and bonds by straight lines. His Professor at L'Ecole de Medecine in Paris delayed publishing his results as he considered them too radical. The German scientist Kekule was then credited with the discovery that allowed organic chemists to make new molecules leading to major advances in drugs, dyes and cosmetics and to the development of plastics. Couper had a nervous breakdown, retreated to Kirkintilloch and never did any serious chemistry again.

★ The relationship between climate change and the earth's orbit: James Croll (1821–90). A self-taught scientist who at one time worked as a janitor in Edinburgh to allow him access to books, Croll was the first person to advance the theory that some climate changes, which can happen very gradually, could be explained by variations in the earth's position as it orbits round the sun. In *Climate and Time*, he postulated that cosmic influences were responsible for warm and cold ages on a global scale and developed concepts like climate feedback. Following the development of his work by a Serb scientist, the Croll–Milankovitch Theory has again assumed significance in the global warming debate.

★ Limelight: invented by surveyor and politician Thomas Drummond

(1797–1840), born and educated in Edinburgh. A surveyor with the Ordnance Survey in Ireland, he invented the 'Drummond Light', a type of signalling system to improve the accuracy of surveying. One of his lights on a hilltop near Belfast was visible in Donegal, 66 miles away. He later adapted his 'Drummond Light' for use in lighthouses. Drummond is jointly credited with the English chemist Goldsworthy Gurney of developing 'limelight' for use in his lights. Burning a block of lime in a hot hydrogen-oxygen flame resulted in an exceptionally bright luminescent light. Limelight became popular as a spotlight in theatres, despite the real risks of explosion, hence the expression 'in the limelight'.

★ The demonstration that water reaches a maximum density at 39.5°F: Thomas Charles Hope (1766–1844), Professor of Chemistry at Edinburgh. Fellow Scot Lyon Playfair and James Joule later set the figure more accurately. An immensely popular teacher, Hope attracted audiences of up to 500, conducting extra-mural classes for ladies which became the fashionable place to be seen.

★ Strontium: Sir Thomas Charles Hope (1766–1844) identified many of the characteristics of the element strontium, although it was left to Sir Humphrey Davy to extract it from the mineral, strontianite.

★ Determination of the mean level of the sea: James Jardine (1776–1858), a civil engineer from Dumfries, who calculated it from observations on the Tay estuary.

★ The demonstration that surfaces with different colours and textures do not radiate heat equally even when at the same temperature: Fife-born Sir John Leslie (1766–1832) devised the Leslie cube and the differential thermometer. He treated the four sides of the cube differently to show that the temperature of the cube varied according to which side was turned towards a source of heat. His differential thermometer, a siphon of liquid enclosed between two bulbs, allowed temperature differences to be measured with unprecedented accuracy.

★ The explanation of capillary action, the force that causes a liquid to rise within a narrow tube: Sir John Leslie (1766–1832). Leslie made this discovery in 1805, the year of his appointment to the Chair of Mathematics at Edinburgh University. This was the occasion of a cause célèbre when local ministers opposed the appointment, accusing Leslie of atheism on the basis of his support for David Hume's view of causality.

★ The proof that diamonds were simply carbon: Sir George Mackenzie (1780–1848). Following his experiment of 1800, he presented a paper *On the Combustion of Diamonds* to the Royal Society of Edinburgh.

★ The observation that the light emitted by metals heated in a flame gives distinctive lines in the spectra, the basis of spectroscopy: Thomas Melvil (1726–53), who observed the effect a year before his early death.

★ The physical chemistry of polymerisation: Sir Harry Melville (1908–2000) a leading authority on the science of polymers. He developed ways of measuring how fast the individual building blocks in giant molecules join on to the end of growing chains, starting work on materials like polystyrene and polyethylene while at Aberdeen University.

★ The theory of streamline flow: William Rankine (1820–72). Rankine's mathematical model of fluid flow is still used in engineering calculations.

★ The first experimental observation of what became known as the Doppler effect: John Scott Russell (1808–82). The Scottish engineer based his observation on the sounds made by fast-moving trains whose sound rose in pitch as they came towards him and fell after they passed.

★ The concept of isotopes and experimental proof of their existence: Frederick Soddy (1877–1956). Although English, Soddy conducted the work, which later won him a Nobel Prize, while a lecturer at Glasgow University.

★ The lowering of the freezing point of water by pressure, the principle that allows skaters to slide easily over the ice: James Thomson (1822–92). The brother of Lord Kelvin, Thomson developed improved water-wheels and steamboat paddles before becoming Professor of Civil Engineering at Glasgow University in 1873.

★ The law of equipartition of kinetic energy among the molecules of a gas: John Waterston (1811–84). In 1843, while a naval instructor of East India Company cadets in Bombay, Waterston published *Thoughts on the Mental Functions*. This included a partial statement of the equipartition theorem, showing that all the molecules in a gas at equilibrium have the same energy regardless of size. Given the book's misleading title, no scientist read it and Waterston's paper on the subject to the Royal Society was also rejected. By the time of its rediscovery in 1891, others had been credited with the theorem.

SCOTTISH SCIENTISTS' NAMES LIVE ON

★ Appleton Layer, the layer in the atmosphere that reflects short wave radio waves: Yorkshireman Sir Edward Appleton, Principal of Edinburgh University from 1949–65.

★ Beilby Layer, the thin layer of atoms responsible for the shine of polished surfaces: Sir George Thomas Beilby (1850–1924). His theory helped to explain the hardening of metals under cold working.

★ Brewster's Law governing the polarisation of reflected light: Sir David Brewster (1781–1868).

★ Brownian motion, the continuous random motion of particles in a liquid when bombarded by atoms and molecules: Robert Brown (1773–1858).

★ Crum Brown's rule, determining the way in which groups attach to a benzene ring: Alexander Crum Brown (1838–1922).

★ Graham's Law of the diffusion of gases: Thomas Graham (1805–69).

★ Higgs Boson particle: postulated by Peter Higgs (1929–), Professor Emeritus of Theoretical Physics at Edinburgh University. If found, the particle would complete the standard model of particle physics. The search continues . . .

★ The Kerr effect concerning the rotation of the polarisation of light by an electric field widely used in opto-electronics: John Kerr (1824–1907).

★ Maxwell's Demon: James Clerk Maxwell (1831–79). To illustrate the relationship between information and entropy, a foundation of information theory, Maxwell envisaged an imp who separated fast-moving from slow-moving molecules, thus extracting energy in apparent contradiction of the second law of thermodynamics. To perform this task, however, the Demon requires information which can only be gained by interacting with the molecules, and so the trick will not work.

★ Rankine cycle, a theoretical cycle corresponding closely to the actual operation of a steam engine: William Rankine (1820–72). Throughout his career, Rankine's goal was to make theoretical developments in thermodynamics accessible to practising engineers.

INSTRUMENTAL TO SCOTTISH SCIENCE

★ The dioptric lens formed of concentric prisms of glass: Sir David Brewster (1781–1868). Perfected by the Frenchman, Augustin Fresnel, it was widely used in lighthouses.

★ The Coddington lens used in simple microscopes: Sir David Brewster (1781–1868). It is named after Henry Coddington, a Cambridge tutor who publicised its use in 1829, nine years after its invention by Brewster.

★ The scintillation counter for measuring radioactivity: Sir Samuel Curran (1912–98). He also invented the pulse-amplifier, a counter used to measure the energy of many types of radiation.

★ The continuous recording pendulum seismograph, the first effective means of scientifically recording earthquakes: Sir James Ewing (1855–1935). Ewing developed the seismograph with John Milne and Thomas Gray while working at the Imperial College of Engineering in Tokyo.

★ The Kelvin ampere balance: an apparatus for the absolute measurement of currents by measuring the force produced by the current's magnetic field developed by William Thomson, Lord Kelvin (1824–1907).

★ The electrostatic voltmeter permitting the measurement of AC or DC voltages without the use of any current: William Thomson, Lord Kelvin (1824–1907).

★ The Nicol prism consisting of two prisms glued together to produce polarised light: William Nicol (1768–1851). Nicol discovered the effect in 1828 by sticking two pieces of Iceland spar crystal together. His prism was the standard means of polarising light until recent times: polarised sunglasses operate on the same principle.

★ The Stevenson screen: still the standard housing for weather station thermometers designed by the author Robert Louis Stevenson's father, Thomas Stevenson (1818–87).

★ The Thomson tide prediction machine: William Thomson, Lord Kelvin (1824–1907). Using it, a tidal curve at a port for a year could be drawn in four hours allowing the production of accurate tide tables.

SCOTTISH FIRSTS

★ **The Thomson binnacle:** William Thomson, Lord Kelvin (1824–1907). Patented in 1876, the binnacle was set about with adjustable magnets to counter permanent magnetism, and with balls of soft iron to counter the induced magnetism of iron ships depending on the ship's orientation. His invention, the model for well-designed binnacles ever since, also reduced significantly the swing of the compass in rolling seas.

★ **The bi-metal thermostat:** Andrew Ure (1778–1857). A doctor and vociferous advocate of free trade, Ure patented his device in 1830 to regulate the temperature in cotton mills, which needed a consistent temperature to produce a uniform product.

★ **Philosopher's bubbles or beads used to measure the specific gravity of liquids:** Alexander Wilson (1714–86). Their main use was in checking the alcohol content of spirits to assess the excise duty due.

MEN OF MATHEMATICS

★ **The first textbook in English on probability:** John Arbuthnot (1667–1735). A noted wit and physician to Queen Anne, whose deathbed he attended, he published a paper in 1710, discussing the slight excess of male births over female births. This paper may be the first application of probability to social statistics, albeit he attributed the sex ratio at birth to divine providence, rather than chance.

★ **Foundations of modern algebra:** Duncan Gregory (1813–44). The Edinburgh-born great-great-grandson of James Gregory spent most of his short career at Trinity College, Cambridge, where he became first editor of the *Cambridge Mathematical Journal*. He produced one of the first definitions of modern algebra, defining it as the study of the combinations defined by the laws of operation to which they were subject. He was a major influence on George Boole on whose algebra much of modern computing depends.

★ **The Ivory theory of the gravitational field of ellipsoids:** Sir James Ivory (1765–1842), mathematician, astronomer and son of a Dundee watchmaker. His other work included the shape of self-gravitating, rotating fluid bodies, the orbits of comets and atmospheric refraction. A difficult character, he fell out with most of the scientific establishment, although this did not prevent him being knighted for his contribution to science.

★ **Maclaurin's theorem, a key result in mathematical analysis:** Colin Maclaurin (1698–1746). He derived it while producing the first systematic exposition of Newton's mathematics, having completed a thesis on the subject at Glasgow University aged only 14. Newton personally recommended him for the Chair of Mathematics at Edinburgh University, even volunteering to pay part of his salary. It says much for Newton's faith in Maclaurin, who had got into difficulties with his previous employer, Aberdeen University, when he absented himself for two years without permission to accompany Lord Polwarth on a Grand Tour of Europe. In 1745, Maclaurin undertook a more dramatic task, organising the city's defences against Bonnie Prince Charlie's Jacobite army.

★ **Rules for establishing the sections of prisms, cylinders and cylindroids:** Peter Nicholson (1765–1844). An excellent teacher, Nicholson taught mathematics at Glasgow University to many future leading Victorian engineers. His work on sections was used in designing bridges with skewed arches. He assisted Richard Trevithick in drawing up his patent application for the high pressure steam engine. As an architect and future father-in-law of Alexander 'Greek' Thomson, he designed Glasgow's elegant Carlton Place and part of the Clyde embankment, a timber footbridge across the Clyde, and the town plan for Ardrossan, as well as being an influential writer on classical architecture.

★ **Compilation of 15 and 26 place logarithmic, trigonometric and astronomical tables:** Edward Sang (1805–90). Admired for their superb accuracy, the tables, which included the logarithms of all numbers between 100,000 and 200,000 to 15 places, took 40 years to compile and fill 47 manuscript volumes. Sang was employed by the Sultan to establish engineering schools and plan railways in Constantinople, where he gained fame by predicting the solar eclipse of 1847. He was also a founder member of the Society of Actuaries.

★ **The Stirling Theorem:** James Stirling (1692–1770). Born near Stirling, his strong support for the Jacobite cause lost him the right to graduate, as he refused to take the matriculation oath. It also lost him the appointment to the Chair of Mathematics at Edinburgh University, as successor to Colin Maclaurin. In 1730, five years before becoming manager of the Leadhills mines, he published his work, which included Stirling's theorem, an approximation for 'n' factorial.

★ The topological classification of knots: Peter Guthrie Tait (1831–1901). Ever since their days at Edinburgh Academy, Tait and James Clerk Maxwell were close friends and gentle rivals, despite Tait's beating Maxwell in 1859 for the Chair at Edinburgh University. He collaborated with William Thomson, Lord Kelvin, on a widely used physics textbook known by students as *T. & T.* Becoming interested in smoke rings, Tait developed the erroneous idea that atoms might be vortices in the ether: a similar concept, however, applied to subatomic particles, is the basis of modern string theory. Drawn into the study of knots in order to classify the possible forms a ring could take, he had an uncanny ability to deduce which knots were in fact equivalent without being able fully to codify the method he used. He also computed the mathematics to improve the golfer's swing.

★ The theory of determinants: Sir Thomas Muir (1844–1934). Lord Kelvin persuaded him to abandon Greek for mathematics at Glasgow University. After teaching mathematics and science at Glasgow High School for nearly 20 years he was appointed Superintendent General of Education to the Cape Colonies, South Africa. In 1882, he published his Treatise on the *Theory of Determinants*, thereafter making his lifework a five-volume *History of Determinants*. At his death, he was working on Volume 6, taking the history up to 1940; had he lived to achieve this, he would have been at least 94 years old.

4

The Minister who Blew Hot Air and the Black Hole: Engineering Solutions

'The life and soul of science is its practical application.' In these words, William Thomson, Lord Kelvin not only summed up his own life as physicist, engineer and inventor, but also described that remarkable synergy between knowledge and practicality that characterised Scottish engineering from the late eighteenth century. In a small country with a love of learning, it was relatively easy for scientists and merchants to swap ideas over a bowl of Glasgow punch, or for teachers to apply their minds to the problems of shipbuilders. The interaction between academic and practitioner bore remarkable fruit.

Scotland's engineers came from surprisingly varied backgrounds: Sir William Fairbairn, the first professional structural engineer, was the son of a farm servant; the young James Nasmyth moved in the artistic circles of the capital; John Scott Russell was a son of the manse. In the centuries before the Industrial Revolution, engineers were purely practical men, devising practical solutions to practical problems. James Smith of Deanston's interest in draining his land inspired him to invent the subsoil plough. Michael Menzies who invented, and Andrew Meikle who perfected, the threshing machine were respectively blacksmith and millwright in their local farming communities. The first generation of professional engineers could fall back on hands-on skills learned from their fathers, those country millwrights and blacksmiths.

GUNS FROM IRON

It was Yorkshireman John Roebuck (1718–94) who set Scotland on the track of using its natural resources to build its engineering future. After training as a doctor in Edinburgh, where he became friendly with Joseph Black and David Hume, Roebuck briefly set up as a GP in Birmingham before being diverted into running a scientific laboratory for local industry. Here he devised the lead-chamber process for making sulphuric acid, used at the time in dilute form as a bleaching agent.

Missing the intellectual stimulus of his friends in the north, Roeback moved back to Edinburgh, setting up a plant in Prestonpans in 1749 to exploit his highly successful process. Unfortunately, he had omitted to take out a patent and his profits dwindled as competitors latched on to his methods. Although moving into making pottery at Prestonpans, he was always on the lookout for another winner. He saw his opportunity when he interested a local landowner, William Cadell of Cockenzie, to invest in a process he was developing for smelting iron with coal. Before Roebuck, iron was smelted in negligible quantities using methods little changed from the Iron Age. Through his own ingenuity and his contacts from his student days with chemists like Cullen and Black, Roebuck devised a means of smelting using coal, a much more efficient and cheaper fuel than the traditional charcoal. This time, Roebuck took care to patent the process when he perfected it in 1762.

Freed from their timber-devouring dependency, iron smelters no longer had to be located in remote Highland glens. The pair looked for a suitable site to set up a foundry, which they found on the river Carron outside Falkirk with plentiful supplies of coal and iron nearby. Importing skilled workers from England, in 1760 the Carron Iron Works started producing iron in quantity. From 1765, it ran a regular goods service between Grangemouth and London, making the Carron Line – its ships immediately recognisable by the cannonball on their mainmasts – possibly the world's oldest shipping line.

Roebuck's next venture led to disaster. In order to secure supplies of coal he bought mines at Bo'ness from the Duke of Hamilton. Drainage was a problem and the mines regularly flooded. Introduced to James Watt by Joseph Black, Roebuck backed Watt's steam engine in the hope that an efficient pump would solve his problems. Sadly the mines were swamped before Watt's experimental engine, which Carron were building, could be made to work. Hit by a trade slump, by 1773 Roebuck was bankrupt and had to sell up. Among his assets, as yet of negligible value, was a two-thirds share of Watt's patent, snapped up by a mutual friend, Mathew Boulton of Birmingham.

The Carron Company survived and grew to become the world's largest foundry. The foundation of its success was the carronade, a light naval cannon, which required fewer men and could fire faster than the weapons of the time. The carronade became the Royal Navy's weapon of choice in the early nineteenth century, even gracing the decks of Nelson's HMS *Victory*. In the twentieth century, Carron switched to making Britain's traditional red telephone and pillar boxes, before switching again to make stainless steel kitchen sinks.

The raw materials of engineering – ample seams of iron, coal and water to drive machinery – helped Scotland win the lead in the Industrial Revolution. From 1760, the speed and scale of economic and social transformation into an industrial nation was unparalleled in Europe. It took ingenuity to turn these resources into suitable forms for the hungry engineering workshops; to mine the coal, smelt the iron and power the furnaces. The Scots responded to the call. One of Roebuck's assets was a mine with a rich band of ironstone, which in the nineteenth century supported a flourishing iron works once another Scot had tackled the problem of how to smelt it.

MEN OF IRON – HEARTS OF STEEL

Born in Dalkeith, David Mushet (1772–1847) started out as an accountant in the Coatbridge Iron Works, ending up as one of the greatest metallurgists of his day. Taking a break from his ledger he started to experiment with the processes involved in making iron and steel. In 1800, he discovered a way of making effective use of the local black band ironstone in smelting. This paved the way for the great iron and steel works around Airdrie, Coatbridge and Motherwell, once initial resistance from local iron masters to his methods had been overcome. Around the same time, he invented a direct process for making steel from bar iron.

He later acquired interests in iron founding in the Forest of Dean in Gloucestershire, where his son Robert Mushet (1811–91) added the vital ingredient to Bessemer steel. In 1859 Henry Bessemer patented his 'basic process', which allowed steel to be mass-produced cheaply. The poor quality of the steel, however, led to the method being dismissed as a flash in the pan or as *The Times* more elegantly put it, as a 'brilliant meteor that had flashed across the metallurgical horizon'. In 1856, Robert Mushet patented the use of a vital ingredient – spiegeleisen – a manganese alloy which drew off the excess oxygen from the melt which had resulted in the steel cracking. To demonstrate the strength of cast steel, Mushet produced the first steel rail, laid at Derby railway station in 1857.

Since Bessemer had separately patented his 'basic process', Mushet failed to profit from his vital added ingredient: the millionaire Bessemer only grudgingly admitted his help when Mushet's daughter appealed to him for financial assistance for her father in his old age. Mushet fared rather better with his second invention, Robert Mushet's Special Steel or R.M.S. as it became known. Disillusioned with patents he preferred to keep the process of making self-hardened tool steel secret, key stages being carried out under the direct supervision of himself or his sons. R.M.S was tungsten steel, the first real tool steel – tougher, able to cut harder metals faster and giving tools five or six times the lifespan of cast steel.

The discovery of the hot blast by Glaswegian James Beaumont Neilson (1792–1865) brought West Central Scotland centre stage as provider of the raw materials of engineering. The local iron industry, by now flourishing thanks to the efforts of Mushet Senior and other pioneers, paid little heed to fuel efficiency, the environment or their workers' health. The flames and smoke that belched from the furnaces, the sight of which caused James Nasmyth to despair that 'Vulcan had driven out Ceres', were due to several erroneous beliefs. Although the ironmasters were aware that 90 per cent of the coke used to fuel the furnaces was wasted, they believed that leaving the mouth of the furnace open and blasting with cold air made better quality iron.

In 1827, Neilson discovered that by heating air before injecting it into the blast furnace, coal, rather than coke, could be used and the amount of coal needed to make a ton of iron could be quartered. Only after a bitter and expensive struggle did Neilson beat off a challenge to his patents from a local ironmaster quick to see the advantages of Neilson's method, but reluctant to pay to use it. By 1860, 90 per cent of British iron was made using Neilson's hot blast.

Raw materials alone were not enough to fuel the Industrial Revolution: efficient means of transporting people and goods had to be in place. Although the new industrialists could now call on professional architects to build them elegant country houses, in order to afford the lifestyle of a gentleman, they first needed roads that were more than cart tracks, bridges that crossed rivers at the nearest point, canals that carried their goods across country and harbours to provide safe anchor for their ships. Spanning the age from horse to iron horse, two Scots imposed the disciplines of science on the craft of building to create a new profession, civil engineering. John Rennie (1761–1821) built three London bridges – Waterloo, Southwark and London Bridge – as well as Glasgow docks and the Kennet and Avon canal. The wide-ranging portfolio of Thomas Telford (1757–1834) won him recognition as the first professional civil engineer.

THE FIRST CIVIL ENGINEER

A shepherd's son from Eskdale in Dumfriesshire, Telford served his apprenticeship as a stonemason before packing his bags for the bright lights of the big city in 1780. He quickly found work building the grand frontages of Edinburgh's New Town, but soon the even brighter lights of London beckoned. Telford cut his teeth as a road engineer when Surveyor of Public Works in Shropshire, the English county, which has since honoured his name in Telford New Town. He then tackled the huge logistical challenge of opening up the Highlands, from 1803 directing the construction of roads, bridges and even churches in an effort to bring the Highlands closer to the Central Belt and improve its economy. Over 18 years he supervised the building of 1,117 bridges and 920 miles of new road. His tightly specified contracts to his 120 contractors would not be unfamiliar to today's civil engineers. Telford's master plan for the Highlands included building the Caledonian Canal between Inverness and Fort William, to save shipping the long and perilous journey round the north of Scotland and through the stormy Pentland Firth.

Telford was innovative as well as rigorous, the outcome being described as 'the Rolls Royce' of roads. He raised the foundations of his roads in the centre to drain off water and analysed everything from the thickness of the stones to the density of expected road traffic to ensure a smooth journey. His chosen route for the new London–Holyhead road, the main route for Ireland, has no slope more than one in twenty, and for alignment and gradient has not yet been surpassed. His achievements were crowned by his finest suspension bridge, over the Menai Straits, which, when built in 1826, was the longest in the world.

Canals were the late eighteenth-century's motorway network and here too Telford excelled. In 1793, he was appointed engineer for the Ellesmere Canal Company, being presented with the almost insurmountable problems of carrying a canal over two deep river valleys. His supreme achievement as a canal engineer was the Pontcysyllte Aqueduct, the longest and highest in Britain, its tongue-twister of a name simply meaning 'connecting bridge'. He carried the canal in a watertight, cast-iron trough supported by 18 piers, the first use of cast-iron in an aqueduct.

As a consultant engineer, Telford's clients ranged from the King of Sweden, who engaged him to plan the Gota Canal, to some of the first railway companies who sought his advice on their proposed routes. As the first civil engineering professional, he was committed to the proper surveying and planning of projects before work commenced and to contractual agreements written in clear, unambiguous English. His approach raised the standards operated by building contractors and attracted able, ambitious young men who, with the credentials of 'Telford trained', became the master engineers of the coming railway age. In 1818, he was a founder member and the first President of the Institution of Civil Engineering.

A DECENT HEAD OF STEAM

Another Scot paralleled Telford's career not only by building bridges over the same waters, this time for the new railways, but by putting structural engineering on the same footing as civil engineering. The life of Sir William Fairbairn (1789–1874) bridged the span from millwright to professional engineer. Brought up in a Kelso farming family, he moved to Manchester as a young man to set up in business as a millwright to the burgeoning cotton industry. He greatly improved the system of driving textile mills by introducing a widely adopted, high-speed transmission system.

His next move was to London to set up a small shipyard in Millwall where he built his first iron steamship, the 68-ft *Lord Dundas*, commissioned in an attempt to beat off competition from improved coach services and the emerging threat from rail. In 1838, Fairbairn began his famous experiments on the use of cast and wrought iron, the first person to undertake a scientific investigation of the properties of metal as a building material. He wrote, 'These experiments embrace almost every known mechanical property of iron and the knowledge thus obtained has furnished data for the construction of ships and other structures.'

This brought him to the attention of Robert Stephenson, the railway engineer, who was in the process of designing the Britannia railway bridge over the Menai Straits in Wales. Fairbairn had already advised Stephenson's father, George, on the design of boilers for his steam locomotives. Theoretical knowledge of the properties of iron as a building material was critical as the success of the railways depended as much on the civil and structural engineering of the route as on the design of the locomotives. The classic set of experiments conducted by Stephenson and Fairbairn to determine the most suitable form of girder for the Britannia Bridge laid the foundations of structural engineering as a scientific discipline.

Their tubular design for the bridge, the forerunner of the box girder, posed another problem. To roll the sections and girders required was beyond the capabilities of the iron masters and the tubes had, therefore, to be made up of small plates and angles riveted together. Fairbairn designed the first riveting machine for metal to handle the sheer volume of work. Although the Britannia Bridge had almost twice as long a span as any bridge previously built, Fairbairn's design of lattice wrought-iron girders was successful, remaining the most popular form of bridge construction until the advent of steel.

Fairbairn's main contribution to the age of steam was his Lancashire boiler, introduced in the mid-1840s and proving the most popular boiler of its day. It met the need for boilers that could withstand high pressures of steam sought by eager manufacturers anxious to apply steam in ever more ambitious ways. With their twin flues and furnaces firing alternately, Fairbairn's boilers were smaller, safer and cheaper, and could get up a much better head of steam than the previous Cornish models.

In his presidential address to the British Association at Manchester in 1861, Fairbairn looked back to when he 'first entered this city, the whole of the machinery was executed by hand . . . Now everything is done by machine tools with a degree of accuracy which the unaided hand could never accomplish.' The man who first made this possible was the same man who provided a steam pump to Thomas Telford when building London's St Katherine's Dock. Telford ordered the pump, driven by two 80 hp engines, from 'my friend, Mr James Watt, and his able and ingenious assistant Mr Murdoch'. Many of the achievements of the nineteenth century – in industry, transport or the acquisition of an Empire – might not have been possible if one man had not sat down to repair a model engine.

FIRE ENGINES

Brought up in Greenock, James Watt (1736–1819) did not have an easy childhood. His mother died when he was in his teens; his four brothers and sisters died young and his father's business all but failed. Watt went south to seek his fortune, but returned after serving only one year of his apprenticeship to a London instrument maker, his health unable to stand working until nine at night. He tried to establish himself as an instrument maker in Glasgow, but he fell foul of the city authorities because his apprenticeship was not complete. Eventually he was appointed instrument maker to Glasgow University, which was outside the control of the city authorities. Here he met Joseph Black and learned of his work on latent heat. After a London instrument maker had failed to mend the university's model of a Newcomen engine, widely used to pump water out of flooded mines, they gave it to Watt to fix, thereby also giving him a unique opportunity to study how it worked and to appreciate its inefficiency and limitations.

One Sunday in 1765, Watt was thinking about the problem as he took a stroll in Glasgow Green when the idea came to him as to how to improve the engine. His solution was the introduction of a separate condenser, a chamber into which the steam could be led and which could be kept cool while the first chamber or cylinder was kept permanently hot. In this way the two processes were not forced to cancel each other out. In 1769, he patented the Watt steam engine that was to power the Industrial Revolution.

Over the next few years Watt made many improvements to his design, going into partnership in 1774 with Matthew Boulton, a wealthy Birmingham businessman, to manufacture steam engines for sale. By 1790, the Watt engine had replaced the Newcomen engine entirely and ten years later, 500 were at work in England. The engine proved so effective that many people give Watt sole credit for its invention arguing that the Newcomen engine was essentially little more than a pump.

Watt's fertile mind powered more than just an efficient engine. In 1784, he used steam pipes to heat his office, reinventing central heating, a luxury forgotten since Roman times. He or his assistant William Murdoch devised mechanical attachments to his engine that converted the up and down movement of a piston into the rotary motion of a wheel. This versatility allowed iron founders to operate bellows and textile manufacturers to drive machinery. He produced the first germ of automation with his invention of the centrifugal governor, which automatically controlled the engine's speed.

Watt has many other claims to fame. He came up with the concept of horse power as a marketing device for his 'fire engines', to demonstrate to mill and mine owners the power of his engine against that of the horse. He invented the revolution counter; was one of the first people to use a slide rule; developed the principle of the gasometer; proposed the screw propeller over 60 years before it came into use; and was even the first person to reverse a marine engine. Sir Humphrey Davy compared him to Archimedes, while Sir Walter Scott described him as:

> this potent commander of the elements, this abridger of time and space, this magician, whose cloudy machinery has produced a change in the world the effects of which, extraordinary as they are, are perhaps only now beginning to be felt.

Watt himself more prosaically boasted: 'My inventions, at present or lately, give employment to the best part of a million people.'

The consequences of Watt's invention were incalculable. He

provided the prime mover for the Industrial Revolution. An English mine manager, John Blenkinsop, put a Watt engine on wheels to allow coal to be carried greater distances. George Stephenson took the idea a stage further and the steam locomotive was born. Henry Bell's and Robert Napier's marine steam engines brought shipbuilding to the Clyde and carried the people and products of Scotland round the world. No longer having to be tied to a source of water for power, factories moved into city centres, housing ever larger and more sophisticated steam-powered machines.

Watt's perfection of the steam engine spawned generations of engines, designed for different applications and power sources. Scottish engineers contributed the Z-crank engine, the two-stroke engine, the oscillating engine, the steeple engine, the Bell-crank engine, the marine compound engine and the triple expansion engine. The fuel efficient, heated air engine came from a more surprising source, a country manse.

HOT AIR BETWEEN SERMONS

Robert Stirling (1790–1878) completed his hot air engine shortly after joining his parish in Galston, Ayrshire, aged 26. Concern for his parishioners may have been the reason for a minister to design an engine as, in the days before steel, steam engines regularly exploded with devastating results. The Stirling engine simply stopped, rather than exploded, if pressure became too high. He moved his prototype from the manse to a workshop owned by his friend Thomas Morton, who shared Stirling's fascination with new ideas and went on to invent a new carpet loom for his weaving business.

The Stirling engine was the first to incorporate the all important 'regenerator', a device which took up heat from the hot air as it flowed one way and gave the heat back to cool air passing in the other direction. Aptly described as a 'heat sponge', it greatly increased the engine's fuel efficiency. Stirling worked with his brother James to improve his engine, the use of two displacers and pressurised air allowing the engine to cope with greater quantities of heat. The brothers converted a steam-powered beam engine at the Dundee Foundry Company, where James worked, into a Stirling engine. Unfortunately, the engine burned out its cylinder bottom every year and in 1847 it was converted back to steam. While Robert Stirling remained a parish minister all his days, four of his children became railway engineers. The most distinguished was Patrick Stirling, who put Doncaster and Kilmarnock on the map as railway engineering towns. His famous 4-2-2s with their 8-ft single driving wheels ran some of the world's fastest passenger trains in the 1870s, including the *Flying Scotsman*.

Stirling engines were originally used for low power, fixed load duties, such as pumping water, but over the years their uses widened to include applications as different as domestic portable fans and submarines. Their relative slowness to warm up and to change power output means that they have as yet never become a mass-market engine. Aware of their thermal efficiency, researchers throughout the world are intensifying their efforts to design a Stirling engine that could replace some of the gas guzzlers of the twentieth century. A Scotsman also pioneered a significant development in those guzzlers.

PUTTING THE ENGINE IN THE LAWNMOWER

Brought up and educated in Glasgow, Sir Dugald Clerk (1854–1932) was a keen follower of European developments in engine design. Particularly impressed by the Otto four-stroke engine, he reckoned that it should be possible to produce an engine with a power stroke for every second stroke. Applying the principles of thermodynamics, Clerk built the first two-stroke engine in 1879, patenting an improved version two years later. The Clerk Cycle engine used two equal-sized cylinders. One cylinder sucked in and compressed the fuel, feeding it to a reservoir from which it passed to the power cylinder. When the piston in the power cylinder began its outward travel, the fuel was admitted through a slide valve. On its inward stroke, the power piston exhausted the spent gas through a poppet-valve.

Glasgow University was one of the first to install a Clerk engine, coupled to a Siemens dynamo. Lord Kelvin used the electricity it produced to light his house, claiming this as a world first. Clerk's understanding of Kelvin's statement of the second law of thermodynamics underpinned his engine. In old age, Clerk, who had become Director of Research at the Admiralty during the First World

War, met a younger man who cast doubts on the validity of Kelvin's law. He fended off his critic by pointing out, 'Why man, I've made my living off it.' Clerk's two-stroke principle lay behind many twentieth-century petrol engines from the motorcycle and the jet-ski to the lawnmower and the strimmer.

'His benevolent countenance and his tall but bent figure made an impression on my mind that I can never forget. It was even something to have seen for a few seconds so truly great and noble a man.' The man was James Watt, the child who never forgot him was James Nasmyth (1808–90), inventor of the steam hammer, which ushered in a new phase of the Industrial Revolution.

USING A HAMMER TO CRACK AN EGG

The son of the Scottish portrait painter, Alexander Nasmyth applied his creativity to the drawing board, rather than the canvas. As a child, he was lucky in his friends: not only did his father share his inventive interests, but James was able to spend Saturdays visiting a chemical laboratory or an iron foundry run by the fathers of his school friends. By the age of fifteen he was making and selling model steam engines, even building a steam carriage capable of travelling a mile with eight passengers. Attracted by the pull of London, Nasmyth served his apprenticeship under Henry Maudslay, the machine tool pioneer, before returning in 1834 to his native city to work as an engineer.

Deciding that his interests lay in industrial engineering, an activity on which genteel Edinburgh had largely turned its back, Nasmyth moved to Manchester, leasing the part of an old cotton mill until the ever increasing weight of his machinery caused its floor to give way. Opening the Bridgewater Foundry in 1836, he combined running a flourishing engineering business with devising and improving machines and machine tools. He invented the safety foundry ladle, which, by being able to be managed by one rather than twelve men, reduced dramatically the risk of accidents from spilling molten metal. His catalogue of machinery innovations was extensive – a flexible drive shaft, the Nasmyth shaper for planing small surfaces, a nut-milling machine, a machine for cutting key grooves, self-adjusting bearings, steam rams, hydraulic presses and a portable hand drill.

In 1839, Nasmyth invented the piece of equipment which proved to be the driving force behind the development of heavy engineering – the steam hammer. He had received a request from Isambard Kingdom Brunel, the railway and shipbuilding entrepreneur, to forge a drive shaft to turn the huge paddle wheels of Brunel's projected iron ship, the SS *Great Britain*. Brunel had scoured the country in vain for a forge hammer powerful enough to make the 30-inch diameter shaft. Nasmyth came up with the steam hammer, a machine that could be controlled and adjusted so precisely that it could break an eggshell in a wineglass without breaking the glass. When the contract came to nothing, owing to Brunel having opted for screw propellers rather than paddle wheels for his ship, Nasmyth filed away his drawings in a drawer. One day when giving a factory tour to Mr Schneider of the Le Creusot Iron Works, over from France to purchase tools, an employee showed him the design. Schneider copied the idea and built the first steam hammer. When Nasmyth saw the Le Creusot hammer in 1840 and discovered that it was built to his own design, he hastened to build and patent his invention.

Nasmyth completed the circle of the Industrial Revolution by making it possible for machines to make machines. With its ability to apply tremendous force under controlled conditions, the steam hammer found applications throughout heavy industry. As large forgings could now be built in one piece, quality improved while production costs were slashed by over 50 per cent. The hammer could be used to to hammer a nail or forge the iron plates for warships. In 1845, Nasmyth applied the principles behind his steam hammer to produce the pile-driver, used in constructing buildings, bridges, quays and harbours from Devonport's naval dockyards to the High Level Bridge in Newcastle.

In 1856, aged only 48, Nasmyth decided, 'I have now enough of this world's goods: let younger men have their chance.' In his retirement he created the world's first space art. In *The Moon*, a large and lavishly illustrated volume that he produced with James Carpenter in 1874, the plates were reproductions of photographs of plaster models of portions of the lunar surface, seen both telescopically from earth and as they would appear to an observer on the moon.

The building of Brunel's final ship, the SS *Great Eastern*, by far the world's largest ship of the time, captured the popular imagination, vying with the Forth Rail Bridge for the title of the greatest engineering feat of the nineteenth century. Its builder was John Scott Russell, (1808–82) who has many claims to engineering greatness as well as elevating ship design into naval architecture.

MAKING WAVES

Brought up in Parkhead, then a weaving village outside Glasgow, Russell was interested in steam power from his earliest days, constructing a model steam coach using the family kettle as a boiler. He attended Glasgow University from the age of 13, intending to follow in his father's footsteps as a parish minister. A change of heart brought him to Edinburgh to teach mathematics and embark on his first engineering venture, the design of a steam carriage. With the backing of a group of Edinburgh businessmen, he established his first route between Glasgow and Paisley. His career as a coach proprietor came to a dramatic end in 1834, when one of his coaches, probably sabotaged by a competitor, crashed leaving four people dead and giving him the somewhat dubious claim as the cause of the first fatal automobile accident.

By this time Russell's interests were turning to shipbuilding and in particular to the little studied subject of hydrodynamics. He built three experimental wave-line vessels for the Union Canal Company. In 1834, as he was walking on the towpath, a boat stopped suddenly causing a single wave to travel along the canal. Immediately, Russell set off on horseback pursuing the solitary wave for several miles. Although he realised that these solitary waves, which he called solitons, were significant in some way and conducted experiments on them, they remained a scientific curiosity until the 1870s when the mathematics explaining this phenomenon was worked out. The soliton remained a minor footnote in Russell's distinguished career until its fundamental role was discovered in the development of radar and opto-electronics.

Russell used his observations to redesign the shape of ships' bows. His subsequent studies of the design of hulls in relation to the water that they travelled through gave shipbuilders their first scientific guide to the pursuit of speed. In 1838, Russell himself entered the shipbuilding industry as manager of a Greenock yard where he produced his first wave-line designs for ships destined for open waters. In 1844, he moved south to take up a completely new career as a journalist on the *Railway Chronicle*, later becoming Railway Editor on Charles Dickens' newspaper, the *Daily News*. In 1847, he was enticed back to the dockside by an offer from a new shipbuilding firm who had taken over Sir William Fairbairn's yard at Millwall. Over the next few years he combined ship design, including the first longitudinal bracing on iron ships, with helping to plan and organise the first World Fair, the Great Exhibition of 1851.

In 1852, Russell entered discussions with Isambard Kingdom Brunel to build the world's largest steamship. Brunel's dream ship was staggering in both scale and complexity, but Russell painstakingly drew and redrew the designs for this mammoth enterprise. After many vicissitudes, including near bankruptcy and an increasingly strained relationship with the ebullient and wayward Brunel, Russell held a party on board the SS *Great Eastern* to celebrate the completion of her building in 1856. On her first sea trials, however, the forward funnel exploded, delaying her maiden voyage for four years. Although Brunel took most of the credit at the time, Russell's abilities as designer and shipbuilder are now seen as outstanding in overcoming the unprecedented problems posed by the sheer size of the *Great Eastern* and its novel structure. Russell's later career as a shipbuilder was increasingly taken up with the problems of running several large engineering businesses, financial speculation and business management, which came less naturally to him than the design of a hull or the shape of a wave as it broke on the bows. He might have achieved even more if, like Watt, he had found his Matthew Boulton.

When the SS *Great Eastern* proved more of a technological wonder than a commercial proposition, it was William Thomson, Lord Kelvin (1824–1907), who paced its decks watching the laying of the first successful transatlantic submarine cable.

THE KELVIN AND THE KELVINATOR

William Thomson's early promise was fulfilled right to the end of his days as Lord Kelvin – engineer, inventor, scientist and polymath. He was a true infant prodigy, attending his father's mathematics lectures with delight at the age of eight. During his teens, he wrote a mathematical paper that was read to the Royal Society of Edinburgh. The reader was an elderly professor, as it was considered undignified for such an august body to be lectured to by a child. From the age of 23, he held the Chair of Natural Philosophy at Glasgow University, being one of the first people to teach physics in the laboratory as well as in the lecture hall. He was immensely popular with his students all his days.

As a young man, his interests lay primarily in the mathematical theory of heat. He collaborated with James Joule to work out what became known as the Joule-Thomson effect, the way in which gases undergo a drop in temperature when they expand into a vacuum. This research proved crucial a generation later to the work of James Dewar in liquefying gases. In 1848, Kelvin calculated the point of absolute zero to be -273ºC, remarkably close to modern estimates, proposing a new scale of temperature with its base at absolute zero and its degrees equal to those on the Centigrade scale. Three years later, he deduced the proposition that all energy tends to dissipate itself as heat, a crucial expression of the second law of thermodynamics. He introduced the terms 'kinetic energy' and 'potential' to the vocabulary of science and, in his honour, more than half a century later one of the first domestic refrigerators was called the Kelvinator.

Kelvin's interests embraced the whole of nineteenth-century physics: in 1859, he collaborated on the definitive textbook known to generations of students as *Thomson and Tait* or *T. & T*. He was always on the lookout for opportunities to turn his discoveries to practical account, patenting and manufacturing many of the instruments he invented in the course of his research. Always happy to act as a scientific consultant, he took a close interest in the proposed project to lay a telegraph cable across the Atlantic, conducting research on the design of cables, developing and patenting instruments and becoming a Director of the Atlantic Telegraph Company. The first Atlantic cable burnt out soon after being laid because the engineer in charge insisted, against Kelvin's advice, in using a very high voltage and poor insulation. The second cable-laying operation on the *Great Eastern* took Kelvin and his advice on board, using his highly sensitive mirror galvanometer to detect the faintest of currents. For the first time instant communication between Britain and America was possible, earning Kelvin a substantial fortune. Lauded in the press as 'the great Electrician', he was created Baron Kelvin of Largs in 1866.

Kelvin combined vision and practicality. He made significant improvements to the ship's compass, by designing the Thomson binnacle, which allowed corrections for the effects of magnetism in the new generations of iron and steel ships. In 1881, he put forward a proposal to harness the energy of the Niagara Falls into hydro-electricity and was the first person to put forward the concept of the heat pump. Used in air conditioning, the pump warms or cools by moving heat from a low to a high temperature, using less energy than direct heating. He was also one of the great all-rounders. He was a keen rower and founded the Glasgow University Musical Society. He was an enthusiast for other people's innovations: his house was the first in Britain to be lit by electricity and he introduced the Bell telephone to the UK.

Sadly, in old age Kelvin demonstrated that even his imagination had limits. He believed that all the major discoveries in physics had been made and all that was left to do was to adjust the decimal point in a number of measurements. He pronounced that 'radio has no future' and that 'heavier-than-air flying machines are impossible'. With almost his dying breath he denounced the first evidence that physics was to be turned on its head again, bitterly opposing the idea that radioactive atoms were disintegrating or that the energy released came from within the atom. Kelvin was the architect of nineteenth-century physics and with his building complete, he rested rather than tearing it down and starting again with the new building blocks of atomic physics and relativity. He did, however, share the same year of birth and death, and the same laboratory, with a Scot whose work pointed firmly forward to the late twentieth century and opto-electronics, although its significance was not recognised for many years.

THE DIVINE RESIDENT OF THE BLACK HOLE

John Kerr (1824–1907), the son of an Ardrossan fish merchant, started his schooling in a village school on Skye. Graduating in physics from Glasgow, he became a research student under Kelvin, with whom he remained friendly all his life. Kerr was one of the first to work in the converted wine cellar known as the 'Black Hole' where Kelvin had his laboratory. Perhaps it was the Black Hole that caused Kerr to turn his thoughts heavenwards. He took a theology degree, but never practised as a minister, instead lecturing in mathematics in the Glasgow Free Church Teacher Training College for the next 44 years. Throughout he retained his interest in science, setting up a small laboratory where he pursued his researches.

His most important work concerned the effect of electromagnetic fields on light. He performed experiments of great precision to measure very small effects. He discovered the magneto-optic effect, the slight change which occurs in the polarisation of light reflected from the pole of a magnet when the magnet is switched on. The effect on the transmission of light of an electric field at right angles to it, which he identified in 1875, is still known as the Kerr effect. He designed what was to become known as the Kerr cell and using it, showed that the effect was proportional to the square of the electric field. Today, the Kerr effect is utilised in very high-speed switching, ultra-fast cameras and in the operation of high speed lasers. It also makes possible the creation of soliton pulses in fibre optic cables, used in twenty-first-century trans-oceanic communications.

ENGINEERED BY SCOTS

★ The hydraulic spade and the hydraulic riveting machine: Sir William Arrol (1839–1913). He designed them for use in building bridges from the Bothwell railway bridge over the Clyde to his masterpiece, the Forth Rail Bridge. He also devised a way of prefabricating cantilevered beams on land, then rolling them out from pier to pier over water, saving time, money and lives.

★ The first successful steam-driven power loom: a Mr Austin of Glasgow in 1789. Although English clergyman Edmund Cartwright had patented similar looms four years earlier, he could not get them to work and his business failed. By 1800, the Monteith brothers, whose father James in 1780 had discovered a way of making imitation Indian muslin from cotton, had erected 200 looms to an improved design by Austin in their Glasgow mills.

★ Forced draught technology in boiler design: James Howden (1832–1913). He set up as a consulting engineer in Glasgow in 1854, moving into manufacturing engines and boilers eight years later.

★ The Houldsworth Differential Gear: Henry Houldsworth (1774–1853). Initially invented to maintain a constant tension on thread, the same principle can be found in car gears today. Born in Nottingham, Houldsworth moved to Glasgow in 1799 to teach spinning in the Woodside Mill, which he bought two years later. By 1831, he had become Glasgow's largest cotton manufacturer. As well as perfecting the bobbin and fly frame for twisting cotton, Houldsworth diversified into iron working initially to repair his machinery. He opened the Coltness Iron Works in 1839 and the Dalmellington Iron Works nine years later.

★ The Kelvin clip: Lord Kelvin (1824–1907). It is still widely used for connecting test wires to electric circuits.

★ The mirror galvanometer: Lord Kelvin (1824–1907). This highly sensitive instrument for reading electrical signals used pulses of electricity to deflect a light mirror which reflected a spot of light onto a scale. By reducing the stresses on the telegraph cable while increasing the speed of transmission from two to twenty words a minute, the galvanometer made the transatlantic telegraph possible.

★ The siphon recorder: Lord Kelvin (1824–1907). A coil moved a siphon of ink to record Morse code messages sent by telegraph onto a moving paper tape as a wavy line.

★ The pneumatic tube: William Murdoch (1754–1839) was fascinated by the potential of transmitting power by compressed air, using the impulse of the air to move packages in tubes. Pneumatic tubes were used well into the twentieth century to dispatch packages, documents and telegrams round shops, factories and, in the case of cities like Paris, whole districts. Murdoch also installed a pneumatic lift at Boulton and Watt's Soho Works to lift castings from the foundry floor to the canal bank. He used compressed air to ring the bells in his house: when Sir Walter Scott heard of this he fitted up his bells at Abbotsford in similar fashion.

★ The slide valve: William Murdoch (1754–1839). The simplicity of operation of the slide valve to admit and distribute steam led to its use in more steam engines than any other type of valve.

★ **The oscillating engine:** William Murdoch (1754–1839). Although Murdoch did not develop it further, his engine was to find its true home in the steamship.

★ **The steeple engine:** David Napier (1790–1869). This compact steam engine was used primarily in paddle steamers.

★ **The continuous rotary printing machine:** Thomas Nelson (1822–92). By allowing paper to be fed continuously, Nelson's machine greatly speeded up printing and allowed paper to be printed on both sides at once. Nelson's machine, which was shown at the Great Exhibition of 1851, allowed him to pioneer mass-market publishing.

★ **The first machine to make fishing nets:** patented by James Paterson, a Musselburgh cooper, in 1820. The inspiration came from watching local fishermen mending nets by hand: by the mid-nineteenth century 800 people were employed manufacturing his machines.

★ **Desalination plant:** Robert Silver (1913–). A former Professor at Glasgow University, he is described as 'the foremost pioneer of industrial scale distillation units'. His first plants to produce distilled or drinking water by evaporating sea-water were installed in Kuwait and Guernsey in 1960.

★ **Nodding ducks:** Professor Stephen Salter, Edinburgh University. Currently being tested off Islay, the Salter's Duck system, first devised in 1974, can extract 90 per cent of the energy from a wave. The 'duck' is a floating chamber which bobs up and down as the waves pass. A row of 25 ducks is pivoted from a fixed platform at the rear, the waggling motion between the two being used to generate electricity.

★ **The movable jib crane:** Robert Stevenson (1772–1850), the lighthouse engineer. It was one of many ingenious devices he came up with in tackling the immense problems posed by building the Bell Rock lighthouse.

★ **The first textile machinery driven by steam:** James Watt (1736–1819). The first person to buy a Watt engine, after he devised a way of making it produce rotary motion, was Richard Arkwright, the cotton pioneer, in 1790. Inventor of the water-powered spinning frame in 1769, the same year that Watt patented his engine, Arkwright had first run it on horse power and then water power before finding the solution in steam.

★ **The double acting engine:** James Watt (1736–1819). Driving the cylinder by steam on both the forward and reverse strokes made for a more compact and powerful engine.

★ **The centrifugal governor:** James Watt (1736–1819). As two balls were spun round on a spindle they controlled a valve which admitted steam, closing it as they spun faster and opening it as they slowed down. This allowed the steam flow and, therefore, the speed to remain steady. Many years later, studying this device led James Clerk Maxwell to deduce the principle of feedback. He named the science cybernetics after the Greek word for governor.

★ **The direct acting feed pump:** James Weir. Founder of the Glasgow engineering company in 1871, his pump dramatically improved the efficiency of steam boilers. In 1880, the company introduced feedwater heating in boilers, thus significantly improving the performance of marine steam engines. In 1896, Weir developed a high-pressure pump capable of withstanding steam pressures of 25 lbs per square foot, which immediately became standard equipment for water tube boilers.

THE ELECTRONICS REVOLUTION

★ **The first non-US computers to be connected to the Internet:** Edinburgh University.

★ **Fibre optics:** John Logie Baird (1888–1946). Baird took out a patent for the transmission of light down a glass rod, the principle behind fibre optics, although limitations in the glass available at the time prevented it from being of practical use.

★ **The computer language POP-2:** devised at Edinburgh University in the mid-1960s, it ran on the UK's second multi-access, interactive computing system and its early development between researchers at Edinburgh and Cambridge was one of the first examples of teleworking in the UK. The world's first artificial intelligence spin-off company, Conversational Software Ltd, was established in 1969 to market the new language.

★ **Microprocessors in word processing:** the Fife company Fortronic in 1974. The Fortronic word processor brightened up the office – the casing housing the monitor was lime green.

★ **Amorphous silicon:** Professor Walter Spear, Dundee University. His team was the first to determine the electronic properties of this material now used throughout the world in a myriad of flat screen display applications including pocket calculators, photocopiers and TVs. The Dundee researchers designed the first experimental amorphous silicon p-n junction, the fundamental building block of such flat screen devices in 1976, their laboratory equipment including tobacco tins, matchboxes and pill cases.

★ **Edinburgh Prolog:** developed in the early 1970s at Edinburgh University, this 'standard' version of the artificial intelligence programming language made Prolog a practicable tool. In the 1980s, the Japanese Government chose it as the programming language in their attempt to build the first 'intelligent' computer.

★ **The 3.5 inch hard disk-drive:** invented by Dr Jack McGinley in 1983 for the Fife company Rodime. It is the standard disk-drive found in personal computers.

★ **The optical computer:** Heriot-Watt University. The Department of Physics under Professor Des Smith achieved the world's first demonstration of the all-optical computer in the late 1980s. The computer was based on nonlinear logic devices operated and powered by light inputs alone.

★ **The practical ultra short pulse laser:** Professor Wilson Sibbett, St Andrews University. A pioneer of ultra-fast science, Sibbett first demonstrated in 1989 the technique called Kerr-lens modelocking, which unlocked the commercial applications of ultra-fast lasers that could work in quadrillionths of a second. These lasers are now widely used in applications such as eye surgery and the micro-machining of metals like titanium and may soon provide the ultra-high-speed data communications needed to resolve the Internet's increasing traffic jams. At one time, St Andrews University held the world record for the shortest laser pulse.

THE MEASURE OF THE SCOTS

★ **The bel (B) or its more familiar tenth, the decibel:** the measure of sound volume was named after Alexander Graham Bell (1847–1922), inventor of the telephone.

★ **The Henry (H):** the measure of magnetic inductance was named after Joseph Henry (1797–1878) the US physicist of Scots descent.

SCOTTISH FIRSTS

★ Horse power (hp): James Watt (1736–1819).

★ The Kelvin (K): the calculation of the Centigrade temperature scale to start at absolute zero was named after Lord Kelvin who identified the zero point as -273°C.

★ The Maxwell (Mx): a measure of magnetic flux named in honour of James Clerk Maxwell (1831–79).

★ The neper (Np): this unit, expressing the ratio of two numbers in a natural logarithm, is often used to compare the amplitude of sounds. It celebrates John Napier (1550–1617), who often spelled his name Jhone Neper.

★ The degree Rankine (°R): the same temperature scale as the Kelvin, but based on Fahrenheit as being a more familiar measure for British engineers was named after William Rankine (1820–72) in honour of his contributions to thermodynamics.

★ The Twaddell (°Tw): a unit measuring the specific gravity of liquids denser than water was named after Scots scientist William Twaddell (1792–1839), who designed a hydrometer to measure it.

★ The Watt (W): named in 1882 at the suggestion of C.W. Siemens, the steel magnate, when President of the British Association, in honour of 'that mastermind in mechanical science, James Watt'. Ironically, it replaced Watt's own 'horse power' as the standard unit of power. Similarly, the kilowatt hour (kWh) is a common metric unit of work representing the energy of one thousand watts delivered for an hour.

5

Charlotte Dundas and the Craigievar Express: Steering the World

James Watt's horse power sounded the beginning of the end for the horse as the steam engine took to road, rail and ocean highway. One Glasgow engineer even tried to take to the air under steam. In speeding up the world from 5 mph to 1,500, making the dream of fast efficient travel a reality, Scots have come up with a host of ideas, from the seminal to the seriously strange, from the first paddle steamer, the *Charlotte Dundas*, to the *Craigievar Express*, the steam tricycle, which postman Andrew Lawson built in 1897 to make his life easier as he delivered the mail round rural Craigievar in Aberdeenshire. The most groundbreaking idea of all was that of an Ayrshire engineer, John Loudon McAdam (1756–1836), who paved the way for tarmac.

LAYING DOWN THE HIGHWAY

As a young man, McAdam worked for his uncle, a New York banker and merchant: together, they helped to found New York's Chamber of Commerce. The Declaration of Independence saw an end to his career in the new United States, but not before McAdam, a staunch Tory, had made the fortune that allowed him to buy an estate in his native Ayrshire and live the life of a country gentleman. The appalling state of the roads, many of which were little more than rutted dirt tracks, resolved him to do something about them. He built experimental road beds on his estate, albeit not without some opposition, and was appointed a Road Trustee for the locality.

McAdam's system of road building used crushed rock, graded to ensure a constant size of chips. He reintroduced the Roman road-building technique of layering the chips with the largest at the bottom, giving precise specifications for the size of chips and the depth at which each layer should be placed. This allowed the chips to lock together when a roller or a cartwheel was passed over them, creating a smooth, non-slip surface. His roads were cambered with proper drainage at the sides to allow for water run-off.

In 1815, McAdam's appointment as Surveyor-General of the Bristol roads allowed him to put his theories into practice. Meticulously, he wrote up his experiences in two books, published to promote his new methods and campaigned tirelessly for the adoption of new and efficient ways of road surfacing. By 1818, he was acting as consulting surveyor to no fewer than 34 Road Trusts, and in 1827 was appointed Surveyor-General of Metropolitan Roads in Great Britain. Turning down a knighthood, he died at Moffat, Dumfriesshire, the journey back to Scotland being a great deal faster and smoother thanks to his own ingenuity.

McAdam's principles were adopted throughout the world in his lifetime, making rapid road transport a reality: they underpin the motorways and runways of today. In 1822, the first highway in the USA was macadamised and two years later work started on the streets of London. By the end of the century, 90 per cent of European roads were tarmac, and pedalling along a macadamised road or more likely a rutted country lane was soon to appear the world's first cyclist.

THE AMAZING DANDY HORSE

In 1837, Dumfriesshire blacksmith Kirkpatrick MacMillan (1813–78) built himself a dandy horse. While riding this contraption, somewhat like a bicycle, but propelled by pushing on the ground with one's feet, he dreamed of taking his feet off the ground and came up with the world's first pedal cycle in 1839. The machine, weighing 57 lbs, was propelled by a crank on the rear wheel coupled to two horizontal pedal levers, which oscillated back and forwards. The wheels had iron tyres and the frame was of wood with a carved horse's head on the front.

MacMillan did not recognise the enormous potential of his personal transport revolution, regarding it simply as an efficient means of travelling the 14 miles from his home to Dumfries. He was surprised when others began to build copies of his machine: 'Aye, man, it's getting to be a real craze now. If you haven't got one of these road machines today, then you'll no be in fashion at all.' In 1842, he ventured as far as Glasgow, taking an evening and part of a day to complete the 70-mile trip. It provided him unwittingly with another claim to immortality as the first person to commit a cycling offence. He accidentally knocked over a child in the crush of Glaswegians who had come to see his novel 'iron horse', being fined five shillings at Gorbals Police Court. In the early 1840s, his niece, Mary Marchbank, took to riding his machine and thus became the world's first woman cyclist.

The inventive mind of the Scots is most closely associated with the sea. Think of the speed of the tea clippers like the *Cutty Sark*, built on the Clyde in 1869, or of the Blue Riband holders steaming across the stormy North Atlantic. Think of majesty and the Cunarder Queens – *Mary*, *Elizabeth* and the *QE2* – gliding down the slipway of John Brown's Clydebank yard. Empresses, Princesses and warriors – HMS *Hood*, *Tiger*, *Repulse* and *Renown* – all started their careers on the Clyde. Given Scottish engineering skills backed by the know-how of the world's first Department of Naval Architecture, it is not surprising that Scottish yards delivered innovation, from the first triple expansion engine to the factory ship. The origins of the mighty steam ship, however, lie not on the Clyde, but on a Dumfriesshire loch where a party consisting of a teacher, a poet, an artist, an engineer and a landowner who loved technology took a pleasure trip on a tiny boat.

ANSWERING MR MILLER'S EXPECTATIONS

The steamboat started off as a toy for the rich. Born at Leadhills, William Symington (1763–1831) became an engineer at the nearby lead mines on graduation from Edinburgh University, despite his father's wish that he should become a minister. In his early twenties, he patented an improved steam engine in which he achieved rotary motion by a system of chains and ratchet wheels, building a working model of a steam car on this principle. Friendship with James Taylor, tutor to the children of retired Edinburgh banker and amateur technologist, Patrick Miller, switched Symington's interests from land to water. Miller had already tested his own design for a ship on the Forth in 1786, a catamaran with paddle wheels between the hulls, which were operated by capstans turned by a crew of 30 on deck.

Although he declared the trials 'a success', Miller realised that there must be an easier way to turn the paddle wheels. Having seen Symington's model 'steamer', he commissioned him to build him a paddle steamer. The result was an unnamed 25-ft-long catamaran steam boat, with the engine to drive two paddle wheels in one hull and the boiler in the other. James Taylor, the poet Robert Burns, who was a tenant on Miller's Dalswinton estate, and Alexander Nasmyth, the landscape painter, were fellow passengers on the vessel's maiden voyage on Dalswinton Loch in 1788, where she reached a speed of 5 mph. According to Taylor, the steamboat, 'answered Mr Miller's expectation fully and afforded great pleasure to the spectators present'.

Miller patented the concept of the paddle wheel and commissioned Symington to build him a steamer with a larger engine, which was tested on the Forth and Clyde Canal in 1789. Although the boat achieved 7 mph, Miller was dissatisfied with the engine's performance and approached James Watt for advice. On being told tartly that he was infringing Watt's patents, Miller abandoned his shipbuilding dreams. Symington, however, was more patient. After Watt's patents expired in 1800, Symington patented his idea for a paddle wheel drive and found a new backer, Lord Dundas of Kerse, who had invested heavily in the new canals. Symington's *Charlotte Dundas*, named after Dundas's daughter, was the world's first practicable steam boat. Propelled by a stern paddle wheel, the 56-ft-long boat, successfully towed two 70-ton barges along a 19.5 mile stretch of the Forth and Clyde Canal in six hours in 1802. Shortly after, however, concerned that the wake from the stern paddle wheel would damage the banks, the canal company banned steam and the *Charlotte Dundas* was abandoned to rust on the bank. Symington drifted to London where he died, a broken man.

The *Charlotte Dundas* had an unexpected visitor from America, Robert Fulton, the engineer of Scots-Ulster ancestry who went on to design the world's first commercial steam boat, the *Clermont*, powered by a Boulton & Watt engine. The *Charlotte Dundas* proved the inspiration for a century of steam, her piston rod coupled to a crank shaft by a connecting rod, becoming the standard design for steamships. In 1812, Henry Bell, an engineer whose wife ran the Helensburgh public baths, launched the *Comet*, Europe's first commercial steamboat. Bell's achievement was recognised in 1851, when a statue was erected over his grave in Rhu churchyard at the behest of Robert Napier, the father of Clyde shipbuilding.

CLARENCE AND THE CUNARDERS

Initially, steamboats were small, had low boiler pressure and consumed vast amounts of coal. It was men like Robert Napier (1791–1876) who turned them into Cunarders. The son of a prosperous Dumbarton blacksmith, Napier chose to hammer the anvil, rather than the pulpit, despite his father's wishes. In 1812, he moved to Edinburgh, often having 'to count the lamp-posts for my supper' until he found work with Robert Stevenson, the lighthouse builder. In 1815, Napier set up in business as a blacksmith in Glasgow although his real ambition was to become a marine engineer like his cousin, David. He started to build marine engines, his first being installed in the paddle steamer, the *Leven*, and proving so reliable that it outlasted three hulls. His reputation was made when in 1827 the Northern Yacht Club promoted a steamboat race for a twenty guinea cup. Although all the Clyde's crack boats entered the two fastest vessels, *Clarence* and *Helensburgh*, had Napier engines. The next year, he established the Vulcan Foundry and his order book for marine engines grew.

From the 1830s, Napier dreamed of a regular and profitable steamship across the Atlantic, being consulted by the government on the feasibility of such a service. Napier's dream was realised when Nova Scotia businessman, Samuel Cunard, approached him to build his first ship, the *Britannia*. Not only did Napier convince Cunard to build larger and more powerful ships, but when Cunard ran into financial difficulties, Napier brought together a group of Glasgow businessmen to float the British and North American Royal Mail Steam Packet Coy. Napier's reputation and proven ability to provide reliable and powerful engines persuaded his fellow Glaswegians to invest in Cunard's high-risk venture: three of the four founders of Cunard were Scots.

In the early 1840s, Napier moved into shipbuilding, his Govan yard soon busy on the contract for the Royal Navy's first iron steamers. One grateful customer, Sir James Melvill of the East India Company, wrote to Napier in 1856 paying tribute to him as:

> the man who, above all other living men, has given practical effect to the inventions of Watt, and has passed to the world the great blessing of steam navigation. I in my conscience believe that the best vessels afloat are those with which you have had to do.

Napier believed in training his men well. Several went on to found some of the other great shipbuilding names of the Clyde – William Denny, John Elder, co-founder of Fairfields, and George Thomson, whose yard as John Brown's was later to build so many Cunarders. Together they turned Napier's quest for excellence into Clyde-built as a synonym for quality. Over the years, Napier's Lancefield yard launched scores of naval and merchant ships including the Cunarder *Persia*, the world's largest ship of its day, and in 1854, the *Leviathan*, the world's first train ferry.

Although the honours for railway development lie chiefly south of the border, it was a Scot who promoted the possibilities of the new technology to investors and the public. In 1824, the founding editor of the *Scotsman* newspaper and one of the few newspaper editors to fight a duel with a fellow professional, Charles Maclaren, wrote a series of articles in which he predicted that it would be possible for locomotives to speed along at 20 mph, four times the speed then achieved. He promoted the advantages of having railway carriages for passengers and envisaged the role that the railway would one day play in the life of the country:

> With so great a facility and celerity of communication, the provincial towns of an Empire would become so many suburbs of the metropolis . . . Commodities, inventions, discoveries, opinions, would circulate with a rapidity hitherto unknown, and the intercourse of man with man, nation with nation, and province with province would be prodigiously increased.

Two Scots tried to direct railways in very different directions – over rough terrain and into the air.

TYRED AND STEAMING

Robert Thomson (1822–73) was a serial inventor. The son of a Stonehaven merchant, he was originally destined for the Church, but a lack of aptitude in Latin persuaded his father to pack him off instead to an uncle in Charleston, South Carolina, to train as a merchant. Two years later, Thomson returned. His first flash of ingenuity was to rebuild his mother's washing mangle so that wet clothes could be passed through in either direction. While working for his cousin, a civil engineer, on the demolition of Dunbar Castle, he suggested a lifesaver – the use of electricity for firing mines. In 1841, he headed for London where his ideas on electricity were taken up by no less an expert than Michael Faraday.

Thomson believed in gaining wide experience. After spells blasting Dover cliffs in preparation for a railway tunnel, working as a civil engineer in Glasgow and as a railway engineer under Robert Stephenson, he became a self-employed consultant, suggesting the adopted route for the Eastern Counties railway. During this period, he kept right on inventing. In 1845, he patented the pneumatic tyre. His 'Aerial Wheels' were leather tyres with India rubber inner tubes covered with rubberised canvas. Fitted on to horse-drawn carriages, they made for a significantly smoother and quieter ride. Owing to the price of rubber, however, the tyres were not a commercial proposition and the pneumatic tyre had to wait over 30 years to be 'reinvented' by fellow Scot, John Boyd Dunlop. In 1849, Thomson patented the first self-acting fountain pen, which had a reservoir for storing ink, the precursor of the modern fountain pen.

While working as an engineering agent in Java in 1852, Thomson turned his mind to improving the machinery in use in sugar plantations. He wished to erect a crane on the waterfront, but the authorities insisted that it would have to be dismantled every night in case the inhabitants fell over it. Undaunted, Thomson came up with the first portable steam crane. Although he retired to Edinburgh in 1862, his inventive mind still brooded over the problem of how to move traction engines round the Java sugar plantations. In 1867, he patented solid rubber tyres for road steamers, the Scotsman patriotically describing his invention as 'the greatest step which had ever been made in the use of steam on common roads'.

Thomson came up trumps again when he designed the first successful, mechanically propelled vehicles for road haulage over long distances, startling the citizens of Leith when his prototype steamer towed a cart, laden with ten tons of flour, round the streets. By the early 1870s, several companies in Britain and the USA were building Thomson steamers under licence. Several steamers were shipped out and assembled for use by the Indian Transport Service as a steam bus. At speeds of 5 to 8 mph, the steamers carried passengers and freight with refuelling stations at 14-mile intervals and a water tank every 7 miles along the 70-mile route.

With their huge tyres like elephant's pads to spread the load, Thomson steamers came into their own in parts of the world where the roughness of the terrain or lack of capital precluded the development of railways. They were also used closer to home, the manager of the Glasgow Tramways considering them so useful that 'no single article weighing over ten tons is ever moved except by one of them'. The engine's ability to plough effortlessly with two double-furrow ploughs led ultimately to the demise of the working farm horse and the birth of the modern tractor.

GLASGOW TO EDINBURGH IN 20 MINUTES

Like Thomson, Glaswegian George Bennie (1892–1957) was a born inventor. His first patent was for a ship's ashtray which would remain stable no matter the degree of list or sway. He conceived the idea for a 'Railway in the Air' while designing diesel engines. In 1930, Bennie launched his Railplane, the forerunner of the monorail, in a field in the prosperous Glasgow suburb of Milngavie. His vision was to separate passenger traffic from slower moving rail freight, thus also freeing up the increasingly congested roads. He built a steel structure with a tiny station 30 ft over the existing railway line. Suspended from the rail, hung a 10-ton, white, cigar-shaped carriage with electrically powered aircraft propellers at each end. The carpeted interior of the carriage was like a private club with armchairs, sliding doors, electric table lamps and curtained windows. Bennie envisaged that 50 passengers could travel in comfort at speeds of up to 200 mph slashing the journey time by rail between Glasgow and Edinburgh to 20 minutes.

Local reaction was divided between 'Bennie's baby' and 'Bennie's folly'. His plans won him a gold medal at the 1922 Industrial Exhibition in Edinburgh, but despite travelling the world and attracting much interest in his new idea, Bennie failed to find financial backers, thanks to the Depression and opposition from the railway companies. He went bankrupt in 1937, ending his days as a herbalist, while his Railplane rusted in a Milngavie field.

William Beardmore, the Glasgow engineering company that built Bennie's Railplane, had an earlier aeronautical claim to fame. At the end of 1917, they started work on 'Tiny', better known as His Majesty's Airship R34, as big as a Dreadnought battleship and twice as long as a football pitch. By then Scots were no strangers to flight. One of Scotland's earliest aviators was the Birdman of Stirling, one John Damian de Falcuis, an Italian alchemist who persuaded King James IV that he could create gold from base metals. Having failed, he then lured the King with the tale that he could fly from Stirling Castle towards France. In 1507, his attempt ended in ignominy: on launching himself from the castle battlements he ended up in a dunghill below with a broken leg. James Tytler (1745–1804) has a somewhat more creditable claim in the history of British aviation.

BRITAIN'S FIRST AERONAUT

Tytler, the fourth child of an Angus parish minister, studied medicine at Edinburgh University, having served his apprenticeship with a local surgeon. Forced to abandon his studies due to shortage of funds, made worse by an early marriage, he regularly switched career from chemist, surgeon, printer and poet, to textbook writer, journalist, apothecary and political agitator, in his search for a quick way to make money. Eventually, his wife despaired of his financial ventures and departed, leaving their five children in his care. Over the next seven years, Tytler's financial bread and butter was the editorship of the second edition of the *Encyclopaedia Britannica*, to which he contributed 9,000 pages. Finances were still tight as he was paid the equivalent of a subsistence wage for a single man. His desperate need for money inspired him to take to the skies.

Tytler had eagerly followed the exploits of the French balloonists, the Montgolfier brothers, writing eight pages on ballooning in his appendix to the *Encyclopaedia*. Seizing the money-spinning potential of such an exploit, in 1784 he constructed a model balloon, the 'Grand Edinburgh Fire Balloon', which he charged the public sixpence to view. The enthusiastic response fired him to build a real balloon, although lack of money meant that his first few widely advertised attempts ended in disaster. On the morning of Friday, 27 August 1784, before a restless and jeering crowd, he finally took off, reaching a height of 350 feet before drifting gradually to land about half a mile north of his starting point. With this flight Tytler succeeded not only in becoming Britain's first aeronaut, but also her first aeronautical engineer, having designed and built his own hot air balloon.

Tytler's career continued on its wayward course. Buoyed by his moment of fame, he made three further balloon attempts in 1784, each of which ended in a fiasco. His attempt to become a political agitator only led to his arrest for seditious libel. Before his case could be brought to court, he fled to Ireland and then Massachusetts to start a new life. Having acquired a third wife and twin daughters and a further string of business failures, he increasingly took to drowning his sorrows, which resulted in his own watery end in a creek at Salem, in 1804.

Scots remained fascinated by the notion of flight. In 1867, Joseph Kaufmann, a mechanical engineer living in Glasgow, thought that steam might be the answer. He designed an 'aerial steam-machine' with a 40 hp, two-ton engine driving a pair of 35-ft wings to flap like a bird. A large ball suspended beneath kept the machine horizontal in flight. Kaufmann envisaged that his machine, with its three passenger gondolas, would fly at 56 mph, take-off being assisted by steam-operated telescopic legs that shot out when the engine was turned on. Although his working model achieved lift-off, its wings could not sustain the strain of the furious flapping, and so ended a bold experiment. By the end of the nineteenth century the race was on to invent the aircraft. One of the few British contenders was Glasgow University lecturer Percy Pilcher (1866–99).

THE GLASGOW DAEDALUS

Born in Bath of a Scottish mother, Pilcher served in the Royal Navy and as a shipbuilding apprentice in Glasgow before, in 1891, becoming a lecturer at Glasgow University. He started to design and build hang gliders with the view one day of developing a powered machine. He launched his first monoplane, which he christened the *Bat* because of its huge wings, from a hill overlooking the Firth of Clyde at Cardross.

Pilcher developed a series of designs – the *Beetle*, the *Gull*, and the *Hawk*. Unlike many pioneers he seldom tested his craft in free-flight, preferring to tow the glider with an attached rope to act as a stabilising force. On 20 June 1897, he held his first public demonstration, partly in the hope of attracting much needed financial backing for his dream of powered flight. After his cousin Dorothy had shown off the machine's tricks, Pilcher took off, flying at 80 ft while being towed downhill by three boys. The knot slipped and suddenly Pilcher was in free flight.

On that occasion he landed safely, but the powered triplane that he was working on in the late 1890s sadly never flew. He proposed to test it during a public demonstration in Leicestershire in September 1898, but rain changed his plans. Instead, he experimented with flying in the *Hawk* towed by a line passing over a tackle drawn by two horses. On the second flight, a tow rope broke and the *Hawk* plummeted to the ground, Pilcher dying from his injuries two days later. The *Hawk* survived to become Britain's oldest aircraft, displayed in the Museum of Flight in East Lothian.

While aircraft now light up the night sky over the oceans, for centuries they remained pitch black until penetrated by the lights beamed out by a remarkable family.

THE OCEAN LEERIES

> But I, when I am stronger
> And can choose what I'm to do
> Oh, Leerie, I'll go round at night
> And light the lamps with you.

115

The poet Robert Louis Stevenson was not the only Stevenson to want to be a lamplighter when he grew up. From 1800 to 1938, five generations of the one family provided eight engineers to the Northern Lighthouse Board and through their innovative ideas made the sea a much safer place for shipping. Lighthouses were crucial in an age when sea was the only means of transporting people and cargo to other continents, and when navigators did not have radar and radio to guide them.

Robert (1772–1850) was the first of the 'Lighthouse Stevensons'. Destined for the ministry, his fortunes changed when his widowed mother married Thomas Smith, consultant engineer to the newly established Northern Lighthouse Board in Edinburgh. He had already perfected a design for a reflecting street lamp. Robert became his stepfather's apprentice, attending university in the winter months when lighthouse work was not possible. Despite studying for 12 years, however, he never graduated, attributing this to 'my slender knowledge of Latin and my total want of Greek'.

In 1800, with Scots engineer John Rennie, he began work on Scotland's greatest engineering feat of the early nineteenth century, the building of the Bell Rock Lighthouse on the much feared reef 12 miles out into the stormy North Sea from Arbroath. Stevenson had to invent many new tools and machines to tackle the unique problems posed by building a 115-ft tower on a rock, including the first movable jib cranes and the first cranes with ball-bearings. While the Bell Rock was under construction, Stevenson moored a temporary lightship offshore, adopting for the first time the standard practice of using one lantern to surround the mast instead of small lanterns hung from the yard-arms. The completion of the Bell Rock Lighthouse made Stevenson a national hero.

As well as building 20 more lighthouses, he perfected the use of reflecting lights, advocated the use of refractive lights, initiated the system of flashing and intermittent lights and invented the hydrophore (an instrument for taking samples of water at given depths). He was the first person to observe that saltwater from the ocean flows up a river in a distinct stream from the freshwater flowing down. He also gave his namesake, George Stephenson, the idea of malleable iron rails on which to run his steam engines.

Whereas Robert Stevenson was pioneer and Jack of all trades, his three sons, Alan, David and Thomas, added the scientific gravitas by refining his techniques and conducting original research in lighthouse optics and meteorology. Skerryvore lighthouse, 12 miles off the coast of Tiree, was the greatest achievement of Alan Stevenson (1807–65). Among the many who considered it the world's most elegant lighthouse was his nephew R.L.S., who described it as 'the noblest of all extant deep-sea lights'. Second son David (1815–86) introduced paraffin lighting in lighthouses allowing a much more intense light. He built several lighthouses in Japan where he devised an aseismatic version to counteract the effect of earthquakes. On his recommendation, the Japanese Government appointed a Scot as Chief Engineer of their Lighthouse Department to supervise the construction of 50 lighthouses.

Thomas Stevenson (1818–87), the poet's father, developed the azimuthal condensing system to intensify the light beam and the Stevenson screen for thermometers. It was one of his greatest disappointments that his son showed no interest in becoming a civil engineer although R.L.S admitted that, 'whenever I smell saltwater I know I am not far from one of the works of my ancestors'. Thomas Junior and David Alan were the last of the 'Lighthouse Stevensons', the latter only retiring from his official post as engineer to the Northern Lighthouse Board in 1938, when in his eighties.

Their younger brother Charles (1855–1950) was the most inventive of all the Stevensons, a demonstration of the newly invented Bell telephone during a trip to the States firing his imagination. He spent the next 15 years striving to find a means of transmitting speech across distance without wires to allow better communications with isolated lighthouses. He managed to solve the problem in principle two years before Marconi started his famous wireless experiments, but could not raise funds for practical trials. In later life, he adapted radio to devise his 'Talking Beacon', which enabled ships to plot their course in fog by means of synchronised radio and fog signals. With Charles's son, D. Alan Stevenson (1891–1971), the association of the name Stevenson with lighthouse building was finally over.

★ 1801 William Symington built the world's first practicable steamboat, the paddle steamer *Charlotte Dundas*.

★ 1812 Henry Bell's *Comet*, built by John Wood of Port Glasgow, was the first commercially successful steamship in Europe.

★ 1814 The *Margery*, the first steamboat on the Thames and the first to cross the English Channel after being bought by a Frenchman in 1816 was built by Archibald McLachlan of Glasgow.

★ 1817 John Wood of Greenock built a small coaster and named it *Tug*. When it turned out to be unsuitable, being used instead for towing, the name 'tug' came to be applied to all towing vessels.

★ 1818 David Napier's *Rob Roy* was the first steamer to cross the Irish Channel, sailing regularly between Greenock and Belfast. Two years later, bought by the French Government to carry the mails and renamed *Henri IV*, she became the first regular Channel steamer.

★ 1818 Thomas Morton (1781–1832), owner of Leith's oldest shipyard, invented the slipway. The Morton's Patent Slip allowed ships to be hauled up for repair rather than having to go into dry dock.

★ 1819 *Vulcan*, constructed by Thomas Wilson of Faskine, was the first iron passenger boat. Going into service on the Forth and Clyde Canal, the 63-ft-long and 13-ft-wide boat could carry 200 passengers and their luggage.

★ 1835 Scots engineer Sir William Fairbairn built the first iron ships to be accepted as seaworthy by Lloyds.

★ 1835 The Forth and Clyde Canal's wagon boats introduced the principle behind modern container traffic. Each boat could carry 14 wagons of coal, loaded directly on to the deck from the end of the Monkland and Kirkintilloch Railway. Around the same time they pioneered a different form of 'roll-on/roll-off' with barges that could take 16–18 carts in order to provide a service for farmers taking goods to market.

★ 1835 The *Wave*, the first vessel constructed on John Scott Russell's wave line system, was built under his direction by Caird and Co. of Greenock.

★ 1838 *Sirius*, built by Leith shipbuilder Robert Menzies, was the first ship to cross the Atlantic by steam power alone, beating

Brunel's *Great Western* by a short head. She was the first steamship to be fitted with a surface condenser, allowing freshwater, rather than seawater, to be used in the boilers.

★ 1839 J. Ruthven patented jet propulsion in shipping. Based on a centrifugal pump, it was installed in marine craft over the next half century.

★ 1839 The schooner *Scottish Maid*, built by Alexander Hall & Co. of Aberdeen, was the first true clipper with its forward curving Aberdeen bow to improve speed and performance and to cheat the tonnage laws. Thanks to the Aberdeen bow, the length of ships is now measured along the deck rather than the keel.

★ 1840 R. Duncan & Co. of Greenock built the first Cunarder, the *Britannia*. Its sister ships, the *Acadia*, *Caledonia* and *Columbia*, were also built on the Clyde and fitted with Napier engines.

★ 1842 Robert Napier (1790–1869), the first person to combine engineering and shipbuilding in one firm, created the first modern shipyard at Govan, Glasgow.

★ 1849 Robert Napier built *Leviathan*, the world's first train ferry. With rails on deck for 40 wagons, she carried passengers and freight across the Forth from Granton, north of Edinburgh, to Burntisland in Fife.

★ 1853 John Hastie of Greenock patented the first self-holding steering gear using opposing screws to hold the helm steady. Improved steering gear was essential in the more powerful steamships, which previously required up to 100 men to manage the helm in rough weather.

★ 1853 John Elder patented the vertical direct acting compound engine adapted to drive a screw propeller. It reduced a ship's coal consumption by 30–40 per cent.

★ 1854 Randolph Elder and Co. of Glasgow fitted the first efficient marine compound engine on the *Brandon*.

★ 1857 The Dundee yard of Alexander Stephen was the first to fit steam engines on a whaler, the *Tay*.

★ 1858 The *Thetis*, built in 1858 by Scott's of Greenock, was one of the first vessels to have a water tube boiler. The boiler was made by Rowan of Glasgow, who pioneered the use of such boilers in the British Merchant Navy.

★ 1859 The world's first steam foghorn, which hoots automatically in foggy weather, was built to the design of Robert Foulis (1796–1866), the Glasgow-born civil engineer, inventor and artist, on Partridge Island off the harbour of St John's, Nova Scotia.

★ 1862 Scotch boilers were first fitted in ships.

★ 1866 Scottish engineer John MacFarlane Gray developed the first successful steam steering gear, installed two years later in Brunel's *Great Eastern*.

★ 1868 Alexander Hall and Co. Ltd, Aberdeen, built the first vessel for the Japanese Navy, *Jho Sho Maru*. The wooden, barque-rigged corvette had a belt of iron armour plating at the waterline and carried eight 64-pounder guns and two 100-pounders.

★ 1869 The record-breaking tea clippers *Cutty Sark* and *Thermopylae*, built in Dumbarton and Aberdeen respectively. In 1872, the two ships raced from Shanghai, the *Thermopylae* arriving in London with her cargo of tea seven days ahead of her rival. Today the *Cutty Sark* is the world's only surviving tea clipper.

★ 1873 Alexander Kirk, working for John Elder and Company, Glasgow, installed the first triple expansion engine in a ship, on the *Propontis*.

★ 1879 *Rotomahana*, built by William Denny and Brothers for the Union Steamship Co. of New Zealand, was the first ocean-going steel ship and the first ship fitted with twin bilge keels.

★ 1881 Robert Napier and Sons fitted the first simple, mass-market triple expansion engine on the *Aberdeen*. Powerful and fuel-efficient, it was the driving force for the full change from sail to steam and ushered in a half century of tramp steamers on the world's sea lanes.

★ 1881 James Weir of Glasgow patented the direct-acting feed pump embodying his principle of regenerative feed heating, which some authorities consider as important to the economy of the steam cycle as James Watt's separate condenser. Soon, most ships had two separate pumps, often nicknamed Jamie and Geordie.

★ 1881 The Cunarder *Servia*, launched from J. & G. Thomson's Clydebank yard, was the world's first ship to be lit by electricity.

★ 1881 *Alaska*, built on the Clyde by John Elder and Company, was the first ship to cross the Atlantic in less than a week.

★ 1881 The *Parisian*, built by Robert Napier and Sons for the Allan Line, was the first steel Atlantic mail steamer.

SCOTTISH FIRSTS

★ 1882 The world's first commercial ship's test tank was built at William Denny's Dumbarton yard. The water tank, as long as a football pitch, is still used for testing ship designs.

★ 1883 James Howden of Glasgow patented the closed ash pit system, essential for the forced draught adopted by the new torpedo boats. It allowed increases in power of 30 per cent.

★ 1888 The *City of Paris*, built by J. & G. Thomson of Clydebank for the Inman Line, was the first vessel to cross the Atlantic in under six days.

★ 1888 The first modern transatlantic liner, the Inman Line's *City of New York*, was launched from J. & G. Thomson's Clydebank yard. She was the first liner to adopt twin screw propulsion and only the second ship to exceed 10,000 tons.

★ 1889 Edinburgh marine engineers, Brown Brothers of Edinburgh, patented the steam tiller and the telemotor. Together they dramatically increased the efficiency of ships' steering gear: all the helmsman had to do was to turn a small hand wheel to transmit instantly the motion of the wheel to the tiller. The system did away with the incredibly noisy and inefficient system of rods and chains between the steering engine and the rudder and allowed steering gear to be moved aft.

★ 1893 Cunard's *Laconia*, launched from Fairfield's yard in Glasgow, was to make the first world cruise in 1922.

★ 1901 The Clyde steamer *King Edward*, built by Denny of Dumbarton, was the first merchant ship to be powered by turbines.

★ 1903 Built by William Denny for the South Eastern & Chatham Railway, the turbine-powered *Queen* was the first steamer to cross the English Channel in under an hour.

★ 1904 The first turbine-powered liner to cross the Atlantic and the first with triple screws was the *Virginian*, built for the Allan Line by Alexander Stephen of Glasgow.

★ 1905 Launched from John Brown's yard, the Cunarder *Caronia*'s quadruple expansion engines were the largest ship's engines ever built in Britain.

★ 1908 The *Otaki*, built for the New Zealand Shipping Company by Denny of Dumbarton, was the world's first merchant ship to be fitted with a combination of reciprocating and turbine engines, a system later adopted by many liners including the ill-fated *Titanic*.

★ 1909 John Brown's Clydebank-built HMS *Brisk*, the first destroyer to be fitted with Brown-Curtis turbines, jointly developed with the US General Electric Company. By the end of the First World War over 300 British warships were powered by Brown-Curtis turbines.

★ 1916 Built by John Brown's, Clydebank, HMS *Repulse* was the first ship with a flying-off platform for aircraft, fitted in 1917.

★ 1929 Alexander Stephen and Sons of Glasgow built the first turbo-electric-driven ship in Europe, the P. & O. Line's *Viceroy of India*.

★ 1934 *Robert the Bruce*, built by Denny of Dumbarton for the ferry service between North and South Queensferry on the Forth, was the first diesel-electric paddle steamer.

★ 1936 Brown Brothers of Edinburgh patented the fin or Denny-Brown stabiliser. It could move 40 degrees in two seconds, assuring passengers of a dramatically smoother journey and reduction in seasickness.

★ 1936 Colin Campbell Mitchell of Edinburgh engineers, MacTaggart Scott and later Brown Brothers, patented the slotted cylinder steam catapult which enabled aircraft to be launched at sea. It was not taken up by the Admiralty until 1946, before which time the Germans were using the same principle to launch their V1 'doodle bugs'. The catapult was rapidly adopted by the world's navies after the war. Mitchell was the first foreigner to be awarded the Newcomen Gold Medal of the Franklin Institute of Philadelphia and later won the United States Medal of Freedom for his invention.

★ 1938 The world's largest passenger liner ever built, the *Queen Elizabeth*, was launched from John Brown's, Clydebank.

★ 1947 The Cunarder *Media*, built by John Brown's, Clydebank, was the first Atlantic liner to be fitted with fin stabilisers.

★ 1951 The *Lord Warden*, launched from William Denny's Dumbarton shipyard, was the first purpose-built drive-on car ferry.

★ 1954 The world's first factory trawler, *Fairtry*, was launched by John Lewis and Sons Ltd of Aberdeen for Christian Salvesen, the Edinburgh whalers who were seeking to diversify. The novel stern trawl enabled ships to haul bigger nets and catch more fish than their traditional side-trawl predecessors. Several times larger than any existing trawler, the *Fairtry*'s combination of powerful diesel engines, large fuel storage tanks, automatic fish-processing machines and freezer allowed ships to stay at sea for two months or more fishing in grounds thousands of miles from home. By the late 1950s, mass-production of factory trawlers based on the *Fairtry* design was under way in the major fishing regions of Europe and North America.

★ 1961 Commercial vertical plate freezers, developed by the Torry Research Station, Aberdeen, allowed fish to be handled and packed more efficiently. They were installed for the first time on the stern trawler *Lord Nelson*.

★ 1966 Grangemouth on the Forth offered Britain's first fully containerised deep-sea liner service, the service sailing between Rotterdam, Bremen, Grangemouth and New York.

★ 1984 Conoco installed the world's first tension leg platform on its Huttom North Sea oil field. Its hull was built by Highland Fabricators' Nigg fabrication yard.

SCOTS IN THE AIR

★ **The first human to walk on the moon:** Neil Armstrong, whose ancestors came from Langholm, Dumfriesshire. He visited Langholm in 1972 to receive the 'freedom of the town'. Alan Bean, the fourth person to walk on the moon, was also the first to take tartan to the moon, leaving a tartan flag to commemorate his clan in 1969. Bruce McCandless, the first person to walk untethered in space, also claims Scots descent.

★ **The first airship to cross the Atlantic:** the R34, built in Inchinnan near Glasgow by engineers, William Beardmore. It set off from East Fortune aerodrome, East Lothian, on 2 July 1919, arriving in New York four days later. It flew back from New York on 9 July, making it the first aircraft to complete a two-way flight across the Atlantic, only a fortnight after Alcock and Brown made their first one-way crossing by aeroplane.

★ **The aerostatic principle of the balloon:** first demonstrated by the Scottish chemist Joseph Black (1728–99), when he showed that the foetal membrane of a calf, filled with hydrogen, would float in air.

★ **The first non-stop Atlantic flight:** achieved in 1919 by John Alcock and

Arthur Whitten Brown (1886–1948), Brown being born in Glasgow of American parents.

★ **The first East–West solo flight across the Atlantic:** achieved by Glaswegian James Mollison (1905–59) in 1932. In the same year, he married the pioneering woman flier Amy Johnson. As a husband and wife team they set the record for flight between England and India in 1934, making the trip in 22 hours. He was also the first person to fly from England to South America in 1933.

★ **The first crossing of the Sahara and of the Alps in a hot air balloon:** made by Glaswegian Don Cameron. In 1990, he made the first balloon flight between the UK and what was then the USSR. Two years later, he took second place in the first ever transatlantic balloon race, in a balloon of his own design.

★ **The first 'special shape' balloon:** designed by Glasgow University aeronautics graduate Don Cameron, in 1975, following on from his leadership of the team that built Europe's first modern hot air balloon in 1965. Cameron runs the world's largest sports balloon company: 80 per cent of the world's 400 sports balloons are Cameron designed.

★ **The first helicopter capable of lifting a man off the ground:** built by the Clyde shipbuilders William Denny and Brothers. The prototype made a brief tethered flight in 1909, followed by a free flight in 1914.

★ **The first people to fly over Mount Everest:** Scots aviators the Marquess of Clydesdale and Flight Lieutenant D. McIntyre, the Marquess being at the controls. As the 14th Duke of Hamilton, he gained further fame in 1941 as the person whom Hitler's Deputy Rudolf Hess was trying to visit in the hope of negotiating a peace settlement when his plane crashed over Eaglesham moor west of Glasgow.

★ **Concorde:** engineer Sir James Hamilton, born in Edinburgh in 1923, and a graduate of Edinburgh University. As first Director General of the Concorde Project he took civilian supersonic flight from concept to the first two prototypes. He later became the first engineer to be permanent head of a UK Government Department.

★ **The first variable incidence rotors to a rotorcraft:** Perthshire engineers David Kay and John Grieve. Their Kay 33/1 Gyroplanes of 1935, precursors of the helicopter, were designed to allow the angle in which the rotor approaches the oncoming airflow to be altered to suit flying conditions.

★ **The combustion chamber for the jet engine:** designed by Edinburgh firm Laidlaw Drew for Sir Frank Whittle. At the 1936 British Industries Fair, Whittle visited the stands of well-known firms specialising in combustion equipment for boilers. When he explained his required combustion intensities – 20 times greater than ever produced before – Mr Laidlaw was the only manufacturer who did not look at him with blank amazement, but agreed to experiment with a design.

★ **The first all-year, regular British air service:** launched in 1933 by Midland and Scottish Air Ferries Ltd between Glasgow and Islay.

★ **The world's shortest scheduled air route:** lasting two minutes between Westray and Papa Westray in Orkney.

★ **The first powered flight in Britain:** Preston Watson (1880–1915), the son of a Dundee merchant. Although history records the Wright brothers as having flown the first powered aircraft in Britain in December 1903, a number of eyewitnesses reported seeing Watson airborne near Errol, Perthshire, earlier that summer. The craft they may have spotted was Watson's ornithopter. Propelled by flapping its wings, it was launched by an ingenious catapult system before its own power took over.

★ **The first two-seater helicopter:** the W-6 built in 1938 by the Glasgow engineers, G. & J. Weir. From 1932, the company financed the development of the autogiro by Spaniard Juan De La Cierva, whose development of articulated rotor blade design played a major role in getting the first successful helicopter into the air in 1936. Weir built a range of autogiros in the 1930s. Some people predicted the autogiro would be the family runabout of the air, the aviation equivalent of Henry Ford's Model T. The onset of the Second World War ended Weir's involvement in flight.

SCOTS ON WHEELS

★ **Vehicle component standardisation:** adopted by Albion Motors of Glasgow in 1903, five years before Henry Ford's mass-production of the Model T. It allowed Albion to switch between manufacturing vans and cars according to demand.

★ **First production car to be fitted with four-wheel brakes:** the Argyll 15/30, first exhibited at London's Olympia in 1911.

★ Europe's largest car manufacturer: the Argyll Motor Company of Alexandria, Dunbartonshire, albeit briefly from 1907, as the company was bankrupt seven years later. Argyll's imaginative approach to marketing included opening a London showroom with female instructresses to teach ladies how to drive their new Argyll.

★ *Perseverance*: designed in 1827 by Timothy Burstall, the manager of a Leith sawmills. Two years later, *Perseverance* joined four other locomotives including the winner, Stephenson's *Rocket*, in the Rainhill Trials, set up by the directors of the Liverpool & Manchester to choose the best locomotive for their new railway. Burstall spent five days trying to repair *Perseverance*, which had been damaged on the way to the trials. On the sixth day *Perseverance* joined the competition but, after only reaching 6 mph, Burstall withdrew, being awarded a consolation prize of £25.

★ The single sleeve valve engine: patented by Glaswegian inventor Peter Burt and adopted in the Argyll motor car. On discovery that a Canadian, J.H.K. McCollum, had independently patented a similar design six weeks before, although the Burt engine was much more advanced, agreement was reached to grant Argyll the rights to both patents. The Argyll 15/30 with the Burt-McCollum engine installed broke world speed records at Brooklands in 1911. The Burt sleeve valve engine later found its true home in aircraft. The Bristol Perseus engine based on the Burt patent made its first public appearance in a British Bulldog at the 1934 Hendon Air Pageant and was put to the ultimate test in the Second World War.

★ The brougham: the two-seater, enclosed carriage, designed by and named after the Edinburgh-born Lord Brougham (1778–1868). Based on a type of carriage that Brougham had seen on the Continent, the brougham, and the clarence, which developed from it, were the most popular types of closed carriage ever built.

★ Britain's first ring road: Dundee's Kingsway opened in 1919.

★ The world's first cable underground railway: Glasgow Underground. Opened in 1896, the 'Subway' was the third underground in the world after London and Budapest. Although it opened on 14 December 1896, a collision on the first day delayed its operation for nearly a month.

★ The first steam locomotive to achieve a speed of 100 mph: the *Flying Scotsman*, designed by Edinburgh-born Sir Nigel Gresley (1876–1941).

★ The world record for speed under steam: the *Mallard* locomotive designed by Sir Nigel Gresley (1876–1941). The record of 126 mph, achieved in 1938, remains unbroken today.

★ The busiest tramway crossing in the world: claimed by Glasgow's Jamaica Street/Renfield Street junction in the heyday of the 'caurs'.

★ The steam car: William Murdoch (1754–1839), although a Frenchman had designed a similar device in 1771 to move artillery. In 1785, Murdoch mounted a steam engine on a three-wheeled frame and drove the vehicle round the streets of Redruth in Cornwall to the citizens' amazement. His employer, James Watt, however, included the steam car in his patent of 1784 so that he could put the idea on ice, as he considered the necessary high pressures for steam engines in road vehicles as dangerous.

★ The Clincher tyre: patented by the North British Rubber Company of Edinburgh in 1890. The now universally adopted Clincher tyre has beaded edges pressed into grooves on the rim whereas early rubber cycle tyres were held in the rims either by wire or cement.

★ Europe's first custom built car factory: established in Edinburgh in 1898 by astronomer William Peck to manufacture his electric car, the Madelvic. The company only survived two years.

★ The pneumatic tyre: invented in 1845 by Robert Thomson (1822–73) and reinvented by Scots vet living in Belfast, John Boyd Dunlop (1840–1921), initially for the wheels of his children's tricycle.

★ The UK's first combined fire engine: designed by Edinburgh's Firemaster Wilkins in 1886. It brought together in one unit, the fire engine, hose carriage and fire escape ladder.

6

Calling Thomas Watson and William Taynton: Making the World Smaller

For a people of so few words, the Scots at home and abroad played a surprisingly large part in the science of conversation. 'By God, it talks' was the opening remark of the first ever royal telephone call. Brazilian Emperor Pedro II's reaction to using the telephone was soon shared by the world. While Alexander Graham Bell changed for ever the way we communicate, John Logie Baird changed for ever the way the world views itself through his invention of television. Scots throughout the centuries have dreamed of making the world smaller – from facsimile transmission to communication by light – even when their ambitions were sometimes far ahead of the technology of the day.

The Scottish contribution to communications goes back to the seventeenth century with the UK's oldest surviving envelope being sent from a Scot to a Scot. In the eighteenth century, the era of letter writing as a means of communication, Joseph Black significantly reduced the cost of writing paper by introducing a way of manufacturing it by bleaching rags, rather than having to use expensive linen. Even by then one individual, known only by the initials C.M., was anticipating the technology of the next century. In a letter to the *Scots Magazine* in 1753, C.M. proposed the transmission of messages over a distance by means of a set of 26 wires, each of which corresponded to a letter of the alphabet. The receiver had 26 pith balls, each with a different letter of the alphabet. When the wires were activated with static electricity, the balls would be attracted to their corresponding charged wires. No one has yet been able to put a name to the person who forecast telegraphy.

THE FIRST BUSINESS COPIER

James Watt (1736–1819) is known throughout the world for his perfection of the steam engine, but less so for his invention of the copier which became a standard piece of office equipment in the nineteenth century. Watt designed what is arguably the first duplicating machine in order to cope with the paperwork of his growing engineering business. He first described his invention in a letter to his friend, Joseph Black. 'I have lately discovered a method of copying writing instantaneously, providing it has been written the same day or within twenty-four hours. It enables me to copy all my business letters.' The letter copier, patented in 1780, consisted of a flat bed press with either a side-arm lever or screw and a horizontal bar. The item to be copied was placed in the press with a piece of transparent tracing or unsized drawing paper, which had first been treated with a fixative of vinegar, borax, oyster shells, bruised Aleppo galls and distilled water. As the ink penetrated the unsized sheet, the reverse impression of the text on the topside could be read through the translucent paper.

The firm of James Watt and Company was formed in 1780 to produce the copier – some of Scotland's greatest Enlightenment figures, Adam Ferguson, Adam Smith and Joseph Black being among the first purchasers. Watt's partner, Matthew Boulton, launched an aggressive marketing campaign, circulating promotional literature to all MPs and arranging demonstrations at Westminster and at Court. Specimens of every kind of writing along with their duplicates were displayed at all the principal coffee houses. Not surprisingly, the Governors of the Bank of England were unenthusiastic, although Boulton dismissed their concerns about fraud, with the remark, 'Some of their Directors are Hogs.'

Some 150 models were quickly sold, a fifth for export. A portable model was produced for travellers and one for the Indian market used springs of 'best steel' to withstand changes in temperature. A special ink, mixed with the gummy substance, mucilage, was developed in powdered form. Within a few years, the copier was a standard piece of business equipment and machines, little different from Watt's original prototype, continued to be used in offices right up to the beginning of the twentieth century and the advent of carbon paper, stencils and later the photocopier. The

Watt copier helped Scots entrepreneur Andrew Carnegie to make his millions:

> It is difficult to name an invention more universally used in all offices where man labours in any field of activity. In the list of modest inventions of greatest usefulness, the modern copying-press must take high rank, and this we owe entirely to Watt.

Another Scot was to make life in the office still easier.

THE FIRST PERSON TO LICK A STAMP

Born in Arbroath, James Chalmers (1782–1853) produced the world's first adhesive postage stamp at his Dundee printing works in 1834, as a sample to illustrate his ideas for standardising the prepayment of postage. At the time, letters were paid for by the recipient rather than the sender, resulting in lost revenue for the Post Office as many recipients refused the delivery. As a businessman, Chalmers had already successfully taken up the cudgels for a more efficient postal service, persuading the Post Office to reduce by a day the time mail from Dundee took to reach London. His stamp was a sepia-coloured square bearing the legend 'General Postage – NOT EXCEEDING HALF AN OUNCE – One Penny' enclosed in a decorative border. His suggestions for postal reform included the now universal system of using different colours of stamp to denote the different rates of postage. He used one of his sample twopenny stamps on a letter posted to the Secretary of the GPO, the first time an envelope bearing an adhesive stamp ever went through the mail.

Independently, Rowland Hill was campaigning for a more efficient postal service, proposing adhesive stamps in 1837 in his *Postal Reform; its Importance and Practibility*. When a Parliamentary Committee, set up to examine Hill's proposals, invited suggestions from the public, Chalmers sent in his proposals backed by the leading businessmen of Dundee. In 1839, parliament approved plans for the penny post and the next year the Penny Black was launched, bringing letter writing within most people's pockets. To this day, there has been controversy as to whether Chalmers or Rowland Hill invented the adhesive postage stamp. It is likely that Chalmers was the first to produce an adhesive stamp in 1834, and Rowland Hill to suggest the idea in print three years later. Rowland Hill was knighted and buried in Westminster Abbey, while Chalmers had to rest content with a plaque to the 'originator of the adhesive postage stamp' erected by his granddaughter on the site of his bookseller's shop in Dundee.

If the world was to communicate and act effectively, people in different places needed to keep to the same time. Three timely Scots helped to synchronise the world's watches.

THE TIME BALL

Vice-Admiral Robert Wauchope of Niddrie, outside Edinburgh, invented the time ball in 1818. From the mid-eighteenth century, ships' captains used chronometers to keep time at sea to navigate accurately. In order to ensure that their chronometers remained accurate, they needed occasionally to check them against the correct time at port. After Admiralty trials at Portsmouth, the first time ball was built at Greenwich. The very first, visible time signal, it dropped down a pole at 1 p.m., giving astronomers an hour to make their time calculations from the midday sun.

Wauchope's time ball enabled ships' captains to check the time by telescope. The system of time balls continued in use around the world until the introduction of reliable wireless signals in the early twentieth century. Ironically, Wauchope's native city was slow to adopt the device, shelving his suggestion to them until 1854. Once convinced, albeit late in the day, Edinburgh believed in doing things in style. In 1861, the famous time gun was added to the time ball, fired by means of electrical signals along a 4,020-ft single span of wire between Calton Hill and Castle Hill, the longest such single wire span in the world. Today, shoppers on Princes Street still check their watches when the one o'clock gun fires from the castle. What Wauchope did for time at sea, another Scot was to do for railway time.

FATHER OF THE FAX

A twin and one of 13 children of a Caithness crofter, Alexander Bain's (1810–77) apprenticeship to a Wick watchmaker gave him an interest in time that remained with him all his life. In 1837, he moved to London to complete his apprenticeship, attending evening classes at the Polytechnic and becoming fascinated with the application of electricity to the transmission of time. His experiments so impressed the editor of the *Mechanics Magazine* that he put Bain in touch with Charles Wheatstone, soon to win universal acclaim as the inventor of the telegraph.

The relationship started off cordially enough with Wheatstone paying Bain £3 for a model of a telegraph, which he had designed, and the promise of a further £50 on its completion. A lengthy and bitter quarrel soon ensued when Wheatstone patented his own telegraph and opposed all Bain's patents, even for items like his mariner's log in which Wheatstone had no personal interest. The quarrel came to a head in 1847, when Wheatstone and his business partner Cooke sought parliamentary approval for their electric telegraph. Bain issued a challenge and the arguments were heard in both Houses of Parliament and the Courts of England, Scotland and Ireland before Wheatstone finally won the day. The most likely conclusion is that Wheatstone and Bain were both working independently towards the same solution, although Bain was convinced that Wheatstone had simply stolen his idea. As compensation to Bain, Wheatstone's Electric Telegraph Company was instructed to make and promote Bain's clock and give him half the profits.

One of the few patents that Bain did succeed in taking out was for the electric clock, having retreated to Edinburgh in 1844 to set up as a watchmaker. Before the advent of the railways, time did not have the same urgency: each region of the UK happily operated to a slightly different time due to differences in the local time of noon. With the railways, guards could glance importantly at their official watches before blowing the whistle to keep the service running precisely to time, but whose time did they keep? Bain developed a weight-driven clock to make and break contacts and by use of a battery to send these impulses to drive various mechanisms connected by wires. He set up a telegraph system for the Glasgow–Edinburgh railway and, in 1846, demonstrated time transmission over this line, with a pendulum in Edinburgh working clocks in Glasgow. His electric clock and electromagnetic pendulum led to Greenwich Mean Time being adopted throughout Britain in 1852.

Bain has truly earned his place in history as the father of facsimile. In 1846, he patented an automatic, chemical recording telegraph, which recorded 282 words in 52 seconds when demonstrated between Lille in eastern France and Paris. He used his synchronised pendulums to scan print on to an electrically conducting surface at one end of a line, reproducing the print at the other – the essential principle of scanning an image for transmission. Bain's last years were sad and disillusioned, although attempts were made to provide him with a pension in recognition of his contribution to telegraphy and time transmission. A third Scot was to make time international.

KEEPING TIME IN KIRKCALDY AND KHARTOUM

Sandford Fleming (1827–1915) emigrated to Canada from Fife at the age of 17. His versatile career in a young country took in surveying, engineering and design. He conducted the initial survey for the Canadian Pacific Railway, the first railway to span the continent. In 1851, he designed Canada's first postage stamp: it cost threepence and carried the design of a beaver.

Fleming's contribution to time was the system of international time zones. His idea was inspired by the difficulties that travellers experienced while crossing the vast distances of Canada by rail:

> The traveller lands at Halifax, in Nova Scotia and starts on a railway journey through Saint John, Quebec, Montreal, Ottawa and Toronto. As he reaches each place in succession, he finds a considerable variation in the clocks by which the trains are run, and he discovers that at no two places is the same time used.

Although Britain had adopted a standard time in 1852, in America and Canada, with their vast distances, the problem was more intractable. Fleming campaigned for his system of 24 time zones covering the world from 1878 onwards. He presented his proposals to the Royal Canadian Institute the next year, and in 1883 the United States railways adopted four standard zones, in accord with his principles, which achieved widespread support among scientists. In 1884, he succeeded in getting a conference in Washington of all 25 then independent nations to establish a universal system of time. In an attempt to outflank nationalistic rivalries, notably from the French, Fleming proposed a prime meridian running down the middle of the Pacific, not meeting any land at all. This would have meant that date in Europe changed at midday. Fortunately, common sense prevailed and the Greenwich Meridian, the de facto standard, was adopted – the French being outvoted. Universal Standard Time is nonetheless essentially Fleming's system and its introduction owes much to his persistent advocacy. Another Scot, whose invention made international time zones even more critical, was Alexander Graham Bell (1847–1922).

GIVE ME A BELL SOMETIME

The Bell family were fascinated by speech. Alexander Graham Bell's grandfather and father studied the mechanics of speech and his father was a pioneer in the teaching of speech to the deaf, using his system of Visible Speech, an alphabet of symbols, which he claimed made it possible to record the pronunciation of every human sound. In 1857, James Murray, a young teacher from the Borders, who later became the first editor of the *Oxford English Dictionary*, attended a summer school in elocution given by Bell senior who introduced Murray to the science of phonetics. Impressed by the young teacher, Bell invited him home to meet his son and the two became close friends. One afternoon, when young Bell asked Murray to explain to him about electricity, Murray made an electric battery and a voltaic pile out of halfpennies and zinc disks. Graham later referred to Murray as the 'Grandfather of the telephone'.

As a young man Bell worked alongside his father at the Edinburgh School for the Deaf until tragedy struck the family in the shape of tuberculosis. Although Alexander, unlike two of his brothers, survived, his health was affected and in 1870 the family emigrated to Canada in the hope of an improvement. From Canada, Bell moved to the United States where in 1873 he was appointed Professor of Vocal Physiology at Boston University. On being issued the challenge by his father to produce a mechanical voice, Bell and his brother devised a system that imitated human sounds using a lamb's larynx, a mock skull and lungs made of wood and rubber. It was the first step towards the telephone.

Falling in love with one of his deaf pupils drove Bell's experiments even harder, especially towards ways of reproducing sound mechanically. He estimated that if sound waves could be converted into a fluctuating electric current, the current could then be reconverted into sound waves identical with the original at the other end of the circuit. In this way sound could be carried across wires at the speed of light. One day, while experimenting with a device that he had developed to test his theory, Bell accidentally spilled battery acid on his trousers. Without thinking, he called out to his assistant, 'Watson, please come here. I want you.' Thomas Watson, working at the other end of the circuit on another floor, heard the command and the rest is history. The two constructed the world's first telephone, known as the Gallow's Frame.

In 1876, Bell's telephone first went on public display at the Centennial Exhibition in Philadelphia, where it became a major talking point. Lord Kelvin, an exhibition judge, was so impressed that he promptly introduced the telephone to Britain. Although Bell could see that, 'the great advantage it possesses over other electrical apparatus is that it requires no skill to operate', he personally was less enthusiastic about his baby, often stuffing his telephone with paper to muffle the bell and claiming, 'I never use the beast.' The telephone rapidly became part of the American way of life and by the age of 30 Bell was rich and famous, thanks to one of the most successful and profitable inventions ever made. In 1915, when the first transcontinental telephone line was inaugurated, Bell repeated the command to his assistant, 'Watson, please come here. I want you.' This time Watson was located at the other side of America.

Although Bell was, by his own admission, a hopeless businessman, he was lucky in his early partners, which included his father-in-law. He made sufficient profit from the telephone to support his growing family and his continued passion for invention for the rest of his life. All his days, he regarded himself as first and foremost a teacher of the deaf and continued to promote the cause, conducting the first US-wide census of the deaf in 1890. On an extended visit to Scotland, he founded a school for the deaf in Greenock, even going back to teaching for three weeks when the tutor recruited from the United States failed to arrive.

Bell just kept on inventing. He worked with Thomas Edison on the phonograph; developed a form of iron lung; designed apparatus for thirsty travellers in the desert to distil moisture from their breath; created a universal language, World English; bred sheep to increase the likelihood of twins and triplets; and even tried to teach animals to speak. He hoped to make a second fortune from his novelty 'adult' spinning top with a swear word recorded in a groove round its side. Unfortunately, the word he chose has not been recorded for posterity. In 1881, his inventive powers were tested when he was asked to devise a metal detector to locate the bullet fired at President Garfield by an assassin. Although it failed to save the dying President, as no one thought to remove the steel-sprung mattress on which he lay, Bell's invention did save several lives before the invention of X-rays superseded it.

One invention of which Bell was particularly proud was the Photophone – a device which transmitted speech by a beam of light – which he patented in 1880. 'I have heard a ray of the sun laugh!' he exclaimed after the first demonstration, although he admitted that his Photophone might be of 'less practical utility' than the telephone. The problem was that the transmitter and receiver had to be in sight of one another. Bell's vision of long-distance communication by light had to wait for the laser and fibre optics. Bell's last enthusiasm was for flight. In 1907, he devised a kite capable of carrying a person. With a group of associates, including the American inventor and aviator Glenn Hammond Curtiss, Bell developed the aileron, the movable section of an aeroplane wing that controls roll and the tricycle landing gear which first permitted take-off and landing. Applying the principles of aeronautics to marine propulsion, the team started work on hydrofoils. His 'hydrodrome' of 1917 reached speeds in excess of 70 mph and for many years was the fastest boat in the world.

The Scots were among the first to pick up the phone, Lord Kelvin being the first person in the UK to install one. Scottish medical professionals quickly realised its business potential with Glasgow installing the UK's first telephone exchange.

DOUGLAS 174

This was the Glasgow Medical Telephone Exchange installed at 140 Douglas Street in the city centre by the Glasgow firm of electrical engineers, Messrs D. and G. Graham, in January/February 1879, over six months before the first exchange opened in London. At first, the service was planned exclusively for the medical profession including hospital doctors, chemists and GPs. Night and Sunday services were available from the outset, allowing doctors to be on 24-hour call.

The service proved so successful that other exchange networks were quickly added – 'Legal', 'Stockbrokers' and 'Commercial' – and soon members of different networks were able to communicate with each other. Graham insisted that subscribers sign five-year contracts, but guaranteed to keep the roofs of all the buildings used for his overhead lines in a reasonable state of repair provided that the subscriber denied access to any competitor.

Graham's were a remarkably switched-on company. They retained Lord Kelvin as consulting electrician and were responsible for wiring his home for electricity, the first in Scotland. They generated the electricity for Joseph Swan's demonstration of electric light to the meeting of the Philosophical Society of Glasgow in 1881, and in the same year fitted out the first mine in the world to be lit by electric light – the Earnock Colliery, near Hamilton. At the same time, they installed telephonic links between the engine room and the pit face. Despite the introduction of the telephone, the telegraph wires still hummed in the offices of the *Glasgow Herald* newspaper where one operator, Frederick George Creed (1871–1957), was to take a different leap forward in making the world smaller.

THE CURE FOR A BATTERED THUMB

The son of Scots emigrants to Nova Scotia, Creed was the next best thing to Scottish. On leaving school at 14, he trained as a telegraph operator, a job which was a passport to travel. He worked in Canada, Chile and Peru where he met his wife, Jeannie Russell, a Free Church of Scotland missionary. Like many operators, Creed suffered from a permanently distorted right hand from the strain of using a Morse 'stick' perforator, a device with three keys hit by hand, which punched paper tape for transmitting Morse code signals. This started him thinking.

On taking a job with the *Glasgow Herald* as a telegraph operator in 1897, Creed tried to interest people in his idea for a teleprinter. Even when Lord Kelvin and the assistant editor of the *Glasgow Herald* remained unconvinced, Creed persevered, purchasing an old typewriter for 15 shillings and spending his spare time converting it into a prototype. This time he won over Kelvin, who gave him technical advice to develop his idea further. Creed now had the confidence to give up his job and rent a workshop. He sold 12 keyboard perforators to the General Post Office and convinced his ex-employers of the practicality of his invention. As well as buying his equipment, the *Glasgow Herald* gave him the freedom of their office to test his next invention. This was a receiver perforator which recorded incoming signals on a perforated tape identical to that used at the other end for the transmission, and a printer that accepted the received message tape and decoded it into plain language characters on ordinary paper tape.

As business increased, Creed took the well-trodden path south. In 1909, he opened a small factory in Croydon on the southern outskirts of London to be closer to potential clients, notably the Post Office. The company went from strength to strength, the newspaper industry being the first to seize on this new form of rapid communication, the teleprinter. Creed continued to develop his invention with Europe's first start-stop, five unit code teleprinter, the automatic tape transmitter and the send/receive teleprinter. Creed's later years, however, were less happy. In 1927, the American multinational, ITT – the International Telephone and Telegraph Co. – bought out Creed's firm, and Creed soon fell out with his new directors, partly because as a strict Sabbatarian he disapproved strongly of the introduction of Sunday sports for employees. He resigned and worked away at new inventions including catamarans and a twin-hulled 'seadrome' for refuelling aircraft on transatlantic flights. None were successful and Creed spent his last years fighting off impending bankruptcy.

The teleprinter helped the journalist to bring the world's news to the breakfast table. With television, the faces in the news could reach their audience throughout the world 24 hours a day.

'MOVING PICTURES BY WIRELESS'

John Logie Baird (1888–1946), a minister's son from Helensburgh, attributed his interest in science to his classical education: 'If they had taught me science at school instead of Latin and Greek I would probably have become a minister like my father. There is nothing like a Classical education to turn a boy's mind into really practical channels.' He was particularly fascinated by electricity, which he installed in the manse while in his teens. He had already connected it to the homes of four of his schoolfriends with a fully operational, unofficial telephone system complete with exchange. The experiment came to a sudden end when one of the cables caught the driver of a passing horse-drawn bus and pulled him from his seat.

Although his father wanted his son to follow him into the Church, he bowed to the inevitable and Baird took up electrical engineering at the Glasgow and West of Scotland College of Technology, the forerunner of Strathclyde University, and at Glasgow University. His training involved placements with local engineering firms, including the Argyll car plant at Alexandria, where he was treated as any other apprentice. Despite chronic ill health, he showed a capacity for hard work, which earned the respect of his workmates. His experience gave him a deep sympathy with the lot of the working man, which he demonstrated by wearing a cloth cap all his life. He escaped the monotony of his first job as a power engineer in a Glasgow electricity substation by dreaming of a future as an inventor. For this, however, he needed money. After an attempt to manufacture diamonds, by passing a high current through carbon set in a concrete block, resulted in blacking out much of the area and the threat of the sack, Baird decided to turn to less ambitious, but more profitable ways of making his fortune.

Baird's own sensitivity to cold suggested the Baird Undersock, designed to be worn under ordinary socks to keep the feet dry and warm. Effective marketing, including the employment of Glasgow's first sandwich-board women and persuading friends to tour shops asking for the Undersock, resulted in a tidy profit. Continued ill health led Baird to seek sunnier climates. When trade in calico and safety pins with Trinidad proved less profitable than expected, Baird turned to manufacturing mango chutney and guava jelly. Returning to the UK, he successfully marketed imported honey and 'Baird's

Speedy Cleaner', a cheap, pale yellow soap. By the end of the First World War, income from these ventures proved sufficient to fund the pursuit of his dream of 'moving pictures by wireless'.

Baird settled in the South Coast resort of Hastings for his health and recruited assistants, paid and unpaid, throughout the UK from Folkestone to Falkirk, to work on particular aspects of development. Only too aware that others were pursuing the same goal, Baird was deliberately evasive about progress, even keeping his assistants in the dark about each other's activities. His first apparatus consisted of a tea chest, a biscuit tin, Nipkow scanning discs of cardboard, darning needles, hat boxes, cycle lamp lenses and discarded electric motors, all held together by piano wire, glue, string and sealing wax. He may have deliberately presented this 'contraption' to keep competitors in the dark. He succeeded in transmitting the shadow of a Maltese cross over a distance of ten feet in 1924, before being evicted from his laboratory after an explosion caused by his 2,000-volt electricity supply constructed out of several hundred torch batteries wired together.

On 30 October 1925, Baird made the first television transmission of a moving image with gradations of light and shade in his Soho attic workshop. While experimenting with a dummy's head he received an image on the screen and rushed down to the office below in quest of a live model, recruiting office boy, William Taynton. Baird later described what happened next:

> I placed him before the transmitter and went into the next room to see what the screen would show. The screen was entirely blank and no effort of tuning would produce any results. Puzzled and disappointed, I went back to the transmitter and there the cause of the failure became at once evident. The boy, scared by the intense white light, had backed away from the transmitter. In the excitement of the moment I gave him half a crown and this time he kept his head in the right position. Going again into the next room this time I saw his head quite clearly. It is curious that the first person in the world to have been seen by television should have required a bribe to accept that distinction.

Baird gave his first demonstration of true television to the Press in

January 1926, the leading scientific journal, *Nature*, reviewing it with enthusiasm: 'This is the first time that we have seen real television and Mr Baird is the first to have accomplished this marvellous feat.' Selfridge's Oxford Street department store held public demonstrations to tempt the public to buy a Baird Televisor set well in advance of any guarantee of programmes. Other developers of television were not far behind. In April 1927, the Bell Company staged a broadcast from New York to Washington. Baird retaliated by broadcasting from London to Glasgow and, in February 1928, by successfully transmitting pictures across the Atlantic. The Bell transmission involved nearly 1,000 technicians, Baird's only eight. As his team sailed back on the Cunarder *Berengaria* they showed the ship's chief radio officer recognisable moving pictures of the fiancée he was going to meet in London.

Other innovations followed. Baird made the first television transmission in colour from the Baird studios on 3 July 1928, showing scarves, a policeman's helmet, a man putting his tongue out, the glowing end of a cigarette and a bunch of red roses. By 1930, he had demonstrated 3D television and television by infra-red light. In 1929, the BBC made its first transmission of 30-line experimental television. Although Baird eventually lost the race to produce a viable system of high resolution television, he had shown others the way. Fellow Glaswegian John Reith, first director-general of the BBC, who personally disliked television, rejected Baird's system, which used a mechanical scanner in both the transmitting apparatus and the receiver, in favour of the Marconi-EMI all-electronic system, the correct decision in the long term.

Not content with television, in 1928 Baird invented Phonovision, the world's first system to record television in the world's first TV recording studio. Baird's idea, which proved too far ahead of its time both technically and for the market, was that the public could purchase the discs and play them back through a simple attachment to their Baird Televisor sets – the world's first video recorder. Even when the BBC's decision went against him, Baird kept working away; in 1935, for example, helping the German company, Fernseh, to start the world's first three-day-a-week television service. A parliamentary committee recommended the adoption of his 3D colour system, but it proved too complex for the BBC. His idea of transmitting programmes to be shown on large cinema screens was just catching on when the Second World War broke out. Sadly, time was running out for Baird. In June 1946, a week after organising a showing of the victory parades at cinemas in London, he died at the age of 58.

Ironically, the concept of television as we know it – scanned, synchronised and displayed by electronic means – can be traced back to another Scot, Archibald Campbell Swinton (1863–1930), who proposed 'Distant Electric Vision' in a letter to the scientific journal *Nature* in 1908. He suggested using cathode ray tubes, magnetically deflected at both camera and receiver, to transmit and receive images. He was also a pioneer of X-rays, opening the UK's first X-ray laboratory. Among the hands of famous visitors he captured were those of Lord Salisbury, the Prime Minister, and Lord Kelvin.

As early as the 1920s, Baird was experimenting with the transmission, reflection and detection of radio waves to determine the distance of an object on a hilltop near Hastings. He also patented several ideas for infra-red rays for night vision. His later life is shrouded in a mystery greater than his own penchant for smokescreens. It is known that he reported to the military authorities on work that remains classified to this day. It is probable that he was working on secret signalling systems for sending pictures through the atmosphere and on the technology later christened radar by Sir Robert Watson-Watt (1892–1973).

BETTER THAN EATING CARROTS

Born in Brechin, Angus, Sir Robert Watson-Watt traced his ancestry back to James Watt. A graduate of St Andrews University, he trained as a meteorologist before joining the Royal Aircraft Factory at Farnborough. His interest in radio led him to attempt to devise a system to allow pilots to locate local thunderstorms by the radio waves they emitted and, in 1916, to propose the use of the cathode ray oscilloscope to display information to pilots.

A colleague once summed up Watson-Watt's ability to bury his meaning in obscurantist language, 'By using unusual words, double negatives and convoluted syntax he was capable of making almost any subject, however simple, difficult to understand.' By now, one of the leading government authorities on the military uses of radio, he was asked to comment on the possibility of a radio 'death ray' as a weapon. He convincingly dismissed the possibility adding that the proposals on the 'still difficult, but less unpromising problem of radio detection and numerical considerations on the method of detection by reflected radio waves will be submitted when required'. His memo on the subject has been called 'the birth certificate of radar'.

As early as 1919, while a young lecturer at St Andrews, Watson-Watt had taken out a patent in connection with radio location by means of short-wave radio. Throughout the 1920s, he improved on his idea and by 1935 had produced a system that made it possible to track an aircraft by the radio wave reflection that it sent back. He christened the system 'radio detection and ranging', soon shortened to radar. With war clouds forming over Europe, the military significance of radar was realised and Watson-Watt's research went underground, with trials held on a remote airfield on the Suffolk coast. As part of the cloak of secrecy surrounding the project, it was described to the public as being about Radio Direction Finding. This deceit turned out in fact to be true: it had not at first been realised that the direction of an aircraft, as well as its distance, could be tracked by the new device.

In 1937, Watson-Watt's wife joined him in his cloak-and-dagger activities as they travelled through Germany posing as tourists to search for signs of radar stations. By 1939, a number of British radar stations were in place and more were hurriedly erected. They made it possible during the Battle of Britain to detect enemy planes in all weathers and as easily by night as by day, an ability that almost certainly meant the difference between victory and defeat. To explain their success in locating enemy planes, the RAF put about the story that they had been feeding their pilots carrots to improve their night vision. Although the United States and Germany had also been developing radar type systems, it was Watson-Watt's research and the pressures of war that gave Britain the lead. In 1941, he helped the US authorities to complete their radar systems, in time to give warning of the onset of enemy planes at Pearl Harbor: tragically, the radar warning was ignored.

In 1940, aided by two colleagues from Birmingham University, Watson-Watt also invented the cavity magnetron. By producing a compact source of short-wave radio waves, this allowed the RAF's Fighter Command to detect incoming enemy planes from a much greater distance, giving pilots more time to prepare themselves. The magnetron operators also found it had another use – it could heat up water. Today, magnetrons are used as the source of heat in microwave ovens.

FIRST WITH THE NEWS

★ The world's second oldest surviving newspaper: the *Aberdeen Press and Journal*, published in 1746 and pipped to the post for the world title by the *Belfast News Letter* of 1737. Founded in 1783, Glasgow's *Herald* is in eighth place, claiming to be the oldest national daily newspaper in the English-speaking world.

★ America's first newspaper: the *Boston News Letter*, published in 1704 by Islay-born bookseller and postmaster, John Campbell.

★ Britain's first serious film magazine: *Cinema Quarterly*, founded by Forsyth Hardy and Norman Wilson in 1932.

★ The world's oldest surviving comic: *The Dandy*, first published by D.C. Thomson in 1937 with *The Beano* hard on its heels in 1938. Both ushered in a new era of comics, with their distinctive style of drawing and wealth of characters. In the 1980s, the *Dandy* was the world's best-selling comic.

★ Last British daily to replace advertisements with news on its front page: the *Dundee Courier* in 1992.

★ Chancellor Gordon Brown's 'compelling reading': *The Economist*, founded by Hawick hat maker James Wilson (1805–60) in 1843 to campaign for free trade.

★ The oldest continuing medical journal in the English language: the *Edinburgh Medical Journal*, founded in 1805.

★ America's leading biweekly business magazine: Founded in 1917 by Scots emigrant, Bertie C. Forbes, *Forbes Magazine* formed the basis of his son Malcolm's $400 million fortune.

★ Britain's oldest local government newspaper: the *Municipal Journal* was founded in 1893 by Banffshire-born Robert Donald (1860–1933). He later became editor of the Liberal *Daily Chronicle*, taking its circulation to that of *The Times*, *Daily Telegraph*, *Morning Post*, *Evening Standard* and *Daily Graphic* combined.

★ The *National Geographic*: Alexander Graham Bell (1847–1922). Although the National Geographical Society and its modest magazine had been founded by Bell's father-in-law, it was Bell, as President from 1898 who, with his son-in-law Gilbert Grosvenor, turned it into one of the world's best-known magazines. Seeking to promote an understanding of life in distant lands at a time when travel was limited to the privileged few, Bell suggested that geography could be taught best through pictures and good writing.

★ First radio coverage of the launch of a ship: *Queen Mary* in Clydebank in 1934.

★ The leading US journal *Science*: Alexander Graham Bell (1847–1922), who was one of its founders in 1883.

★ The first British newspaper to produce a separate weekend supplement: *The Scotsman* in 1962.

★ The first British newspaper to deliver editions by special train: *The Scotsman* in 1872. The time between publication in Edinburgh and delivery in Glasgow was reduced to 70 minutes, allowing Glaswegians to read the news at the same time as the citizens of Edinburgh. The *London Times* followed the Scottish lead with a delivery to Birmingham in 1873.

★ The first British newspaper to insert 'stop press' news without halting the presses: *The Scotsman*, thanks to a device invented by works manager Edgar Smith, in 1926.

★ The UK's oldest surviving monthly magazine: the *Scots Magazine*, founded in 1739.

★ World's first colour picture of a news event printed during the normal production process: the newspaper was the *Scottish Daily Record* ; the photo, Mrs Simpson during the abdication crisis of 1936. The same year, the *Record* published Britain's first coloured newspaper advertisement.

★ The oldest continuously published weekly magazine in the English language: *The Spectator*, founded by Robert Stephen Rintoul in 1828. Previously editor of the *Dundee Advertiser*, Rintoul aimed to produce a magazine of what he called 'educated radicalism'.

★ The UK's first newspaper crossword: introduced in 1924 by Dundee-born John Rutherford Gordon, editor of the *Sunday Express*. Sundays would never be the same again.

★ Canada's largest selling newspaper: the *Toronto Globe*. Its Alloa-born founder, George Brown (1818–80), emigrated to Canada in 1843. Entering politics, he formed a coalition government for a few days in 1858. For the last seven years of his life he served on the Senate, eventually being killed by a disgruntled employee fired from his newspaper.

7

The Man with a Wooden Top Hat and Wellies: Creating Home Comforts

Scotland's contribution to everyday life is more than haggis, bagpipes and the kilt – none of which were invented here. Scots did, however, patent the water closet, and gave it one of its best-known brands – Shanks – and one of its most popular names – the loo. They may not have come up with the dishwasher, the deep freeze or breakfast cereal, but they did discover the process for water softening and the principle of refrigeration, and they were eating oatmeal porridge centuries before Will Keith Kellogg invented corn flakes. They also added two staples to the English breakfast table – tea and marmalade.

ANOTHER CUP OF TEA, DEAR

The tea that everyone associates with the British breakfast comes from India where three Scots helped to pioneer its growth. Before Hugh Falconer (1808–65) from Forres, Moray, was appointed Superintendent of the Saharanpur Botanic Gardens in 1832, tea was almost exclusively imported from China. The search was on to break the Chinese monopoly by finding a cheaper source of tea. Selecting the north-western Himalayan foothills as a suitable area for tea plantations, Falconer succeeded in growing some plants brought in from China.

To improve the stock he commissioned plant collector Robert Fortune (1812–80), from Berwickshire, to travel into China, recently opened to foreigners after the Opium Wars. On a previous expedition, he had survived angry mobs, pirates and killer storms in the Yellow Sea in his search for new specimens. Although speaking no Chinese, he disguised himself as a peasant with a shaved head, ponytail and local dress and called himself Sing Wah. His second trip was more fruitful, if less adventurous. Commissioned by the East India Company for whom Falconer worked 'for the purpose of obtaining the finest of the tea plant for the government plantations in the Himalayas' and with a 500 per cent pay increase, Fortune supervised the transporting of nearly 24,000 young tea plants and 17,000 seedlings along with eight Chinese tea growers over the Himalayas to the tea plantations of Assam and Hakkim. Dr William Jameson, an army surgeon and Falconer's successor at the Botanic Gardens, used the plants to improve the crop and scale up production to a level where Indian tea displaced Chinese on the British breakfast tables.

Thomas Lipton (1850–1931) helped to turn tea into the everyday cuppa. On his 21st birthday, he opened his first shop in Glasgow's Stobcross Street. His bold advertising posters caught the fancy of the Glasgow public and once he had branches throughout his native city he moved into England and the USA. Increasingly, Lipton's became known for teas, buying plantations in Ceylon to supply the shops direct. What distinguished Lipton's teas was their price, attractive packaging, light-hearted advertising and the fact that he blended teas for different regions depending on the chemical analysis of the local water supplies. He was the first to package tea in small, convenient tins to keep it fresh and preserve its flavour. Lipton played a major role in the revival of tea drinking in the UK from the 1880s and in challenging the popularity of coffee in the USA.

THE SOUR SMELL OF SUCCESS

Although there are strong associations between Scotland and marmalade, the Scots did not invent it. It first appeared in Scotland as a solid, sugary jelly of marmelos – quinces – exported from Portugal as 'marmelada' at the end of the fifteenth century. Mary Queen of Scots is reputed to have eaten it for her health, giving rise to the medical pun 'Marmelade pour Marie malade'. What Mrs

Keiller did two centuries later was to put marmalade on the world's breakfast tables by working out a way to manufacture it in quantity.

When James Keiller (1775–1839), a Dundee merchant, mistakenly purchased a consignment of bitter Seville oranges from a ship that had put into port, his wife Janet decided to make the oranges into a jelly similar to her quince jelly. While most early marmalades were beaten to a puree, Janet decided to take a short-cut using a French recipe she knew, which involved cutting the peel into chips. With a shrewd eye on economy, she also worked out that since this 'marmalade' was not concentrated into a thick paste, it would go further and require less cooking time. Using her bitter oranges, which had been introduced to Spain by the Arabs as a medicine, she changed marmalade from a sweetmeat to a morning aid to digestion.

In 1797, realising that his wife had created a winner out of a disaster, James Keiller set up a company to manufacture the new product. His nephew, Wedderspoon Keiller, invented a machine to cut the peel, previously done by hand. By the 1860s, Keiller's was Britain's largest confectionery, producing jams, jellies, candied peel and sweets from lozenges to gums, as well as marmalade. When the British Trade Mark Registry was set up in 1876, Keiller's Dundee Orange Marmalade, which by then graced the breakfast tables of Australia, New Zealand, South Africa, India and even China, was one of the first products to be registered. A later member of the family, Alexander Keiller, in the 1930s invested his share of the family fortune in uncovering and preserving the wonders of the Stone Age Avebury Circle in Wiltshire.

Until the mid-nineteenth century, however, marmalade was harsh and bitter. James Robertson, a Paisley grocer, realised that the taste was due to the pith and cellulose of the oranges. He and his wife spent months trying to discover a way of blending orange juice and sugar so that after cooking it would set into a jelly-like marmalade, to which they added parings of orange peel. Robertson christened it 'Golden Shred'. In 1859, sales of the new marmalade in Robertson's shop took off and he was soon ready to open a factory: by 1914, there were four throughout the UK. Initially sold in stone jars with parchment lids, Golden Shred later had paper wrappers right round the jar. The infamous golliwog was introduced in 1910, after John Robertson, James's son, had seen children playing with black rag dolls on a visit to the USA. He claimed that 'golly' was simply their mispronunciation of 'dolly'. In 1928, the first character in a range of golly brooches – the Golly golfer – appeared: these could be collected in return for coupons from the marmalade jars. By the end of the twentieth century, more than twenty million gollies had been dispatched.

THE FIRST FRUIT SQUASH

Rose's put the lime in marmalade, but the company's founder took it out of rum when he invented the first branded fruit drink. Edinburgh doctor James Lind first recommended the juice of citrus fruit as a specific against scurvy. The lime ration was served to sailors unsweetened, laced with a 15 per cent measure of rum as a preservative and sweetener. In the same year as the Merchant Shipping Act made a ration of lime or lemon juice compulsory for all sailors, Lachlan Rose, a Leith ship's chandler, removed the need for alcohol as a preservative, patenting his process in 1867.

Inspiration came while Rose was watching wine casks being fumigated with burning sulphur on the quayside. He discovered that salts of sulphur acted as an effective preservative for fruit juices. A shrewd businessman, he also realised that by sweetening the fruit juice and packaging it in attractive bottles, he could increase sales. The branded soft drinks industry was born with Rose's Lime Juice Cordial. His company went from strength to strength, introducing more exotic drinks with names like Ginger Brandy, Rum Shrub and Orange Quinine Wine. In 1893, the company purchased its own estate on Dominica in the Caribbean to guarantee a regular supply of limes. In 1955, Rose's merged with Schweppes, which continues to make Lachlan's lime juice.

Today, the world's best-selling soft drink, even in Scotland, is of course Coca-Cola. Was it the Scots, however, who put the Cola into Coca-Cola?

KOLA

The first reference to kola-type soft drinks is in an article in the *Mineral Water Trade Review* of 1873 recommending manufacturers to use the seeds of the kola nut to make syrup flavouring for lemonade. It is thought that Scottish manufacturers may have introduced the Kola flavour. By 1880, the drink was extremely popular in Scotland with more than seven bottlers producing it: a recipe still survives for 'Edinburgh Kola'. Scotland is probably the only place where Kola, traditionally known in the trade as 'Scotch Kola', survives to this day.

In 1879, an American journalist wrote in a trade magazine:

> In Scotland they have a drink called Kola in which extracts from the nuts and leaves of the African cola tree are used. It is much thought of by the natives and is flavoured in various ways after the fashion of meads, sherberts and sherries. It could presumably be tried in the United States of America by any enterprising bottler.

About this time, American soft drink manufacturers were starting to produce coca-flavoured drinks from the leaves of the Brazilian coca shrub, two chemists conducting an acrimonious correspondence in the press with each claiming to be the originator of coca-flavoured drinks. An Atlanta chemist, John Pemberton, was trying to devise a new blend of soft drink to be sold through soda fountains as a pick-me-up. He hit upon the idea of combining the flavours of coca and cola, making his first sales in May 1886. Had he read the article in search of inspiration?

Until very recently, Scotland was the only country in the developed world not to put Coca-Cola at the top of its favourite soft drink list. The drink that regularly topped Coke is Irn-Bru, Scotland's other national drink, manufactured originally under the name of Iron-Brew by the Glasgow soft drinks company A.G. Barr from 1901. Like Coca-Cola, the recipe for the drink 'made in Scotland from girders' remains a secret known only to a handful of people. Also like Coca-Cola, a Scottish butcher recognised the importance of branding, making his meat extract drink the generic, like Hoover did for its vacuum cleaner.

ALAS! MY POOR BROTHER!

John Lawson Johnston (1839–1900) trained as a butcher in Edinburgh before emigrating to Canada where, in 1874, he first manufactured his 'fluid beef' on a commercial scale. Ten years later, he returned to the UK producing his meat extract in a factory in Trinity Square, London. Determined to make it a household name, he hit upon the name 'Bovril', a combination of 'bos', the Latin word for ox, and Vrilya, the name given to the life force in a little-known novel by Bulwer Lytton. The first advertisement for Bovril read:

> ONE OUNCE of the nutritious constituents of JOHNSTON'S FLUID BEEF, brand BOVRIL, contains more real direct nourishment than FIFTY OUNCES of ordinary meat extract, and FIVE HUNDRED GUINEAS will be forfeited if this statement can be refuted.

Advertising played a large part in Bovril's success. A former Bovril factory manager, S.H. Benson, founded a London advertising agency with Bovril as its first client. One classic advertisement showed an ox mourning over a small jar of Bovril with the line, 'Alas! My poor brother!' When fellow Scot David Ogilvy came on board, the agency became the world leader, Ogilvy Benson and Mather. In the 1890s, Bovril survived an attack by the Scottish chain store millionaire Sir Thomas Lipton, who decided to manufacture his own version and undercut Bovril's prices by 35 per cent. By 1914, however, Bovril was back in Lipton's stores when Lipton managed to negotiate a large enough trade discount with Bovril to render the continued production of his 'own brand' uneconomic.

While Rose and Johnston enhanced the minor pleasures of life, other Scots concerned themselves with the basics like heating the home and lighting the streets. In 1892, to celebrate the centenary of gas lighting, Lord Kelvin unveiled a memorial at the Wallace Monument in Stirling to the son of an Ayrshire millwright who lit his home with gas.

FANNY BY GASLIGHT

As a child, William Murdoch (1754–1839) was fascinated by the new steam engines. In 1777, he walked 300 miles to Birmingham to persuade James Watt to take him on as an apprentice. At the start of his interview he laid his hat on the table with a thud. When Watt's partner, Matthew Boulton, commented on the noise, Murdoch replied, 'I turned it myself.' He was determined to look the part even if lack of funds meant having to make his hat out of a piece of wood. Impressed by the young man's skill and enthusiasm, Boulton and Watt dispatched Murdoch to Cornwall to supervise the installation of their engines in the local tin mines. He prospered and by 1800 had been made a partner in the firm.

Although Murdoch introduced many improvements to the steam engine, including the sun and planet wheel, the bell crank engine and the slide valve, his contribution to everyday life lay in a different direction. Fascinated from childhood by coal, he was the first person to see in it something more than a simple solid fuel. He heated coal in a kettle and ignited the gas that issued from the spout, which he had closed off by a thimble with holes drilled in it. In 1792, heating coal, peat and wood in the absence of air, he stored the gases given off and used them to light his house. By 1805, his factory was lit by gas. Although he met some initial scepticism – Sir Humphrey Davy asked Murdoch if he planned to turn St Paul's Cathedral into a gasometer – the huge potential of his discovery was quickly realised with some London streets being lit by gas as early as 1807. For the first time it was relatively safe to go out at night.

Ten years earlier, Archibald Cochrane, 9th Earl of Dundonald (1749–1831), had lit Culross Abbey in Fife by gas from his coal tar retorts. As he was in touch with James Watt about his experiments it is possible that Murdoch came to learn of the discoveries of this aristocratic experimenter. Cochrane laid the foundations of many processes that were to provide the bulk chemicals demanded by nineteenth-century industry, including the manufacture of gas. In 1781, he patented the distillation of tar from coal, yielding tar, varnish, lamp black, coke and gas, but was only interested in the tar. Although today admired as an industrial chemist, Cochrane's interest was only in inventions that would benefit the navy. He hoped to persuade the Admiralty to use tar as a wood preservative for ships' bottoms, but his words went unheeded. The Admiralty also rejected another of his many ideas – the smokescreen – on the grounds that it was considered an ungentlemanly way of conducting naval warfare. Dundonald's formula lay dormant in their files for a century until used in the First World War. Due to bad luck and poor business sense, Cochrane saw few of his ideas bear fruit in his lifetime.

THE FIRST GAS FITTER

Murdoch's original gaslight was a simple affair, nicknamed the cockspur, as the three small holes at the end of the tube were arranged to produce three divergent jets of flame. Like Murdoch, the son of a millwright, James Beaumont Neilson (1792–1865), was the first superintendent of Glasgow's first gasworks, being chosen out of 20 applicants, despite having seen gaslight only once in his life. Although better known as the inventor of the hot blast in iron and steel making, while a gas engineer Neilson devised a way of removing sulphur from gas and invented the swallowtail, or union jet gas burner, the standard gas fitment of the early Victorian household. The swallowtail burner was so called as it was arranged to cause two streams of gas to mingle and flatten out into a narrow, high sheet of flame. The flame was less vulnerable to draughts than previous burners and could be used with a globe light shade. Poor as the light from his burner was by modern standards, it was a vast improvement on earlier means of lighting and in its small way contributed to the marked increase in literacy over the period.

SIR PARAFFINE

Some miners in east central Scotland used a more unusual light to read by. James 'Paraffin' Young (1811–83) explored the source of this light and founded the oil industry. Until gas lighting, tallow and whale oil were the main sources of light. Tallow, processed from animal fat, was smelly and gave out a poor light, whereas whale oil was expensive, involving long and hazardous journeys to the world's whaling grounds. Phenomenal population growth in the early nineteenth century and the new demands of the Industrial Revolution spurred a number of people to look for a better light: James Young was one. While training to join his father as an undertaker, Young attended evening classes at the Andersonian Institution, the forerunner of Strathclyde University, held by Thomas Graham, the most noted chemist of his day. Here he met two students who became lifelong friends, the explorer David Livingstone and chemist Lyon Playfair.

Impressed by Young's enthusiasm and ability, Graham invited him to become his assistant when he moved to University College, London. Young soon left for a better paid career in industry, his second job as scientific adviser to Tennant's Chemical Works in Manchester being one of the first posts of industrial chemist to be created. This experience was invaluable in teaching Young large-scale production techniques. In 1847, Playfair, now a professor, wrote to him about a very unusual underground spring which he had found in his brother-in-law's Derbyshire coal mine from which there flowed daily about 300 gallons of a thin treacly liquid. When distilled it burned 'with a brilliant illuminating power'. Playfair concluded, 'Perhaps you could make a capital thing out of this new industry.'

Young was on to a winner. From the liquid, he prepared paraffin wax, naphtha, light oil and lubricating oil. One of the first things he made was a pair of candles which Playfair used to illuminate his reading desk at a Royal Institution lecture. Until his dying day, Young kept the stump of a candle as a memento of the origin of what was to become one of the largest chemical industries in modern times. When his employers showed no interest in his discovery, Young handed in his notice and used his savings to open a factory to process the oil, but as demand started to outstrip supply, he had to search for a new source of his lucrative oil. Believing erroneously that his oil had been naturally distilled from coal, he sought samples of coal from his many friends and soon parcels arrived from all over the UK. One parcel from Bathgate, to the west of Edinburgh, contained a substance which local miners called 'cannel coal' because, when burnt, its light was as bright as a candle's.

Young anticipated the drilling of the first oil well in the US by nine years when, having devised a process for extracting oil from cannel coal 'artificially', in 1850 he patented his method for the heating, distillation and processing of bituminous coal to form paraffin. In this patent he used the word 'cracking' to describe the process of splitting the oil into its component substances and modern petrochemicals complex still have 'crackers'. Although it is now believed that the patent was wrong, cannel coal not being coal at all, but a geological freak, probably an unusually rich seam of oil shale, it gave Young a worldwide monopoly over the next 15 years despite constant challenges.

With great speed, Young opened the world's first oil refinery on the outskirts of Bathgate. Surrounded by a high wall, the factory was run as a 'secret works' with employees required to take an oath of confidentiality. Production of oil and paraffin started in time for samples to be displayed at the Great Exhibition of 1851. Young extended his patents to North America where coal-oil or kerosene companies used his processing technology in return for a royalty. During a visit to the States to chase up slow payers, Young declined partnerships in several oil concerns, offered in exchange for him waiving royalties. Had he taken up an offer, Young, rather than Rockerfeller, might have become the name associated with the legendary wealth of the oil tycoon.

Ironically, it was partly the increasing scarcity and cost of cannel coal – whose price was inflated by the demands of the US processors of kerosene by his methods – that forced Young to look for another source of oil. Although shale gave a much lower yield than cannel coal, it was available in West Lothian in almost unlimited quantities. By 1864, when his original patents ran out, foreseeing oil mania, Young had already secured some of the best seams for himself setting up Young's Paraffin Light and Mineral Oil Company and even diversifying into the design of lampshades. Oil mania did sweep the country with, by 1870, 97 oil companies operating in West Lothian alone. At its peak, Scotland's shale oil industry employed 40,000 people making everything from household cleaners to Scotch petrol. In the long term, however, it was doomed to fail in competition with the more easily extractable mineral oil. The last shale mine closed in 1962, less than a decade before the first North Sea oil was brought ashore from the rig Seaquest in an old pickle jar.

Young never forgot his introduction to the science of petrochemicals. He became President of, and benefactor to, the Andersonian Institution and founded the Chair of Technical Chemistry in honour of Thomas Graham. In his retirement, Young continued his varied scientific pursuits – from a Channel tunnel to light waves – in the laboratories which he installed in two of his many houses. He also provided financial backing for the African expeditions of David Livingstone, his lifelong friend who had nicknamed Young 'Sir Paraffine'. He acted as guardian to Livingstone's children and financed a search party when the famous missionary was finally reported missing.

Joseph Swan and Thomas Edison, both of distant Scots ancestry, have their supporters in the fight for the title of 'Father of the Electric Light'. Could the prize, in fact, belong to a little known inventor from Dundee, who claimed to have produced continuous electric light half a century before?

WHAT WAS LINDSAY'S LIGHT?

There is little doubt that James Bowman Lindsay (1799–1862) achieved some form of electric lighting, which he demonstrated to the public in a series of evening lectures at the Thistle Hall, Dundee, in 1835. The reporter sent along by the local paper to cover the event wrote enthusiastically the next day:

> Mr Lindsay, a teacher in town, succeeded on the evening of Saturday July 25 in obtaining a constant electric light . . . The light in beauty surpasses all others, has no smell, emits no smoke, is incapable of explosion and, not requiring air for combustion, can be kept in sealed glass jars . . . It can be sent to any convenient distance and the apparatus for producing it can be contained in a common chest.

In a letter to the newspaper Lindsay shed a little more light on his invention:

> I am writing this letter by means of it at six inches or eight inches distant; and at the present moment can read a book

at the distance of one and a half feet. From the same
apparatus I can get two or three lights, each of which is fit
for reading with. I can make it burn in the open air or in a
glass tube without air and neither wind nor water is
capable of extinguishing it.

What did Lindsay actually discover? Little more is known of his
invention and none of his apparatus has survived. Was it simply an
unusual form of arc lighting or was it the true forerunner of the
electric light bulb? Lindsay himself could see the day when:

its beauty will recommend itself to the fashionable: and
the producing apparatus, framed, may stand side by side
with the piano in the drawing room . . . and being capable
of surpassing all lights in its splendour it will be used in
lighthouses and for telegraphs.

Having achieved his ambition of creating continuous electric light,
Lindsay moved on to one of his many other projects, the production
of a *Pentecontaglossal Dictionary* – the Lord's Prayer in 50 languages –
more a monument to tireless perseverance than a contribution to
philology. Lindsay's life in general is divided between flashes of
genius and diligent pursuit of pointless goals, such as his mammoth
'Chrono-Astrolabe', a set of astronomical tables intended to assist
in the calculation of chronological periods. For a time he became
interested in wireless telegraphy, succeeding in transmitting
messages for some miles across the Tay. His system depended on
using sea-water as a conductor for the signal. Although his methods
were unlikely to work, his willingness to try earned him a footnote
in the history of telegraphy as the first person to propose linking
Britain and America through the new medium.

While Scots were trying to introduce better forms of heat and
light into the home, one Edinburgh tradesman was busy cleaning up
after them.

CLEAN CHIMNEYS WITHOUT CHILDREN
In 1803, George Smart of Edinburgh invented a machine to clean
chimney flues to replace the appalling practice of employing

children as young as five to crawl with their brushes through the narrow sooty twists and turns, at risk of life and limb. Smart's device consisted of hollow wooden poles, the ends fitting within each other. The lead pole had a brush made of whalebone splinters, fastened to a cord that passed through the poles connecting them together. A sweep could push the device up the chimney: once the end protruded out the top the rope was pulled and the brush would expand like an inverted umbrella. The brush was then pulled down to scrape the soot off the inside of the flue. Even after a Bristol engineer, Joseph Glass, improved Smart's design, introducing in 1828 the system that is universally used today, the machine was slow to catch on, many sweeps preferring the simpler, cheaper but crueller option of sending children up the chimney, a practice not outlawed until 1864.

Smart is also credited with the invention of the traditional sweep's outfit. His closest friend was an undertaker who passed on his worn-out mourning clothes to Smart, to be used as overalls when sweeping chimneys. Old top hats and ragged formal coats with tails quickly became associated with the new breed of sweeps, universally popular at weddings as bringing good luck. In more recent times, sweeps have adopted more practical waterproof clothing to protect them from the weather.

THE MAC

Charles Macintosh (1766–1843) was the son of a Glasgow chemical manufacturer producing cudbear, a dye from lichens, which he used to colour silks and wools. Inspired by a series of lectures by the chemist Joseph Black, Macintosh established his own works making sal ammoniac and Prussian blue dye and introducing to Britain the manufacture of lead and aluminium acetates. He moved into alum production in 1797, becoming Britain's largest producer of this substance, which is used to fix colours in dyeing. To manufacture alum, he needed aluminium sulphate, potassium and ammonia. He obtained potassium by toasting seaweed, thereby helping to develop the Highland kelp-gathering industry and he sourced ammonia from stale human urine. Every local farmhouse had a barrel outside to which all workers and visitors were invited to contribute. As the industry prospered, demand outstripped supply and urine was shipped in from Newcastle and London. Men with barrels came around once a week to collect it from street corner buckets. It was well known in the trade that the urine from the poor was much better than that of the wealthy as they did not partake of so much strong drink.

Macintosh was an economical Scot. Nothing was wasted in his chemical works and as soon as gas was introduced, its waste products were added to the pile. One such waste product was naphtha. Experimenting to find a use for it, he came up with a waterproof fabric consisting of two layers of cloth glued together with a solution of India rubber dissolved in the naphtha. It proved impossible, however, to tailor such an unwieldy sandwich. Edinburgh medical student James Syme discovered a more practical method of dissolving rubber using a by-product of coal tar. Macintosh patented the process in 1823 and gave birth to the garment that bears his name.

Important early commissions for the new fabric included the outfitting of Sir John Franklin's expedition to the Arctic in 1824, for which Macintosh made the world's first inflatable lifejacket and the first rubber airbed. At first, Macintosh produced the waterproof cloth for individual tailors to make up, but from 1830, when he joined up with the Manchester firm of Thomas Hancock, he moved into the ready-to-wear market. The timing was unlucky. The comforts of the railway carriage soon superseded the stage-coach where the Mac offered ideal protection against the elements. There were complaints about the ungainliness of the garments, their peculiar smell and their tendency to melt in hot weather. They also fell apart in cold weather when the rubber cement, which was affected by the natural oils in woollen cloth, crumbled. The Mac was not even guaranteed to be waterproof, as rain could penetrate the holes made when sewing up the garment. Some of the problems were solved by the rubber hardening process, known as vulcanisation, which Hancock patented in England in 1843. Over the following decades, other manufacturers cracked the problems of shape and smell, ensuring that the Mac continues to honour its Scottish inventor. Hancock's patent, however, had some surprising results.

THE WELLY BOOT

Although Hancock took out a patent on his revolutionary technique for manufacturing rubber in England eight weeks before Goodyear, Goodyear beat him to it in Scotland, which at the time had separate patent protection. An American, Henry Lee Norris, obtained the right to manufacture rubber under the Goodyear patent in Scotland, setting up Scotland's first overseas manufacturing plant in Edinburgh in 1856.

For more than a century the North British Rubber Company made Edinburgh a world centre for rubber goods, from golf balls to hot water bottles. One of its earliest and most enduring products was the rubber wellington boot, a design made popular half a century earlier by the Duke of Wellington. One of several US manufacturers to experiment with making rubber, rather than leather, wellington boots, Norris brought his design to Scotland along with four New York employees to train the workers who would make the boots. Production of wellies was limited until the First World War when the War Office approached the company to produce a sturdy boot that could cope with conditions in the flooded trenches of Flanders. Working day and night, the factory produced 1,185,036 pairs. While the First World War moved the boot from fashion item to functional necessity for farmers, building workers and school children, the Swinging Sixties and the Yuppie Eighties brought it back into high fashion.

Charles Macintosh not only produced the first Mac, but helped another Glasgow entrepreneur, Charles Tennant (1768–1838), to produce bleaching powder.

DANTE'S INFERNO

In the days of soap powders that wash whiter than white, it is difficult to imagine that, until the late-eighteenth century, the only effective way to bleach cloth was to expose it to sunlight, often having first soaked it in an acid like sour milk or urine. Every small village had its bleaching green to cope with domestic linen while giant bleaching fields were used to prepare cloth for dyeing. The search was on to find a more reliable source than the sun. In 1778 ,James Watt demonstrated the power of the recently discovered chemical chlorine as a bleaching agent. Tennant and Macintosh went one step further.

Born in Ochiltree, Ayrshire, Robert Burn's 'Wabster Charlie' was apprenticed as a weaver before setting up his own bleaching fields in Paisley. With the help of Charles Macintosh, who owned a nearby chemical works, in 1798 Tennant patented a liquid mixture of chloride and lime as a way of bleaching textiles. A powder version of this compound revolutionised the textiles industry, freeing it from the need for organic materials, such as seaweed and buckets of pee. From its beginnings as a soap works in 1803, Tennant's St Rollox Chemical Works in Glasgow grew to be the world's largest chemical factory by 1830, making soda and sulphuric acid as well as soap. Known locally as Dante's Inferno, the 50-acre plant was surrounded by piles of greyish-white solid waste and standing tanks of urine, still needed as the cheapest source of ammonia. The 435-ft high Tennant's Stalk, built in 1841 in an attempt to dispose of gaseous waste, dominated Glasgow's northern skyline until the 1920s.

GOLD IN THE GORBALS

'Waste not want not' could have been the motto of the entrepreneurial Tennants. Son John acquired pyrite mines at Tharsis in southern Spain as, being nearly 50 per cent sulphur, pyrites – fool's gold – were a valuable source of the sulphur needed by the chemical works. His son Charles became interested in the other products of the pyrites mine – silver, gold, copper and iron. By 1872, he had bought seven companies to extract metal from the ore and purchased gold mines in India. One of his employees was John MacArthur who, from the basement of a Gorbals clinic run by Drs Robert and William Forrest, developed a process for extracting gold by cyanide. The MacArthur-Forrest process involves three steps: contacting the finely ground ore with the cyanide solution, separating the solids from the clear solution and recovering the precious metals from the solution by precipitation with zinc dust.

Tennant bought the patent of 1887 and his Cassel's Cyanide Co. charged a royalty to licence the process to other companies, although the patent was successfully challenged. MacArthur-

Forrest cyanidation, still the standard means of extracting gold, doubled the world's output of the precious metal in just 20 years and made South Africa one of the world's leading gold producers.

Three Scots were to contribute to the typical entertainment of the Victorian drawing room although the first, John Broadwood (1732–1812), would, as a young man, be more familiar with the fiddle round the cottage fireside.

THE GRAND PIANO

John Broadwood took up his father's trade as carpenter and joiner to the farmers round Oldhamstocks in East Lothian before setting off at the age of 29 to seek fame and fortune. In his pocket was a letter of introduction from the local laird to the Swiss harpsichord maker in London, Burkhard Shudi. Broadwood proved such an excellent apprentice that soon he gained not only the hand of Shudi's daughter, but also a partnership in the firm, renamed 'Burkhard Shudi et Johannes Broadwood'. In 1771, Shudi handed over the running of the business to his son-in-law.

In the late 1770s, Broadwood and his assistant, Scotsman Robert Stodart, were working on what became known as the English Grand Action. This was the basis of the grand piano, patented in 1777 in the name of Stodart. For some time Broadwood was content to leave the development of the grand in Stodart's capable hands while he concentrated on improvements and modifications to the square piano. He took out the first patent for 'piano and forte pedals', to do away with the awkward hand and knee levers of existing models.

Satisfied with his improvements to the square piano, Broadwood moved on to developing the grand. In order to improve the quality of the tone of the notes he introduced a separate bass bridge, an adaptation soon adopted by all piano makers. He extended the range of the piano, introducing the first six octave grand in 1794. By the mid-1790s, such was the success of the piano that the company gave up harpsichord manufacture altogether. Handel, Haydn and the child prodigy Mozart had played Shudi harpsichords; Beethoven, Liszt and Chopin were to play Broadwood grands.

Another Scot added a lighter touch to entertainment in the nineteenth-century drawing-room.

THE KALEIDOSCOPE

Sir David Brewster (1781–1868) was a kaleidoscopic figure – scientist, university principal, writer, journalist and founder member of The British Association for the Advancement of Science. His father, headmaster of Jedburgh Grammar School, was also a formidable character, insisting that all four of his sons train for the ministry. While at university, Brewster's interest in science developed as his enthusiasm for the Church waned. When nerves led to him fainting in the pulpit, he abandoned the ministry for journalism as editor of the *Edinburgh Magazine*. He continued to pursue his scientific interests, which lay in the theory of light, optical instrumentation and the relationship between colour and temperature. To the scientific world he is best known for the law of polarisation of bi-axial crystals that bears his name and for laying the foundations of the study of crystallography and experimental optics.

Brewster loved experimenting and in the pursuit of his investigations invented several new types of micrometer and the dioptic lens, which greatly improved the effectiveness of lighthouse lamps. He married the daughter of James MacPherson, the Scottish poet and literary fraudster who stunned the European cultural world with *Ossian*. Although he claimed *Ossian* was a translation of legendary poems about Celtic heroes, in fact he composed the poems himself. In 1831, Brewster was knighted for his scientific achievements, but only after he received a royal assurance that he would not have to pay the fee of £109 for the honour. In later life he became Principal of St Andrews University where he took up photography, introducing the painter David Octavius Hill to Fox Talbot's calotype photographic process. In 1859, having fallen foul of the St Andrews professors by treating his post as more than a sinecure and attempting to reform the university administration, he became Principal of Edinburgh University at double the salary.

Brewster is best remembered as the man who brought entertainment into the nineteenth-century drawing-room. He hoped to make his fortune from his kaleidoscope, but his patent of 1814 was not watertight and soon every instrument maker was copying it. On a visit to London, he wrote home to his wife:

> You can form no conception of the effect which the
> instrument excited in London. Infants are seen carrying
> them in their hands, the coachmen in their boxes are busy
> using them . . . and thousands of poor people make their
> bread by selling them . . . Had I managed my patents
> rightly, I would have made £100,000 by it.

In 1849, Brewster's interest in photography resulted in his
designing a stereoscopic camera and viewer, and a second craze was
born. His stereoscope was the grandfather of virtual reality. The
viewer looked at two almost identical pictures mounted side by side
through two lenses. As the viewer's eyes merged the two images, the
picture appeared in three dimensions. After Queen Victoria
expressed her approval on seeing a stereoscope at the Great
Exhibition of 1851, sales were unstoppable and by the mid-1850s
over a million homes owned a Brewster stereoscope. Although most
Victorians amused themselves with 3D views of the Pyramids or
French cathedrals, the stereoscope had its darker side, being
admirably suited to erotic photographs and fuelling trade in
pornography.

SCOTS AT HOME

★ **The coin-op gas meter:** invented around 1900 by the Edinburgh gas
  fittings company, Alder & Mackay.
★ **The world's hardest biscuit:** Bickiepegs developed in 1925 by Aberdeen
  paediatrician Dr Harry Campbell, to provide the correct exercise
  for teeth and jaw development while easing the pain of teething.
  Royals have since cut their teeth on them.
★ **Cornflakes:** first produced in the UK by Brown & Polson of Paisley
  in 1934 from a recipe using pearl maize, malt and sugar.
★ **The rubber wringer roller:** invented by Peter Burt of the Acme
  Wringer Co., Glasgow. He replaced wood with rubber to make
  the Acme Wringer a must in every 'modern' kitchen. A classic
  inventor, Burt also designed washing machines, mangles,
  perambulators, stoves, mincing machines and ice cream freezers.
★ **Cotton reels:** introduced by James Clark of Paisley as a more
  convenient way to supply cotton thread than the skeins which
  the firm had first used.

SCOTTISH FIRSTS

★ Cotton sewing thread: invented by Patrick Clark of Paisley in 1805. Spurred by the need to replace the supply of silk threads used in weaving looms during the Napoleonic wars, Clark invented a cotton thread that was strong and smooth enough to replace it. Much cheaper than linen thread, his cotton thread was soon adopted for sewing.

★ Sewing machine thread: developed by Sir Peter Coats who produced the strong fine cotton needed by sewing machines in the 1850s. Its success helped his company, J. & P. Coats, to become one of the world's largest manufacturing enterprises.

★ The first British patent for a water closet: in 1775 Alexander Cumming, an Edinburgh-born watchmaker, invented his loo which flushed on the pull of a lever.

★ 'French cakes': introduced to Britain by Glasgow baker James Craig. He imported craftsmen from Europe to teach local bakers the art of French confectionery at the beginning of the twentieth century. It is arguable whether the French would recognise Scottish 'French cakes' with their brightly coloured icings and sweet 'cream' fillings.

★ *Lemmings*: one of the world's most addictive computer games, created in 1991 by DMA Design in Dundee. They hit the top of the world bestsellers list again with *Grand Theft Auto*.

★ The seasonal greetings card: designed by Charles Drummond, a printer in Leith. In 1841, he published a card of a fat laughing face and the legend 'A Guid New Year An' Mony o' Them' two years before Henry Cole in London published the first Christmas card.

★ Fingerprinting: discovered by Henry Faulds (1843–1930), from Ayrshire, while working as a doctor in Tokyo's Tsukiji Hospital. In a letter to the scientific journal *Nature*, published on 28 October 1880, he was the first person to suggest the use of fingerprints as a way of catching criminals because of their unique patterns. Faulds failed, however, to interest the Police Commissioners in his discovery. Shortly before his death he turned down the post of personal physician to the Crown Prince of Japan. Little honoured in his native land, he is commemorated by a statue in Japan.

★ The recipe for Rodine rat poison: dreamed up by Perth chemist Thomas Harley in the early twentieth century.

SCOTTISH FIRSTS

★ Golden Syrup: invented by Abram Lyle (1820–91). A lawyer's apprentice from Greenock, Lyle established the Lyle shipping line, one of whose cargoes for many years was sugar from the West Indies. Having moved into sugar refining, his response to a bumper sugar beet crop in 1882, which depressed the price of processed sugar, was to develop a new product, Golden Syrup, which soon established itself as a staple of British larders.

★ The first commercially successful spinning reel for fishing: patented by Peter Malloch of Perth in 1884. It was immensely popular, as it made fishing easier for beginners and could be used to catch anything from salmon to sharks.

★ The Jaffa cake: invented around 1927 by Edinburgh baker McVitie and Price. The sponge, orange and chocolate confection remains Britain's most popular everyday treat today.

★ Patterned linoleum: first made in the 1850s by Michael Nairn of Kirkcaldy. By 1870, his factory was the largest producer of floor cloths in the world. His invention of the process of printing patterns in different colours on linoleum went a long way to brightening up the living-rooms of those who could not afford carpets.

★ The vacuum coffee machine: invented by Glasgow marine engineer Robert Napier (1791–1876) in 1840. The 'Napierian', a vacuum pot with two detachable glass globes, was the first coffee machine to operate like the modern Cona or Bodum Santos.

★ Paisley pattern: the teardrop pattern, today used on everything from pyjamas to tea trays, takes its name from the cotton town of Paisley, which was at one time the world centre for Paisley shawls. The design itself can be traced back thousands of years to several Indo-European cultures. Kashmir shawls using the pattern were first introduced to Britain in the eighteenth century and rapidly became a fashion accessory. In 1812, Paisley weavers introduced an attachment to the handloom which enabled five different colours of yarn to be used, better imitating the genuine Kashmir shawls at a very much lower cost. Paisley shawls remained in fashion until the introduction of the bustle in the 1870s.

★ The gutty golf ball: invented by the Rev. James Paterson of Dundee in 1845. While a missionary in Asia, he shipped back a statue in a crate packed with rubbery gutta percha. The elastic substance encouraged him to try out different ways of fashioning golf balls. His 'Paterson's Patent' ball had a smooth surface engraved with lines to look like the seams of a traditional feathery ball. Given that they invented the game it is no surprise that the Scots were behind many golfing inventions: the first balls with surface patterns, developed by Robert Forgan of St Andrews in the 1860s; the rubber core ball patented in 1876 by Captain Duncan Stewart of St Andrews; moulded golf balls which ushered in mass-production invented by William Currie of the Caledonian Rubber Works, Edinburgh from 1878; the hickory shaft, introduced when Robert Forgan received the wrong delivery of wood for his clubs. They got round a peculiarly Scottish problem with the Sabbath stick. Golf addicts could use this walking stick with a golf-club head for a quick game if no one was watching during the widespread ban on golf on Sundays until well into the twentieth century.

★ Cornflour: John Polson, starch manufacturer of Paisley. In 1854, he patented the means of extracting edible starch from maize, setting up in business with his partner William Brown to manufacture it. Sauces never tasted the same again.

★ The first power machinery for dry cleaning: introduced by Pullars of Perth in 1869.

★ The first washable distemper paint: invented by Glaswegian John Bryson Orr (1840–1933). He patented lithopone, or 'Orr's Zinc White', a mixture of zinc sulphide and barium sulphate, in 1874. Significantly cheaper and more light-fast than other white pigments, lithopone was widely adopted in the paint and paper industries. Marketed as Duresco, it provided a popular alternative to whitewashing for both interior and exterior walls.

★ Unshrinkable underwear: Peter Scott and Co. Ltd, Hawick, the first company to guarantee that their woollen underwear would not shrink in the wash. Their Pesco range kept troops warm in the trenches during the First World War, as well as Ernest Shackleton and the crew of the *Endurance* when trapped for months in the Antarctic ice.

★ The first modern lawnmower: designed by Arbroath engineer, Alexander Shanks (1801–45). Commissioned by a local landowner in 1841 to design a mower for his two-and-a-half-acre lawn, Shanks came up with a machine which could be pulled by a small pony without leaving hoof marks on the grass. Previously, lawn mowers had to be pushed and often churned up the ground that they were intended to smooth. Shanks' mower not only cut, but rolled the grass.

★ **The world's first liquid coffee essence:** produced by the Edinburgh chemists T. & A. Smith in 1840.

★ **The deep fried Mars Bar:** invented sometime in the 1990s by an east coast chip shop, most likely in Stonehaven. This Scottish delicacy is now enjoyed on a stick in Australia's Bondi Beach or with cream and strawberry sauce in a Paris restaurant. Cadbury's creme eggs and Twixes have also gone under batter cover.

★ **Bakelite:** patented by Sir James Swinburne (1858–1958), a pioneer of the UK plastics industry. Unfortunately, he filed his patent application outlining a process for producing synthetic resin in 1907, one day after the Belgian chemist, Leo Baekeland, who was working in the USA. By agreement, the resin was produced in the US by Baekeland and the liquid lacquer was made in England by Swinburne. By the 1920s, everything from domestic plugs to telephones was being moulded in hard black or brown bakelite.

★ **Affordable Persian carpets:** first produced by James Templeton, a Paisley shawl manufacturer who, in 1839, set up a carpet factory in Glasgow to produce Persian or Turkish carpets without hand knotting. His chenille process simulated the rich quality of hand-knotted rugs, but could weave room-sized seamless rugs and runners. In 1880, William Gray of Ayr introduced seamless Kidderminster carpets.

★ **The self-acting fountain pen:** patented by Robert Thomson (1822–73) in 1849 with a separate reservoir for storing ink. The ingenuity of this precursor of the modern fountain pen won it a place in the Great Exhibition of 1851.

★ **Tapestry carpets:** first produced by Richard Whytock of Lasswade. In 1832, he patented the pre-printing of colours on carpet yarns and a loom to weave his tapestry carpets. Instead of using a number of short threads each of a different colour, Whytock worked out the number of loops taken by each colour and dyed each part of a long thread according to the length needed. People could buy a carpet that looked like a Brussels carpet without having to pay the price.

8

'Dismal Johnnie' and the Original Green:
Shaping the Future

The vision of some remarkable Scots has helped to shape the way we live our lives. Some have expressed their vision in words, which have changed the way we think about our world, acting as an inspiration to others. Some have themselves acted on their vision, whether of a world without hunger or a landscape protected from human depredation. Some have changed the way the world looks by translating their vision into buildings whose revolutionary style has made an impact on our culture. Some have simply explored new worlds.

Although there have been visionary Scots in every century, Scotland stepped firmly centre stage during the latter half of the eighteenth century in the outpouring of intellect that was the Scottish Enlightenment. Ideas drawn from different disciplines and points of view fed on each other to produce a new understanding and new ways of doing. Men dared to think the unthinkable and to debate the very nature of society in the taverns of the cities where merchant drank with scientist and professor shared a pint of claret with physician. Together they helped to lay the foundations of the modern world. One of these giants with his feet firmly on the ground was Adam Smith (1723– 90).

THE PATRON SAINT OF FREE ENTERPRISE
Adam Smith from Kirkcaldy was very much an only child. He never knew his father, who died six months before he was born and, never marrying, he stayed with his mother all her days. The most dramatic event in his life occurred when, only four years old, he was briefly

kidnapped by gypsies. As a student at Glasgow University he came under the influence of the charismatic Professor of Moral Philosophy, Frances Hutcheson, who broke with tradition by lecturing in English rather than Latin and whose teaching stressed the value of 'common sense' and individual freedom.

After spells at Oxford – where the authorities confiscated his copy of David Hume's *Treatise on Human Nature* as dangerously radical – and Edinburgh, Smith became a philosophy professor at Glasgow from 1751. Despite his hesitant manner of speaking and tendency to digress, his lectures proved very popular. The biographer James Boswell recalled attending Smith's lectures: 'Mr Smith's sentiments are striking, profound and beautiful. He has nothing of that stiffness and pedantry which is too often found in professors.' A congenial drinking companion, Smith rubbed shoulders with the merchants who were building Glasgow's trade with the American colonies, helped young James Watt to set up in business and played cards with Joseph Black and David Hume, who became lifelong friends.

In 1759, Smith published an edited version of his lectures in *The Theory of Moral Sentiments*. The brilliant psychological insight, which he applied to attributing moral behaviour to enlightened self-interest, attracted the interest of, among others, the politician Charles Townshend, who recommended him as tutor to the young Duke of Buccleuch. In 1763, Smith accompanied the Duke on the Grand Tour of Europe, spending two and a half years mainly in Paris where they met many great thinkers including Voltaire and Quesnay, the French economist who coined the term 'laissez-faire'. The tour had its dull moments. On 5 July 1764, Smith wrote to Hume, 'I have begun to write a book in order to pass away the time.' That book, *An Inquiry into the Nature and Causes of the Wealth of Nations*, was to change the world.

Although the tour ended unhappily when the Duke's younger brother died in mysterious circumstances, far from blaming Smith, the Duke rewarded him with a pension for his services which enabled him to spend the next ten years quietly at his Kirkcaldy home completing and revising his *magnum opus* to the point that he told his publisher, 'I had almost forgot that I was the author of an inquiry concerning *The Wealth of Nations*.' A laborious 27 years in the writing, in Smith's large, round, childish hand, *The Wealth of Nations* was published in 1776 and was an immediate success, the first edition selling out in six months. The massive volume was translated into several languages and banned by the Spanish Inquisition. Delighted by the book's success, the Duke arranged for the lucrative, if undemanding, post of Commissioner for Customs to come Smith's way. This enabled him to enjoy the society of Enlightenment Edinburgh. He was looked after by his mother until her death at the age of 90 and thereafter by a cousin.

Smith's *Wealth of Nations* laid the foundations of modern economics and provided the framework for the Industrial Revolution. It ranks alongside the Bible, Newton's *Principia*, Darwin's *Origin of Species* and Marx's *Das Kapital* as one of the most important books ever written. The book contained a devastating and detailed attack on the existing economic system of government intervention, monopolies, trade restrictions, colonies and slavery. It went on to argue with clarity and precision that removing all artificial restrictions to trade and allowing individuals to pursue their interests as freely as possible, far from leading to disaster, would bring about the best possible result for everyone. It introduced the concepts of the modern market economy and challenged the belief that an economy could not work without government intervention.

> Every individual ... neither intends to promote the public interest, nor knows how much he is promoting it. By preferring the support of domestic to that of foreign industry he intends only his own security; and by directing that industry in such a manner as its produce may be of the greatest value, he intends only his own gain, and he is in this, as in many other cases, led by an invisible hand to promote an end which was no part of his intention.

Smith argued that a nation's wealth depended not on its gold and silver, but on the labour of its citizens, made productive through the division of labour, with everyone doing what they did best and exchanging the results through fair trade. Government should ensure that competition was fair, but otherwise should intervene as little as possible except to protect the most vulnerable in society. To the frustration of posterity, Smith summoned his friends, James Black the chemist and James Hutton the geologist, to his deathbed and made them promise to burn 16 volumes of his manuscripts.

Smith's vision was of economic liberty showing that the way to achieve peace and prosperity was to set individuals free. His lifelong friend and Scotland's greatest philosopher, David Hume (1711–76), took freedom one step further.

'LE BON DAVID'

From his earliest days, above all else, Hume valued truth even if it meant trouble. When the teenager passed wind during a dinner party, he felt compelled to own up to the smell even although the company were blaming his dog, Pod. The son of a Berwickshire landowner, he studied law at Edinburgh from the age of 11. It was philosophy, however, that caught his interest. He reckoned that by living very frugally, he could survive on his small inheritance until he either found a job that gave him time for study or made money from his writing. He embarked on an intensive course of study spent partly in France. The result was the anonymous publication of his three volume *Treatise on Human Nature* in 1739–40.

The *Treatise* was an original and generally sceptical voice, questioning conventional wisdom on everything from cause and effect to morality and religion. He argued that nothing other than logic and mathematics could be deduced by thought alone: everything must be tested by observation and experiment. It was in effect the basis of a revolution in thinking which Hume naively hoped would take the world by storm. To his intense disappointment, the work 'fell deadborn from the press, without reaching such distinctions even to excite a murmur among the zealots'. Even a 16-page summary of his main arguments sank without a ripple of interest. It took a later generation to recognise a philosophical masterpiece.

Undaunted, Hume concluded that it was his explanation rather than his philosophy itself that was at fault. In 1741–2, he published two volumes of *Essays, Moral and Political*, presenting his views in a more accessible style. Although this was sufficiently well received to make him a strong candidate for the Chair of Moral Philosophy at Edinburgh in 1744, it also established his reputation as an 'atheist'. In modern terms he was an agnostic, arguing that there was simply no valid evidence for or against the existence of God. Despite strong support for Hume in some quarters, the Church and the Town Council mobilised their opposition, giving him no option but to withdraw as a candidate rather than lose the election.

After serving as secretary to General St Clair on an unsuccessful military expedition, Hume returned to Edinburgh and reworked his philosophy in *An Enquiry Concerning Human Understanding* published in 1748. This was followed by *Political Discourses* in 1752, which promoted many of the ideas so effectively developed by his friend, Adam Smith. Hume's candidacy for the Chair of Moral Philosophy at Glasgow also failed: it is not to Scotland's credit that through bigotry both her leading universities preferred nonentities to her greatest philosopher. In 1752, Hume at last obtained employment as Librarian to the Faculty of Advocates, valuable to him not so much for the small salary, as by now he was earning enough from his writing, but for access to one of Scotland's largest libraries. He settled down to write his six-volume *History of England*, finally producing the bestseller that made his fortune.

In 1763, Hume was invited to join the British Embassy in Paris, the new Ambassador, the Earl of Hertford being anxious to foster friendly relations after the recent wars with France. He was enthusiastically received in French intellectual circles and in the Paris salons where his fame as a philosopher was far greater than at home. 'Le bon David' was tempted to stay in this congenial society rather than return to the constant sniping at his 'atheism', but he could not leave his beloved Scotland for long. In 1767–8, he held the government post of Under-Secretary for the Northern Department, his duties including advice on patronage to the Church of Scotland and drafting the royal address to its governing body, the General Assembly. Taking on these duties must have given Hume the 'atheist' a certain degree of satisfaction.

A lifelong bachelor and generous host, Hume retired to enjoy the company of his wide circle of friends, practice his hobby of cookery and continue to revise the works that were to change the way the world thought. Hume's private life totally belied his ungodly reputation, his easy manners and engaging innocence charming all he met. His belief in benevolence to mankind meant that he helped friends in need: his tolerant views of human nature led him to forgive injuries. He remained, however, a controversial figure to the end. After his death from cancer in 1776, religious people refused either to believe that he had died unrepentant and unconcerned at the absence of an afterlife or thought that he deserved to remain without honour.

Hume laid the foundations not only of the Enlightenment with its emphasis on rational thought and practical experiment, but of our modern way of thinking in philosophy, psychology, sociology, economics and even religion. He took nothing on authority, pursuing the truth wherever it led him and whatever the consequences, even if it meant questioning the sacred 'truths' of religion. On making his fortune from his *History*, Hume resigned as Librarian to the Faculty of Advocates in 1757 in favour of a younger friend more in need of the money. Adam Ferguson (1723–1816) had a view of human nature as acute, but less benign.

THE MAN WHO INTRODUCED SCOTT TO BURNS

Born in Logierait in Perthshire, Ferguson studied divinity at St Andrews University and served as Chaplain to the Black Watch regiment before gradually losing his faith through his friendship with David Hume and Adam Smith. After two years as Librarian of the Faculty of Advocates, he was appointed Professor of Physics at Edinburgh, transferring to the more congenial Chair of Moral Philosophy in 1764. Three years later he wrote his classic work, the *Essay on the History of Civil Society*, in which he argued that humans were by nature social and had always adapted to and been influenced by, the society in which they lived. He argued 'that civilisation is the result of human action, but not the execution of any human design'. How society is organised could be deduced not by theory, but only by observation. His emphasis on society earned him the title 'Father of Sociology'.

Although he advanced the same idea as Adam Smith of the division of labour as a function of an industrial society, he adopted a much more pessimistic view of its effects, from inequality to behaviour influenced by envy or servility. He had a profound influence on the social theories of Karl Marx. Ferguson took a less benign view of human nature than David Hume, attributing motivation not just to the pursuit of pleasure and self-interest, but to a desire for domination resulting in aggression, animosity, conflict and corruption. Unlike Hume, he optimistically believed in inevitable progress towards civilisation. Although Hume considered that Ferguson had 'more genius than the rest', he dismissed his work as superficial.

In the early 1770s, Ferguson went on the Grand Tour as tutor to the young Earl of Chesterfield, and in 1778 he was appointed to the commission to negotiate peace with the American colonies. In 1792, in his retirement, he published his collected lectures, *Principles of Moral and Political Science*, drawing together the views of the Scottish philosophers and adopting a stoical standpoint. A sociable character, who 30 years before had founded one of Edinburgh's most famous clubs, the Poker, Ferguson hosted the evening when the two greatest literary Scots, Robert Burns and Sir Walter Scott, met for the first and only time. In the early 1790s, while Ferguson was enjoying the convivial company of the capital, a very different Scot was putting his theories into practice by compiling what may be the world's first social survey.

THE FIRST CENSUS

Sir John Sinclair of Ulbster (1754–1835) was one of the Scots who took up the new Enlightenment thinking and ran with it. Born in Thurso Castle into a prominent landowning family, he attended university at Glasgow, Edinburgh and Oxford, qualifying as an advocate in both England and Scotland and travelling extensively abroad. After becoming an MP in 1780, he was appointed as the first President of the Board of Agriculture in William Pitt's Government, thus effectively founding the Department of Agriculture. A man of considerable energy and strong views, his interests ranged from writing a *History of the Revenues of the British Empire* in 1784, to Highland dress, on which he argued that trews rather than the kilt was the correct apparel for a Caithness soldier.

His interest in agriculture was as much that of the farmer as the bureaucrat. By the time he was 50 'Agricultural Sir John' could look at the view from Thurso Castle with a degree of pride: it had changed out of all recognition, thanks largely to his own endeavours. The marshy land had been drained, enclosed and seeded with grass on which the Cheviot sheep that he had introduced grazed productively. Unfortunately, with hindsight, he enthusiastically conveyed his view that 'under sheep the Highlands would be six, if not ten times more valuable than under cattle if proper breeds were introduced' to the Countess of Sutherland whose factor, Patrick Sellar, became responsible for some of the worst excesses of the Highland Clearances. The town of Thurso, which had been stagnant for decades, now boasted a grid of wide, paved streets around a central square and a new harbour was planned. Thanks to his strategy, the nearby town of Wick was destined to become a major fishing port. His designs for the Highlands' first planned town at Halkirk were starting to be realised. Unfortunately, the nightingales which he had tried to introduce to Caithness by putting eggs in the nests of local birds had flown to sunnier climes.

In 1791, Sinclair started out on the mammoth task of compiling the first statistical survey of a country. At the time, 'statistics' was a very novel concept which Sir John had heard of from Germany where the word was used to refer to a collection of facts about a country's political strength. In seeking to collect information about the natural, economic and social resources of his native land, Sir John took the concept much further. His aim was not only to gather and order knowledge for its own sake in accordance with the spirit of the Enlightenment, but to gain a measure of 'the quantum of happiness' of communities as a 'means of future improvement'.

He sent a questionnaire to the ministers of Scotland's 938 parishes asking for details about their locality. Despite everything from climate to morals being covered in the original 160 questions, he added a further 11 questions in the light of the first replies. Not surprisingly, some ministers missed the deadline, but Sinclair pursued them relentlessly by letter and even by sending out 'statistical missionaries' to persuade the reluctant to cooperate. By 1799, he had elicited some sort of response from everyone. The result is, in Sinclair's own words, 'an unique survey of the state of the whole country, locality by locality', published in the years up to 1799 in a massive 21 volumes as the *Statistical Account of Scotland*. The value of the survey was recognised even before his death and in 1834 a second Statistical Account on an even more ambitious scale was undertaken with contributions not only from ministers, but also from doctors, schoolmasters and landowners in each parish. While the First Statistical Account took Sinclair eight years, the Third Statistical Account, started in 1951, took over five times as long. A twentieth-century Scot was to share Sinclair's passion for statistics, but was to use them for a very different end.

'DISMAL JOHNNIE'

At the beginning of the twentieth century the sight of Glasgow's slum children – pale, undernourished and vulnerable – so moved a young medical student, John Boyd Orr (1880–1971), that he made it his lifetime mission to use science to rid the world of poverty. His single-minded zeal won him the Nobel Peace Prize in 1949. His carefree childhood in Kilmaurs in Ayrshire belied his later nickname of 'Dismal Johnnie', prophet of the consequences of unchecked population growth without a matching increase in the food supply. Boyd Orr was a man who attracted nicknames. His crusading zeal led to 'Sir John and the Twelve Disciples' while his family called him 'Popeye' because of his distinctive appearance and love of sailing. When he was offered a peerage, a friend suggested that he should take the title of 'Lord Either Orr Else', his own jocular preference being 'Baron Soil'. These nicknames hint at what Boyd Orr brought to the science of nutrition: a warm friend, a fearless enemy and, most of all, a man who cared passionately about the future of the world.

While training as a teacher and then as a doctor in Glasgow, Boyd Orr's Saturday night walks through the slums gave him 'an intense hatred of unnecessary hunger and poverty'. His brief experience as a locum made him realise that he was unsuited to general practice, due to lack of confidence in his diagnostic skills and not being able to smoke his beloved pipe. His research in physiology was soon interrupted by the First World War and life in the trenches. After the war he became the first Director of the Rowett Research Institute outside Aberdeen where he pioneered the era of scientific farming. Through careful survey work he established the links between the chemical nature of different soils, the resulting nutritional make-up of pastures and the health of grazing livestock.

Boyd Orr was among the first to make the direct link between the prosperity of agriculture and the health of cities, believing that it was impossible to correct deficiencies in diet without increasing agricultural wealth. In the late 1920s, he conducted large-scale surveys to demonstrate the value of providing milk to school children in order to supplement their meagre diet at home. He showed that with a proper diet, poor children began to grow as quickly as rich children, who previously had been on average four inches taller by the age of 14. Over the next few years he lobbied and fulminated against politicians and civil servants who were literally pouring milk down the drain because people could not afford it. His recommendations went unheeded.

During the Depression of the 1930s, Boyd Orr explored the link between health, income and food consumption, carrying out the first quantitative study of the state of nutrition of the British people. The results were political dynamite. They showed that a diet adequate to meet health standards required an income above that of half the British population. The government appointed economists and statisticians with the brief to disprove his figures, but his scientific method could not be challenged. In the end an embarrassed government yielded to public pressure to introduce free school milk and acknowledged Boyd Orr's efforts by awarding him a knighthood. It was thanks to Boyd Orr, working with Lord Woolton, the Minister of Food, that Britain's health improved dramatically despite the shortages and rigours of the Second World War.

During the war, Boyd Orr forecast an even gloomier future of worldwide famine due to a combination of over population and inefficient agriculture. His ultimate equation was simple. Half the population suffer from lack of food: farmers suffer if they produce too much food: therefore the two evils have to be cancelled out by political and economic adjustment. His ceaseless campaigning to interest world leaders in taking action against impending world starvation largely led to the setting up of the United Nations Food and Agriculture Organisation in 1945. Reluctantly, Boyd Orr agreed to become its first Director. Although world politics conspired against the adoption of many of his practical measures to increase the efficiency of agriculture and realise his vision of a world without hunger, in 1949 he was awarded the Nobel Peace Prize. Although Patrick Geddes (1854–1932) shared Boyd Orr's concerns about hungry children, his vision of a new world was very different.

EDINBURGH, SCOTLAND, EUROPE, THE WORLD

The son of a soldier, Geddes was born in Ballater and brought up in Perth. After only a week of studying biology at Edinburgh University, he left for London and the more progressive lectures of T.H. Huxley, the brilliant populariser of Darwin's theory of evolution. Geddes was employed by the British Association for the Advancement of Science to set up a zoological research facility at Stonehaven at the age of 24 before going on a research mission to Mexico. There he contracted a disease that left his eyesight too weak to use a microscope and so, on his return, he became a demonstrator in botany at Edinburgh University.

Although, as Professor of Botany at University College, Dundee, from 1889, he co-authored a book on *The Evolution of Sex*, his creative energies had long since moved on from plants and procreation to people and how they lived in towns and cities. Always a nonconformist, Geddes thought that respectable Edinburgh was 'as if frozen in an ice-pack' while hating London culture for its 'Cockneyfication'. He conceived the idea of recreating among the insalubrious slums of Edinburgh's Old Town a university quarter in which a community of researchers and students would live and interact as in the great days of the Enlightenment. In pursuit of his vision, in 1885 he took his new bride to live in the Old Town while he built professors' houses in Ramsay Garden next to the Castle and student residences in the adjacent Mylne's Court. As a centrepiece he bought the Outlook Tower where, around a camera obscura, he mounted an exhibition to illustrate his theories on the development of the city and its relation to the country and to the world.

Geddes was a man of grand visions, describing his task as 'that of planning the cultural future of Edinburgh – a renascent capital – and of Scotland as again one of the great European powers of culture'. His approach was summed up by his three Ss: Sympathy for people and the environment; Synthesis of all factors relating to a case; Synergy, the combined cooperative action of everyone involved. He was concerned not with the technical problems of expanding cities or the creation of brave new utopias, but with the task of inspiring communities to participate in their own cultural and social renewal.

He took a close interest in town planning, a topical subject around 1909 when Britain's first planning legislation was passed, promoting his ideas in an award-winning exhibition which toured the UK and abroad. He prepared strategic plans of towns and cities, and wrote *Cities in Evolution*, which emphasised the preservation of historical traditions, the involvement of the people in their own environment and the rediscovery of past city building traditions. He laid the ground rules for the new profession of planner, earning him the title of 'Father of Town Planning'. One of the first people to describe themselves as a landscape architect, he designed parks and urban spaces including Edinburgh Zoo and Pittencrieff Park, donated by multi-millionaire Andrew Carnegie to the citizens of his birthplace, Dunfermline.

'Scotland embraced Europe and his Europe embraced the world.' So the great American urban theorist Lewis Mumford described Geddes' radical ideas which he carried with him round the world, most notably to India where he introduced community-sensitive town planning, met Mahatma Gandhi and became Professor of Sociology at the University of Bombay until 1925. In the new state of Israel, he conducted a survey of Jerusalem and planned its Hebrew University. Knighted in 1931, Geddes, died in Montpelier in the south of France in the midst of planning an international college, a revival of the city's pre-Reformation Scottish college. A friend said of Geddes that he had 'a tendency to light a candle and walk away to the next thing leaving you holding it in your hands'. Although few of his projects turned out quite as he had hoped, as biologist, planner, landscape architect, sociologist, ecologist and educator, his ideas were immensely influential. Patrick Geddes' romantic vision for Edinburgh's Old Town was to revive its medieval turrets, turnpike stairs and gargoyles, a style far from the cool Classicism of Robert Adam's New Town.

ADAM STYLE

Robert Adam (1728–92) had architecture in his blood. His father William started out as a Kirkcaldy builder and ended up as a highly successful architect and designer of country houses in the increasingly fashionable Classical style. Profiting, as was then the normal practice, not only as architect, but also as building contractor for his commissions, he was able to purchase the estate of Blairadam on the Fife–Kinross border. In these comfortable and cultured circumstances, Robert Adam, whose fame would far surpass his father's, grew up with his three brothers, John, James and William, who also all became successful architects.

Robert's time at Edinburgh University was cut short by serious illness and the 1745 Jacobite rebellion, but his father's extensive practice gave him and his brothers the best possible training. Accompanying Charles Hope, younger brother of his father's client the Earl of Hopetoun, on the Grand Tour gave him the opportunity to study the best Classical architecture. Realising that the fashionable Palladian architecture of the day was based on Roman public buildings, Adam decided to study the dwellings in which the Romans had actually lived, exploring Diocletian's Palace in Split, Yugoslavia, well off the beaten track of Grand Tour tourism. This not only gave him material for a successful book of drawings, but also inspired the style, still Classical, but lighter in feel and more colourful than Palladian, that came to be known as Adam.

With the book acting as effective promotion, on setting up his architect's practice in London, Adam rapidly acquired a large and aristocratic clientele whose houses he designed or remodelled. Country and town houses rolled off his drawing board – Syon, Kenwood, Osterley Park, Kedleston, Harewood, Culzean Castle, Mellerstain – while he graced the capital of his native land with General Register House, the Old College of Edinburgh University and Charlotte Square. The brothers' venture into speculative property development in 1772, a large residential and office development by the side of the Thames called the Adelphi, from 'brothers' in Greek, was less successful, nearly bankrupting Robert and James and seriously damaging their reputations.

The Adam style from the most successful architect of his time influenced buildings throughout the world, including the White House in Washington, whose workforce included Scottish masons who had previously cut their mark on Adam's Edinburgh New Town. His style continues to be copied to this day. Two Glasgow architects were to play their part in pioneering a very different style, the Modern Movement.

GLASGOW STYLE

Alexander 'Greek' Thomson (1817–75) and Charles Rennie Mackintosh (1868–1928) were very different in personality, style and approach although they both came from large families. Thomson, a son of the bookkeeper at a cotton mill in Balfron, Stirlingshire, was the seventeenth of twenty children, while Mackintosh was one of ten children of a Glasgow policeman. There the similarity ends. While Thomson was self-taught, Mackintosh attended Glasgow School of Art, one of the leading institutions of the time. By the time that Thomson started designing buildings at the age of 32, Mackintosh was well into his most productive period including Glasgow School of Art. Thomson was a pillar of his profession while Mackintosh remained outside the architectural establishment. Thomson was the the God-fearing paterfamilias: Mackintosh lived the bohemian life of the artist.

What the two had in common was an ability to produce architecture which was modern without losing sight of the traditional values and style – in Thomson's case, of Classical Greece and Egypt, in Mackintosh's, of Scots vernacular. Thomson constantly asked himself the question, 'How is it that there is no modern style of architecture?' He rejected the Victorian Gothic fashion, attacking the decision to employ the English arch-medievalist Gilbert Scott to design the new University of Glasgow. Mackintosh encouraged future generations of students to remember that 'there is hope in honest error, none in the icy perfections of the mere stylist' as they entered the portals of his School of Art.

Thomson revelled in the latest technology, pioneering the use of iron frames for his shops and warehouses, which were both functional and imposing with their large sheets of window glass. Although his work was largely confined to Glasgow, Thomson's influence as a pioneer of the Modern Movement spread to the United States and architects there like Frank Lloyd Wright. Mackintosh, whose solution to the School of Art's brief to design a 'plain' building was to produce a masterpiece, was too far ahead of his time for his fellow citizens. While Thomson died wealthy, Mackintosh died poor. During his lifetime and beyond, Europe recognised his genius long before Glasgow, whose City Fathers in the 1960s threatened to demolish some of his buildings to make way for motorways.

Mackintosh first gained his European perspective when awarded a Travelling Scholarship funded in memory of Alexander 'Greek' Thomson, who never went to Greece. Today thousands of overseas tourists flock to see their buildings as part of their Scottish tour, thanks to the man who put Scotland on the tourist map.

THE MAN WHO INVENTED ROMANTIC SCOTLAND

Although brought up in Edinburgh, the son of a lawyer and a professor's daughter, it was the holidays that Sir Walter Scott (1771–1832) spent on his grandfather's farm which inspired his love of the Borders and its ballads. While practising law, he published the three-volume collection of ballads *The Minstrelsy of the Scottish Border* in 1802–3. Next came his own narrative poem, the bestselling *Lay of the Last Minstrel*, followed by *Marmion* and *The Lady of the Lake*. Set in the Trossachs, *The Lady of the Lake* and his later novel *Rob Roy* introduced the wider public for the first time to the romantic scenery of mountain, glen and legend. Scott's writing brought the first tourists in significant numbers to the shores of Loch Katrine and the wooded slopes of the Trossachs, more accessible and less daunting than the Highlands proper, whose stark wilderness did not accord with contemporary ideas of romantic beauty.

Financial necessity largely drove Scott into becoming the world's first historical novelist. Until 1827, he did not put his name to his novels, fearing that this might not be seen as a suitable pursuit for a lawyer, although the author behind the novels became an increasingly widely known secret among his friends. Although he set some of his Waverley novels, published from 1814, in England and even the Holy Land, most of Scott's characters were Scottish and their exploits based on romanticised incidents in Scottish history. The number of tourists to his 'romantic Highlands' continued to grow. In his book for children, *Tales of a Grandfather*, he published a more systematic account of Scottish history, one that remained the popular interpretation of the country's past throughout the nineteenth century.

Scott himself was passionate about his country's past and separate traditions. He published a pamphlet successfully defending the right of the Scottish banks to issue their own bank-notes. In 1818, he rediscovered the Scottish crown jewels lying forgotten in a chest in Edinburgh Castle. He decorated his house at Abbotsford, itself reflecting his vision of Scotland's baronial past, with fragments of medieval stonework and welcomed his many visitors' contributions to his collection of memorabilia of his heroes, Mary Queen of Scots, Rob Roy and the Young Pretender.

When, in 1822, George IV proposed to make a visit to Scotland, the first by a reigning monarch for over 150 years, Scott was the obvious man to stage-manage the event. He decided that it should be a pageant of the loyalty of the Highlands to the rightful king. Chiefs were encouraged to wear 'their' traditional clan tartans: when some had difficulty identifying their 'tartan', enterprising firms were only too happy to suggest an appropriate design. Scott did George IV proud. Edinburgh rapturously welcomed its monarch, tartan was everywhere and the portly king sported a Stuart kilt – only 75 years after tartan had been banned as a badge of rebellion – over fetching pink tights. Singlehandedly, Scott had created the romantic view of Scotland as a land of clans and tartan that has been the mainstay of the tourist industry ever since. All that remained was to erect the Gothic rocket of Edinburgh's Scott monument in his memory for the shortbread tin image of Scotland to be complete.

Less than a century later, the dramatic growth of people, cities and leisure resulted in increasing pressure on the world's wild places. A corn merchant's son from Dunbar took on the mantle of 'father of ecology'.

FIVE HOURS TO MYSELF

As a child John Muir (1838–1914) roamed the East Lothian countryside, developing an empathy with the natural world, which remained with him all his life. On emigrating with his family to Wisconsin, aged 11, he found time to observe a very different natural environment while helping his stern and overbearing father in the backbreaking work of clearing the forest to create a smallholding. There was no time for school, but Muir made time for learning by getting up five hours before the work of the day began. One of his many inventions was an 'early rising machine' which, triggered by an alarm clock, tipped him out of bed.

In 1867, an accident changed Muir's life. While working as a mechanic, his file slipped, rendering him blind for several months. As his sight gradually returned he vowed to devote his life to drinking in the sights of the wild places that he loved. He set off on a 1,000-mile trek from Kentucky to Georgia, intending, thereafter, to seek the wilds of the headwaters of the Amazon. An attack of malaria in Florida changed his plans and he ended up in San Francisco where, on asking where the nearest wilderness was, he was directed to Yosemite.

There he continued his study of nature as he worked as shepherd, sawmill manager and guide to the increasing number of tourists seeking out the wonders of the Sierra Nevada. In 1880, Muir married and settled on the coast outside San Francisco, growing pears and grapes. He satisfied his restless yearning for the wild places by his writing and occasional visits. Each time he went back to Yosemite, however, he noticed how grazing pressures were eroding the pristine wilderness he had discovered in 1868. Having struck up a friendship with Robert Underwood Johnson, editor of the magazine *Century*, Muir started a campaign in 1889 to have the area round Yosemite declared a National Park. Muir's inspirational writing and Johnson's effective lobbying resulted in Congress passing the relevant legislation a year later.

When Muir wrote to Johnson, 'Let us do something to make the mountains glad', the result in 1892 was the world's first significant organisation dedicated to preserving wild nature, the Sierra Club, and the birth of the ecology movement. The aim of the club was to give people access to the high places, while protecting it against the pressures of commercialisation. At first, the movement grew slowly until the threat by the San Francisco city authorities to build a dam made Yosemite and conservation front-page headlines. Until his death from pneumonia, Muir wrote and campaigned to open the eyes of America to the value and the fragility of the wilderness and to make people aware of the need to place checks on the unbridled commercialism which was so much part of the American way of life of that time.

Muir is a man much honoured in his adopted land. Californians celebrate 21 April as John Muir Day in honour of the 'Father of the American National Parks'. In 1976, the California Historical Society voted Muir 'The Greatest Californian'. The US Geological Survey is unlikely to approve any more mountains or lakes being named after him as the map is already overcrowded with Muirs. Perhaps the greatest tribute of all came when two great mountaineers were debating why American mountains remained relatively uncluttered with developments, from resorts to funiculars, compared with the Alps. Rheinhold Messner gave a three-word answer to his American companion, 'You had Muir.' Muir's contribution lay in establishing the need for a balance between protecting wild nature and allowing people to share his wonder at its beauty.

While Muir summed up his goal as 'I care to live only to entice people to look at Nature's loveliness', other Scots had different reasons to seek out the world's unexplored places, from the challenge of exploration and the sheer joy of discovery to enhancing the developed world with the fruits of their journeys. David Douglas (1798–1834), one of the world's great plant collectors, was to bring back something that was arguably to make the most dramatic impact on his native landscape over the next 200 years.

THE MAN OF GRASS

Born in Scone in Perthshire, Douglas left school aged 11 to work as a gardener on a local estate before moving to Glasgow's Botanic Gardens. There he met Sir William Hooker, Professor of Botany at the university, who asked him to lead a plant-hunting expedition to North America on behalf of the Horticultural Society of London. Douglas's first expedition to the relatively settled eastern regions in search of new fruit and vegetables was such a success that he was recruited to undertake a more ambitious venture to the north-west seaboard.

After an eight-month voyage round Cape Horn and an exploration of the region round Vancouver, Douglas travelled over 7,000 miles inland. He became the first European to climb the northern Rockies, where he named a mountain after his mentor, Hooker; another peak is now named after Douglas. He sent back seeds of over 800 species, of which 250 were new introductions and 130 flourished well in Britain, the two areas sharing a temperate maritime climate.

Returning to Britain in 1827, Douglas could not settle despite the hardships of his journeys and weakened eyesight from snow blindness. By 1829, he was back on his travels, this time further south to the region around the Columbia River. From there he travelled up to Monterey, exploring the Sacramento Valley and Santa Lucia Mountains. He aborted his attempt to reach Alaska after about 1,000 miles as too ambitious and decided instead to return to Vancouver by canoe down the Fraser River. Unfortunately, he lost his seed collection and instruments when his canoe capsized. His final journey – exploring Hawaii – was in 1833, when he met his mysterious death in a pit trap dug for wild cattle into which a wild bull had already fallen. Gored to death by the maddened bull, whether Douglas fell as a result of his damaged eyesight or foul play was never proven.

Two hundred plants are called after Douglas including the Douglas Fir, the greatest number ever associated with one person. Other seeds he brought back included the Sitka Spruce, the mainstay of the forestry industry, the Noble Fir, the Grand Fir and the Radiata or Monterey Pine, now widely planted in Australia and New Zealand and forecast to become the most important timber tree of the twenty-first century. Flowers he introduced to the West include the California poppy, five species of monkey flower and eighteen of lupin. Three Douglas Firs in Scotland, each higher than London's Nelson's Column, regularly battle it out for the title of the tallest tree outside America's western seaboard. On expedition, Douglas lived under the boughs of trees, in tents or under his upturned canoe. He shared his life with the native Indians whose trust he won and who called him the 'Man of Grass'. The native companions of a Scot who opened up another continent were to call him 'the great master' while the *New York Herald* nominated him 'Man of the Century'.

THE SMOKE THAT THUNDERS

Brought up in a single room in Shuttle Row, Blantyre, David Livingstone (1813–73) was sent to work in the local cotton mill aged ten. Determined to better himself by becoming a medical missionary in China, he attended evening classes until he had saved enough money to study medicine. By the time he qualified, however, China was inaccessible to missionaries as a result of the Opium Wars. The words of Robert Moffat, 'the smoke of a thousand villages, where no missionary has ever been', fired Livingstone's imagination and decided where his future lay. In 1841, he joined Moffat at his mission station at Kuruman, 700 miles north of Cape Town in South Africa.

Livingstone was fascinated by the lifestyle of the local African tribes, learning their languages and growing to understand their customs. He discovered the joy of exploration when travelling over 700 miles to heal, spread the gospel and find a site for a permanent mission of his own, which he established in the Mabotsa valley in 1843. Among the hazards he faced were marauding lions, one of which he shot but failed to kill, leading it to attack in maddened retaliation, permanently crippling his arm. Regarding his lack of pain during the attack as an example of God's providence, Livingstone stoically commented, 'I wondered what part of me he'd eat first.'

In 1844, on marrying Moffat's daughter Mary, he moved further north to Kologeng where they had four children in the space of five years. When the water dried up in 1849, they headed off into the unknown again, discovering Lake Ngami. Three years later, Livingstone, deciding that the rigours of African life were too much, dispatched his family home. Convinced that opening up the country to trade was the way to bring the benefits of civilisation, including Christianity, to the Africans, he set out with 27 tribesmen to find a possible trade route to the west coast of Africa. Six months and 1,500 miles of hazardous and uncomfortable travel later he reached the coast at Luanda. Rejecting it as a trade route he turned back, despite being offered a passage to England, feeling obliged to see his loyal men safely back home.

Although the journey back in the wet season was even longer and more uncomfortable, Livingstone was still determined to find a route to the east coast by the Zambesi River. Only 50 miles into the journey, he came upon 'the smoke that thunders' – the great Victoria Falls that he named in honour of his Queen. He followed the river to the sea, convincing himself that this was his long sought highway to the interior. On his return to Britain in 1856, he found himself a celebrity as the first white man to cross the 'Dark Continent', using his fame to expose the evils of the African slave trade. The one group who were unenthusiastic about his achievement were his employers, who wished for mission work, not exploration. Convinced of the urgent need to open up Africa, if only to combat the slave trade, Livingstone reluctantly resigned, being appointed Consul for the East Coast to develop the route he had discovered.

The next expedition was a disaster. Although brilliant at inspiring the loyalty of Africans, Livingstone was too shy and dour to lead an inexperienced team of Europeans. The prefabricated boat he christened the *Ma Robert*, after the African name for his wife, was so underpowered as to be near useless, the Europeans squabbled and the Zambesi proved unnavigable. A relatively small detour on his previous journey meant that he had bypassed the impassable Kebrabasa Rapids. Livingstone did succeed in exploring the Shire River, discovering Lake Malawi and realising his dream of establishing an inland mission.

The worst blow of all was the death of his wife within months of her rejoining him. Broken-hearted, Livingstone threw himself into work. He decided to sail another prefabricated boat, the *Lady Nyasa*, to India, despite its obvious unseaworthiness, to keep it from falling into the hands of the slavers. Arriving at Bombay against the odds after a hazardous six-week voyage, he set sail for Britain where once more he campaigned against slavery. The puzzle of Africa, however, continued to nag. With the backing of the Royal Geographical Society he determined to return alone with his loyal Africans to solve the mystery of the sources of the three great rivers of Africa – the Congo, the Zambezi and the Nile.

In 1866, he set out for the interior. Desertion by many of his staff, illness, tribal wars and the ravages of the slave traders slowed his progress and the mystery of the rivers' sources proved intractable. Deep in the hinterland, Livingstone was lost to the outside world. When rumours started to circulate that he was dead, the enterprising editor of the *New York Herald*, James Gordon Bennett, decided that finding him would sell newspapers. In 1871, Henry Morton Stanley obliged, with the immortal greeting, 'Doctor Livingstone, I presume.' Although welcoming the company, Livingstone, by now seriously ill, refused to leave, his quest uncompleted. A second search party, financed by his friend James 'Paraffin' Young, arrived too late. In 1873, his devoted bearers found their 'Great Master' dead at prayer. They carried his body 1,000 miles to Zanzibar where it was shipped for burial in Westminster Abbey. They buried his heart where he died, in Africa.

The second person to be awarded two medals from the Royal Geographical Society was a very different character, the first European to cross Australia.

WHISKY, NOT GOLD, IN THEM HILLS

John McDouall Stuart (1815–66) was born the youngest of nine children of a Customs Officer in Dysart, Fife. Although he attended a military academy, when his height at only 5ft 6ins, his slight build and uncertain health ruled out a career as a soldier, he sought a new life in South Australia. He surveyed the virgin lands of the interior for sheep ranching and tried farming for himself, but could not settle. In 1844, he was invited to join Charles Sturt's expedition into the deep interior to find the inland sea that was thought to exist in the centre. They penetrated north for 250 miles, but found only stony desert. After the second in command died and Sturt partially lost his sight, Stuart drew the maps of their discoveries.

Stuart was bitten with the exploration bug. With one companion and food for only six weeks, which he made last four months, he discovered 40,000 square miles of potential sheep country; an official expedition at the same time only managed 40 miles. Although the reward of a 1,000 square mile ranch by a grateful government did not materialise, Stuart bore no grudge; his first priority on his return being to find some whisky and get gloriously drunk. He spent any money he was given on wild living to have an excuse to return to the bush. His third expedition, only 600 miles away from a full crossing of the continent, revealed a route well supplied with water.

Seeking a route for a telegraph, the Government of South Australia offered a reward for the first person to cross Australia. Stuart took up the challenge although he had difficulty finding men willing to travel under his Spartan regime. His fourth expedition reached beyond the centre and identified the mountain later named after him. His fifth, backed by the government, achieved five-sixths of the crossing, but failed to find a way across the arid Sturt plains. While Stuart was in the outback, news broke that the rival Wills and Burke expedition had perished and the interior was an empty waste of no economic value. Government enthusiasm evaporated.

Stuart was undeterred. Government support was eventually won on condition that he took along a scientist, whom he found to be a constant thorn in his flesh. On 24 July 1862, he at last reached the north coast after an arduous journey. The way back was even tougher and Stuart, desperately ill with scurvy, had to be carried in a litter slung between two horses for part of the way. By the time he reached civilisation, however, he had recovered sufficiently to enjoy his customary bender before facing a jubilant reception in Adelaide. The 14-year-old son of a sheep station owner whose land he had crossed wrote to a friend: 'Oh, he is such a funny little man, he is always drunk. You won't be able to have him at your house.' Although fêted, financial rewards were few and Stuart retired to London to live with his sister, broken in health, but not in spirit.

BUILT BY THE SCOTS

★ **The Aswan Dam, Egypt:** brought up in Inverness, Sir Murdoch MacDonald (1866–1957) was resident engineer during the building of Egypt's Aswan Dam. He was also responsible for its first heightening in 1912 and for much of the irrigation and drainage of the Nile. He was the MacDonald of today's global structural engineers, Mott MacDonald.

★ **Coventry Cathedral:** the icon of post-war Britain was designed by Sir Basil Spence (1907–76) who, in 1951, won the competition to replace the cathedral, which had been bombed in the Coventry Blitz. Although born in India, Spence trained and spent much of his working life in Edinburgh. He is rather less famous as the designer of the notorious Hutchie B multi-storeys in Glasgow's Gorbals.

★ **The Forth Rail Bridge:** the world's first all-steel, long span bridge and its longest bridge when opened in 1890. It ushered in the age of great cantilever bridges, holding the world record until 1917. The Forth Rail Bridge was built by Sir William Arrol (1839–1913), the Glasgow engineer who also designed the steelwork of Tower Bridge, London, and the Khedive Abbas Bridge, near Cairo.

★ **New Scotland Yard, London:** the most famous building of Edinburgh-born Norman Shaw (1831–1913), who was the most influential architect of the late nineteenth century and set the style for twentieth-century suburbia. Shaw pioneered the Old English and Queen Anne styles.

★ **Pavlosk Palace, St Petersburg:** Charles Cameron (c. 1740–1812). The son of a prosperous master builder, Cameron completed his training in Rome, possibly at the court of the exiled Young Pretender, before accepting an invitation in 1779 from Catherine the Great, who had been impressed by his book on Roman antiquities. In St Petersburg he built, remodelled and extended many royal and aristocratic buildings. Although virtually unknown in Britain, he produced work of as high a quality as Robert Adam and played a significant part in the revival of Greek and Etruscan styles in Europe.

★ The Royal Festival Hall, London: opened as part of the Festival of Britain in 1951, it was masterminded by the Edinburgh architect Sir Robert Matthew (1906–75). His father was a partner of Sir Robert Lorimer, who introduced the Arts and Crafts movement to Scotland. Matthew, the first Professor of Architecture at Edinburgh University, also designed Pakistan's new capital of Islamabad and founded the architectural practice, RMJM.

★ Skyscrapers: invented in Edinburgh centuries before New York to solve the same problem, a shortage of building land. With no room to spread out, the only way was up. In the seventeenth century, the tallest tenement, behind Parliament Square, was 14 storeys high.

SCOTS AT THE EXTREME

★ The Beardmore Glacier: named by Ernest Shackleton during his 1908–9 Antarctic expedition after Eliza and William Beardmore (1856–1936). In 1906, Shackleton briefly worked for Beardmore, the Glasgow engineering magnate and his wife who encouraged him to plan his own British Antarctic Expedition. They met while Shackleton was Secretary of the Royal Scottish Geographical Society in Edinburgh from 1904–10. James Caird (1837–1916) of the Dundee jute family was a major sponsor of Shackleton's 1914–17 expedition to cross the Antarctic continent coast-to-coast. The tiny whaling boat in which Shackleton sailed from Elephant Island to South Georgia to seek help, after the expedition had been trapped in the ice, was the *James Caird*. One of the six men who sailed on her was carpenter Henry 'Chippy' McNish from Glasgow. When a professor at Cambridge, fellow Glaswegian Sir James Wordie, who had been the ship's geologist, first aroused an interest in Polar exploration in his student, Vivian Fuchs, and helped him plan the trip which led to Fuchs realising Shackleton's ambition of crossing the Antarctic continent, in 1957–8.

★ **The world's first scientific research ship:** RRS *Discovery* built in Dundee for the 1901 National Antarctic Expedition led by Captain Scott. She is now the last vessel of her type afloat. The *Terra Nova*, also built in Dundee, carried Scott on his second ill-fated Antarctica expedition. Scott planned this expedition with scientist Dr Edward Wilson on the verandah of a cottage in Glen Prosen, Angus, overlooking what he called 'his favourite view in the whole world'. One of the last three to die after Scott was beaten to the Pole was Henry Robertson 'Birdie' Bowers (1883–1912), born in Greenock in a house on the Esplanade known as 'Bowers' Folly'. Although moving to Kent as a child, Bowers' mother later returned to live in Rothesay, where on regular visits Bowers used to swim daily across Rothesay Bay, even in December.

★ **The first European to discover the source of the Blue Nile:** James Bruce (1730–94). Born in Stirlingshire and educated at Harrow and Edinburgh University, it was while Bruce was Consul in Algiers, broken-hearted after the death of his young wife, that he started on his African travels to find the source of the Nile. In 1770, he found the source of the Blue Nile, later tracing it to its confluence with the White Nile. His stories of his travels, although written up in five volumes and later verified, were widely disbelieved by his contemporaries.

★ **Lake Chad:** discovered by Hugh Clapperton (1788–1827) when he crossed the Sahara in 1823. Born in Annan, Clapperton was press-ganged into the navy where he rose to rank of lieutenant before retiring on half-pay. He was selected for a small British expedition to open up a trade route from Tripoli across the Sahara. He failed in his other goal, dying while on an expedition to trace the course of the Niger.

★ **The first European to cross Equatorial Africa:** James Grant (1827–92) from Nairn, with fellow explorer, John Speke. They were the first to report the discovery of the source of the Nile in Lake Victoria, although Sir Richard Burton bitterly disputed their claim.

★ **The first British climber to conquer the North face of the Eiger:** Dougal Haston (1940–77), who learned to climb on the railway bridge at Currie, outside Edinburgh. As well as the Eiger in 1966, Haston's achievements included being the first to climb Changabang in India, in 1974, as well as being a member of the UK team who conquered the south face of Annapurna in 1970, made the first ascent of the south-west face of Mount McKinley in 1975 and the first ascent of the south-west face of Mount Everest in 1975. He died in an avalanche in Switzerland while on a skiing trip.

★ The first European to cross the American continent: Alexander Mackenzie (1767–1820).

★ The course of the River Niger: largely traced by Mungo Park (1771–1806). Born near Selkirk, he trained at Edinburgh, becoming a surgeon with the East India Company. He reached the headwaters of the Niger via the Gambia River, tracing much of its route. On marriage he became a GP in Peebles, but preferred exploration to writing prescriptions. His later expedition, to complete the mapping of the course of the Niger, met with disaster, all 40 Europeans on it, including Park, dying from disease or native ambush.

★ The first explorer to reach the earth's magnetic north pole: Scotsman Sir John Ross (1777–1856), who joined the navy aged nine. He led an expedition to look for the Northwest Passage during which his nephew, Sir James Clark Ross (1800–62), discovered the magnetic north pole in 1831. When James Clark Ross went on a quest to find its pole's southern equivalent, he claimed Antarctica for Queen Victoria in 1841, named Mount Erebus and Terror after his ships, and discovered the sea and huge ice shelf now called after him.

★ The Weddell Sea, Antarctica: named after James Weddell (1787–1834), born in Ostend to a Lanarkshire father. He commanded the sailing brig *Jane* of Greenock on three privately organised voyages during the third of which, in unusually open ice conditions, he reached the furthest south in the sea later named after him. The record for the furthest journey south would not be broken for nearly 100 years.

SCOTS AND THE NATURAL WORLD

★ The first dissection of an elephant in Britain: carried out by Dundee doctor and botanist Patrick Blair in 1708. He also wrote the first treatise in English on the sex of plants.

★ The world's greatest rhododendron collector: Falkirk-born George Forrest (1873–1932), Scotland's Indiana Jones. After a decade as a gold panner during the Australian gold rush, Forrest was employed by seed merchant A.K. Bully to collect plants. He made seven expeditions to China and Tibet bringing back hundreds of new species – identified by the suffix *forrestii* – including orchids and primula to the Royal Botanic Garden, Edinburgh, where he was appointed Keeper of the Herbarium in 1902. Thanks to the network first established by Forrest, the Royal Botanic Garden has the world's largest collection of rhododendrons and the world's largest collection of Chinese plants outside China.

★ *Forsythia viridissima*: one of the 120 new plant species including *Rhododendron fortunei*, *Jasminium mudiflorum* and *Dicentra spectabilis* introduced by Robert Fortune (1812–80) from Berwickshire during several trips to China and Japan from where he also brought back the art of bonsai.

★ The Fraser Fir: named after John Fraser (1750–1811), a Scots botanist who made several plant-collecting expeditions to North America, one of his sponsors being Tsar Paul of Russia. He was responsible for introducing many favourite shrubs to Europe, including *Magnolia fraserii*, *rhododendron catawwbiense* and *Pieris floribunda*.

★ The Gardenia: named in 1761 after Dr Alexander Garden, an Aberdeenshire doctor who, on emigrating to Charleston, South Carolina, classified local plants according to the Linnaean system.

★ Grant's gazelle: named after James Augustus Grant (1827–92) from Nairn. After serving in the Indian Army during the Mutiny, he joined Speke's expedition to find the source of the Nile, tracing the river to Lake Victoria.

★ Lawson's Cypress: named after the Edinburgh nurserymen P. Lawson and Son, who were the first firm to receive the seed of the tree on its introduction from Oregon in 1854.

★ The lechwe: named by explorer David Livingstone (1813–73), who took the name for the swamp antelope from the native Shona language

★ Gardenesque: the style introduced by John Claudius Loudon (1783–1843), who shaped the Victorian garden with its manicured lawns, circular flower beds and use of the exotics like rhododendrons and other flowering shrubs that the plant collectors were introducing to Europe. His massive gardening textbooks and his wife's six-volume *The Ladies' Flower Garden* did much to inspire the growing suburban middle classes with an interest in gardening.

★ **The terrarium:** A.A. Maconochie. Although Nathaniel Ward, a London surgeon and gardening enthusiast, gave his name to the miniature greenhouse for transporting plants, known as the Wardian case, the Scottish botanist Maconochie invented the same device independently four years earlier. In 1839, he went public with his terrarium, but chose not to press his claim of prior invention. The Wardian case proved invaluable in bringing back the spoils of plant-collecting trips: before then many exotic species failed to survive the journey.

★ **The monkey puzzle tree:** introduced to the northern hemisphere by Archibald Menzies (1754–1842), a surgeon-naturalist with the Royal Navy, who first recorded many species now commonly grown in the UK. His most bizarre find resulted from dining out one night in Chile. Unable to identify some nuts on the table, he popped a few in his pocket. Several sprouted on the voyage home and led to the weird and wonderful-looking monkey puzzle tree taking root in Europe.

★ *Hopea,* **the genus of tropical trees:** named by William Roxburgh (1751–1815), the Edinburgh doctor who became Superintendent of the Calcutta Botanic Garden. He named it after his mentor, John Hope (1725–86), Professor of Botany at Edinburgh University, who introduced rhubarb to Scotland and was the first person in Britain to use Linneaus' system of botanical classification. Roxburgh also gave the name *Boswellia* to the frankincense family either after James Boswell, the biographer, or his uncle, John, a doctor. Roxburgh catalogued the many Indian plants he discovered in his magnum opus *Flora Indica*. This included the first major treatment of the ginger family, most of the species known at that time being native to India.

★ **Sibbald's Rorqual, better known as the blue whale:** named after Sir Robert Sibbald (1641–22), the first Professor of Medicine at Edinburgh University, founder of the Royal College of Physicians in Edinburgh, co-founder of the Edinburgh Botanic Garden and author in 1694 of *Observations on some Animals of the Whale genus* *lately thrown on the Shores of Scotland*, the first scientific study of the whale.

★ Thomson's gazelle: named after Joseph Thomson (1858–95), the son of a Dumfriesshire stonemason, who joined an expedition to East Africa led by Keith Johnston. When Johnston died, the 22-year-old Thomson assumed command and successfully completed the exploration of an area between Lakes Nyasa and Tanganyika. He led several other expeditions, including the first crossing of the East African Masailand by Europeans.

★ *Westlothiana lizziae*, the world's earliest known reptile: discovered by Stan Wood, the fossil hunter, in 1988 in a West Lothian quarry and nicknamed Lizzie because she looked a bit like a modern lizard. The most intriguing creature found in the quarry is *Eucritter malanolimnetes*, 'the beautiful creature from the black lagoon', possibly a common ancestor of both modern amphibians and reptiles.

★ The Bearsden Shark, *Akmonistion zangerli*: excavated by Stan Wood in 1981 in a Glasgow suburb. It is the best preserved fossil shark of its time in the world. Even the partly digested remains of its last and now 330-million-year-old fish supper can be seen in the bowels of the one-metre-long fossil, housed in Glasgow's Hunterian Museum.

9

Macs and Taipans: Making their Mark on the World

In his rectorial address, playwright Sir James Barrie reminded the students of St Andrews, 'You come of a race the very wind of whose name has swept to the ultimate seas.' The nineteenth-century English historian J.A. Froude concluded that 'no people so few in number have scored so deep a mark in the world's history as the Scots have done'. The US President Woodrow Wilson, one of the 31 US Presidents to claim Scots blood in their veins, stated, 'Every line of strength in American history is a line coloured with Scottish blood', and Sir Winston Churchill went a step further: 'Of all the small nations of this earth, perhaps only the ancient Greeks surpass the Scots in their contribution to mankind.' Of course, there have been voices of dissent. English novelist Anthony Powell wrote of the Scots:

> In two Qualities they stand supreme,
> Their self-advertisement and self-esteem.

Even Sir James Barrie had to admit that 'there are few more impressive sights in the world than a Scotsman on the make'.

There is a saying that 'the Scot is never so much at home as when he is abroad'. Flora Macdonald, who emigrated to America after helping the Young Pretender escape following the Battle of Culloden, gave a clue to the reason why when she described her motive as being 'to begin the world again, anew, in a new corner of it'. Refuge from political and religious oppression was just one of the many reasons why Scots left their homeland to leave their mark on the world. Geography was another. The unyielding terrain and uncertain climate, especially of the Highlands, persuaded many to abandon a subsistence living from the hostile soil for the opportunities of the big cities and of the young countries of North America, Australia and New Zealand.

Emigration quickened after the 1745 Rebellion when the British Government adopted stern measures to subdue the fighting spirit of the Clans. The new landowners saw the potential of the Highlands in terms of sheep rearing and deerstalking rather than of people. Often the only hope for the future lay in the advertisement offering a cheap passage across the Atlantic. For some this was the road to prosperity and fame; for others the struggle to survive in the Frontier backwoods was little different than the life they had left. Some did not survive the crossing, herded like cattle in insanitary holds, others did not even get that far. The bell of Robert Owen's New Lanark community is inscribed 'Hoggers Town . . . Maryland, 1786'. It belonged to would-be emigrants from Caithness who, stormbound on their journey to Greenock, decided to seek work in New Lanark instead.

For centuries, Scotland's main export has been its intellectual capital. From parish school to university, its educational system was far in advance of that of most European countries, but a small, relatively poor and inaccessible country could not provide the opportunities to keep the enterprising at home. The world was to benefit from Scotland's centuries-old brain drain, with 'Mac' the engineer on every ship and an Edinburgh-trained doctor hanging up his certificate in swamps, savannahs and suburbs throughout the globe. For those with little to offer except a strong arm and a brave heart, the wars of Europe and Empire provided endless opportunities for mercenaries or soldiers.

As early as the mid-fifteenth century, the French King had a Scots Guard whose bravery was proverbial: '*Fier comme un Ecossais*' was 'proud as a Scot'. When one of them, Jacques Montgomerie, accidentally killed King Henri II during a tournament, Mary Queen of Scots briefly became Queen of France as the wife of his successor, Francois II. In the ensuing centuries, Scottish mercenaries fought in the armies of Sweden, Russia and Prussia, or as soldiers in the British Army throughout the Empire. The 93rd Sutherland Highlanders earned immortal fame as the Thin Red Line, when they repulsed a massed Russian cavalry charge at Balaklava during the Crimean War, while the Royal Scots have 149 battle honours for heroism overseas. Few Scottish families were left untouched by the carnage of the First

World War, for which Earl Douglas Haig (1861–1928), Edinburgh-born commander of the British forces in France, must bear no small responsibility.

From earliest times, Scotland has been an exporting nation and where its people traded they also settled. As early as 1297, Sir William Wallace thanked the citizens of Lubeck and Hamburg for their 'friendly and helpful counsel' to Scottish merchants, offering safe conduct to any of their merchants who might venture to a Scottish port. Until the advent of good roads and the railway, eastern Scotland looked as much to the Baltic and the Low Countries as to England as places with which to do business. A Scot built Norway's first shipyard and founded the world's fifth oldest gentleman's club, the Royal Bachelors' Club in Gothenburg. By the seventeenth century, 30,000 Scots were living in Poland, although by no means all had made their fortune. 'Scot' in Polish means a commercial traveller, and there is a Polish proverb 'as poor as a Scots pedlar's pack'.

Scots were found wherever trading opportunities opened up. King James VI was the first overseas royal to write to an Emperor of Japan. Many of the early Indian 'Nabobs' were Scottish and many of the great Far East trading houses were founded and run by Scots. From the seventeenth century, Scots looked west and saw gold in the sugar plantations of Jamaica and the tobacco fields of Virginia, in the forests of Canada and the prairies of the Mid West. From 1821–70, nearly two-thirds of the commissioned officers of the Hudson Bay Company were of Scots origin. Dundee fabric covered the wagon trains carrying pioneers into the American West and during the Klondike the Canadian Pacific Railway, itself largely financed and built by Scots, hired ships from the Clyde to transport miners to the Alaskan goldfields.

Money and skills followed in the path of the traders. Scottish investment lay behind three key stages of the nineteenth-century American economy: ranching, mineral mining in the West and the opening up of the Great Plains to agriculture. The first large joint stock venture in cattle ranching in Texas, the Prairie Cattle Company Ltd, was based in Edinburgh, although much of its capital came from Dundee, which in the 1880s invested in the USA ten times as much as the value of its own real estate. Three-quarters of the overseas investment in US ranching came from Scotland, the rebuilding of

Chicago after the fire of 1871 and the draining of the Sacramento swampland in California being just two examples of US endeavour backed by Scottish capital. One historian has attributed the Scots willingness to invest to 'romantic, speculative inventiveness, crossed with the mentality of a chartered accountant'.

Scots exported skills as well as money. Scottish textile workers in Spain may have introduced the country to its national game of football, while Clyde shipbuilding expertise helped build the floating docks of Java and Saigon and the shipyards of Japan. Dundee, the city of 'jute, jam and journalism', provided an eighth of the investment to develop India's jute industry, which eventually bit the hand that fed it. Scots found a ready home for their industrial skills in late nineteenth-century North America. Five thousand Scottish Mormon miners emigrated to Utah to establish the industry there while the US thread industry owes its development almost exclusively to Scots. Canadian banking and business were largely modelled on Scottish practice and a third of the country's business élite were of Scots origin, leaders in fur, timber, mining and civil engineering. Scottish enterprise flourished in the wildest places, from the Antarctic stations of Christian Salvesen of Edinburgh, at one time the world's largest whaling company, to the sheep farms of the Branders family on Easter Island.

The Scots left their mark on the places where they settled, on its communities, place names and institutions. It is not possible to estimate how many people in the world today trace their ancestry back to Scotland, but proud claims of Scots blood range from Bonnie Dunbar the astronaut to Mickey Rooney the pint-sized film star, from Joan Baez the folk singer to 37 of the members of the American Baseball Hall of Fame. One measure is the popularity of all things Scottish, with Highland Games in Japan, Burns Clubs in Russia and St Andrews and Caledonian Societies chequering the globe from Brazil to Brunei. A harder measure comes from statistics. Scots form the third largest ethnic group in Canada and the second largest West European ethnic group in the United States, with 25,000 people tracing their origins to before the Revolution. In 1984, the US Census Bureau provided the official stamp on what Scots had known for centuries: that they were an educated, employable, prosperous and uxorious people, scoring top out of the eight European ethnic groups selected for study.

Few would dispute that many Scots come from Scotland, but what about the Escots and Lescaux from France, the Scoti and Scuotto from Italy, the Schottes and Schottles of Germany, the Schots of Flanders or the Skotte of Norway? There is only a one letter switch between 'Greig' and Grieg, Norway's most famous composer who claimed Scottish roots. Scots mercenaries and traders in Europe stayed on to found the clans of Stuarts and Colquhouns in Sweden, the Drummonds, Crawfords and Moncrieffs in France, and the Taits, Ramsays, Mackays and MacKinnons in Finland. One in ten Australians has a Scottish surname and a third claim a line of Scottish ancestry in their family tree.

A quick glance at a US atlas shows the wealth of cities and counties called after Scots or Scottish place names. In Georgia, Highland Hills, Donaldsonville, Lennox, McIntyre and Stewart are a reminder of the Highlanders who defended the border against the Spanish in the eighteenth century, while in Carolina, Highlanders fleeing the aftermath of the Jacobite rebellions set up a Gaelic-speaking community: one Highland emigrant, on arrival at Wilmington, was amazed to hear two blacks speaking Gaelic. Names recall pockets of Scottish immigration in Massachusetts and Texas where workmen were recruited from Aberdeen to work the local quarries. There are fourteen Aberdeens worldwide, seven of which are in the United States, from Aberdeen, Mississippi, previously called Dundee, to Aberdeen, Idaho, the 'heart of Idaho's potato country'. There is of course a two-way traffic in names with Scotland having its Houston, Dallas, Waterloo and Moscow.

Scots also made their mark on the institutions of the countries in which they settled or invested. Montreal's McGill University was set up in 1821 thanks to a bequest from James McGill, a wealthy Glasgow fur trader, and its medical school was founded by four graduates from Scottish universities, two of whom were native Scots. Montreal's main teaching hospital was financed by the gift of Donald Smith from Moray, who rose from a clerk in the Hudson Bay Company to be its top man in North America: the building was created from the same architectural plans as used for the Edinburgh Royal Infirmary. Scots carried with them their love of learning. John Witherspoon, the only cleric to sign the Declaration of Independence, developed Princeton from a local theological college to one of the top three American universities. William and Mary College, North America's second oldest university, Adelaide University, the medical schools of Melbourne and Sydney and the first three universities in India all trace their history back to the influence of the Scots.

Scots have performed on the world's stage as prime ministers, presidents, admirals, generals, bankers, industrialists, doctors, scientists and stars. From the nine signatories of the US Declaration of Independence from Scottish families to the founders of the navies of Russia, Japan, Chile and the United States, wherever there was a challenge, there also was a Scot. Meet just 50 of them.

FLYING THE SALTIRE ROUND THE WORLD

★ Founder of the *New York Herald*: James Gordon Bennett (1795–1872) from Keith, who decided to emigrate rather than take holy orders in 1819. The many firsts he introduced to the USA after the launch of the *Herald* in 1835 included: first society page; first to print a Wall Street financial article; first to regularly employ European correspondents; first to publish the story of a sex scandal; first to publish stock quotations; first significant use of the telegraph for news; and the first illustrations. His son inherited a news empire and the wealth to cultivate a playboy lifestyle. His outrageous exploits gave rise to the slang expression of surprise – 'Gordon Bennett!' He was a great sports enthusiast, funding the James Gordon Bennett Cup for international yacht racing and the Gordon Bennett Motor Car Road Racing Trials, the precursor of the TT races on the Isle of Man.

★ Founder of America's second oldest university: Rev. James Blair (1656–1743). Son of the Minister of St Cuthbert's, Edinburgh, he was sent to America as a missionary rising to be the representative of the Anglican Bishop of London in Virginia. Blair promoted the foundation of the College of William and Mary, the oldest university in America after Harvard and the only university with a Royal Charter. When fundraising he received one £300 donation from three grateful privateers for whom he had interceded when they faced a charge of piracy. As the university's first President, he created the Christopher Wren Building, the oldest surviving building in the USA. The first true American bishop, Samuel

Seabury (1729–96), attended Edinburgh University and was consecrated in Aberdeen by bishops of the Episcopal Church of Scotland, as no English bishop would do so in fear of government displeasure.

★ The first Buick car: designed by David Dunbar Buick (1854–1929). Emigrating from Arbroath to America at the tender age of two, Buick made his first and only fortune from his invention of heat-bonding porcelain or enamel to cast iron to make the white bath tubs that were all the fashion. Bitten with the auto bug, in 1899 he sold out and set up a company to manufacture petrol engines. The first Buick car was either built by Buick himself or by Walter Marr, his gifted machinist to whom he sold the car in 1901 for $225. The next year the Buick Manufacturing Company developed Marr's 'valve-in-head' engine that would become the standard in the industry for power and efficiency. More of an inventor than a businessman, by 1906 Buick was out, ending his days as a penniless clerk. In 1937, General Motors, who had bought the Buick plant in 1908, adopted the ancestral crest of the Scottish Buicks for its cars. To date the Buick name has been stamped on over 25 million cars, only 120 of them built by David Buick.

★ Founders of Dunedin, New Zealand: Rev. Thomas Burns (1796–1871), nephew of the Bard, and Captain William Cargill (1784–1860), Edinburgh-born soldier, wine merchant, banker and the New Zealand Company's agent in Otago. Following the breakaway of the Free Church from the Church of Scotland at the Disruption of 1843, Burns sought to promote a Free Church colony in New Zealand. Unable to find enough recruits, as emigrants had to pay for their passage, Burns joined forces with Cargill who was also recruiting colonists, some of them English Anglicans. Through the New Zealand Company they arranged to buy land from the Maoris and lay out a settlement round Otago Bay in the south of South Island.

In 1847, the colonists set sail, 97 with Cargill in the *John Wickcliffe* from Gravesend and 247 led by Burns in the *Phillip Laing* from Greenock. After 117 days at sea, they arrived to discover that little had been done to prepare 'New Edinburgh' other than laying out some streets and naming them after the streets of Scotland's capital. The prosperity of the town, finally named Dunedin after an old name for Edinburgh, was assured when gold was found in 1861. The canny Scots settlers invested their new-found wealth in education, setting up high schools and New Zealand's first university with Burns as its chancellor. Cargill, the province's first Superintendent from 1853–59, did all in his power to preserve Dunedin's Scottish character.

★ **The first railway to cross the American continent:** the Canadian Pacific Railway, completed in 1885. Its building was an epic of engineering, crossing the intractable rock and swamp of the Canadian Shield and the wild canyons and gorges of the Rockies to unite the scattered provinces of Canada and ensure Canada's future as an independent nation. The railway was largely a Scottish achievement. The political driving force was Glaswegian, John A. Macdonald (1815–91), Canada's first prime minister. In order to persuade British Columbia, threatened with absorption into the USA, to join the Canadian Dominion, he promised a railway across the continent within ten years. The work of surveying the line, under the direction of chief engineer Sandford Fleming (1827–1915) from Kirkcaldy, was interrupted in 1873 when it emerged that the consortium contracted to build the line had bribed Macdonald's Conservative Party. Disgraced, Macdonald resigned and was replaced by the Liberal Alexander Mackenzie (1822–92), from outside Dunkeld, in Perthshire.

Progress on the line was slow until Macdonald returned to power in 1878 and formed a consortium of experienced Scots to take over the venture. Donald Alexander Smith (1820–1914) from Forres, Governor of the Hudson's Bay Company and later Lord Strathcona, recruited his cousin to promote the scheme. George Stephen (1829–1921), later Lord Mountstephen, the son of a carpenter from Dufftown in Banffshire, was a financier of skill and daring who had risen to be President of the Montreal Bank and one of Canada's leading businessmen. The entirely Scottish consortium signed a contract in 1880 to complete the railway within ten years; they achieved it in five, although they had to commit their personal assets to save the project from bankruptcy. On one occasion things were so desperate that Stephen cabled Smith from London – 'Stand Fast Craigellachie' – the rallying cry of Clan Grant. In 1885, at Craigellachie, British Columbia, Smith drove in the last spike.

★ **Teacher of the founder of the Chinese Republic:** Sir James Cantlie (1851–1926) from Banffshire. Cantlie trained as a surgeon in Aberdeen before being appointed Dean of the Hong Kong College of Medicine for Chinese in 1888. One of his pupils was Sun Yat-Sen, who was so inspired by Western ideas of order and society that he decided to be a reformer rather than a doctor on graduation, 'All my revolutionary thoughts originated from Hong Kong.' Shortly after Cantlie returned to London in 1896, he saved his former student who was being held against his will in the Chinese Legation. Cantlie alerted the media who secured Sun Yat-Sen's release. San went on to introduce reform to China, overthrow the Emperor and found the Chinese Republic. Less eventfully, Cantlie continued his pioneering work in tropical medicine, co-founding the Royal Society of Tropical Medicine and Hygiene in 1907, and playing a leading role in the training of ambulance crews during the First World War.

★ **Sri Lanka's first department store:** opened by two young Scots, David Sime Cargill and William Milne. After setting up a trading post in Kandy in 1844, they expanded into the former governor's house in the centre of the capital, Colombo, where they opened Cargill's, the county's first and largest department store. Business boomed and branches were opened throughout Sri Lanka to satisfy the European tastes of the tea planters. In 1896, Cargill bought out Milne on his retirement to Glasgow. The store, still trading today, moved into a purpose-built building with lifts and air conditioning in 1906, 'the finest of its kind east of Suez'. In 1886, Cargill divested £1.5m of his wealth by founding Burmah Oil. The first two decades proved so successful that by 1909, when the Anglo-Persian Oil Company, later BP, was founded, Burmah Oil was able to purchase 90 per cent of the shares.

★ **The world's greatest philanthropist:** Andrew Carnegie (1835–1919), the richest man in the world of his day and the embodiment of the American Dream. The son of a Dunfermline weaver who emigrated to Pittsburgh, Carnegie started out as a telegraph message boy in his teens. Working his way up as a railway manager, Carnegie never forgot to save part of his salary. His shrewd investments gave high returns, enabling him to start companies on his own account often then selling out at a substantial profit.

Visiting Britain, he saw the Bessemer process and introduced it to his steel works in the US: by 1892, Carnegie Steel was the largest in the world.

Carnegie believed that 'a man who dies rich dies disgraced' and in 1901 he sold out his businesses for the equivalent of £100 billion today. Devoting the rest of his life to philanthropy, he disposed of virtually all his fortune. He financed 2,811 Carnegie libraries in America, Canada and the UK, funded museums and research institutions, established scholarships, built New York's Carnegie Hall and set up an Endowment for International Peace, financing the building of the Peace Palace in the Hague, which houses the UN's International Court of Justice. Carnegie never forgot the influence on his life of Colonel James Anderson, who opened his library of 400 books every Saturday to any poor boy who wanted to borrow a book. He remained passionate about the land of his birth, richly endowing his home town of Dunfermline and building Skibo Castle overlooking the Dornoch Firth as a retreat.

★ **The man who bought Ceylon:** Hugh Cleghorn (1751–1836) of Stravithie in Fife. Although Professor of Civil and Natural History at St Andrews University from 1772, he was asked to resign 20 years later as he spent most of his time on the Continent. There he had made friends with the Count de Meuron, the Swiss commander of a mercenary regiment which, in 1795, was garrisoning Colombo in Ceylon for the Dutch. When the French invaded Holland, Britain sought to take over the Dutch colonies in the East. Cleghorn volunteered to 'buy' the garrison through Meuron, ensuring that Ceylon would fall to the British without bloodshed. He smuggled a note announcing the transfer to the commander in a Dutch cheese. He later served as secretary to the governor, compiling a report on the management of the island, which has since become notorious as forming the basis of Tamil claims to the north.

★ **The man who blew the whistle on deforestation:** Hugh S. Cleghorn (1820–95) who, after graduating in medicine from Edinburgh, spent most of his career with the East India Company. He became increasingly concerned about the flagrant misuse of India's scarce timber resources, Rajahs happily selling off cedar plantations for railway sleepers. At the Edinburgh meeting of the British

Association for the Advancement of Science, Cleghorn alerted the world to the dangers of deforestation to species diversity and warned against the economic consequences from climate change and resource depletion. As a result of Cleghorn's report, the East India Company set up the Forest Department of Madras, which eventually controlled forestry throughout the subcontinent with Cleghorn as Inspector-General from 1867. His work in establishing forestry in India earned him the title of 'Father of scientific forestry in India'.

★ **Freedom fighter extraordinary:** Thomas Cochrane, 10th Earl of Dundonald (1775–1860), aristocrat, admiral, radical MP, inventor, naval tactician and liberator of four countries. During his first career in the Royal Navy he delivered crushing defeats on the French during the Napoleonic Wars, including destroying a French fleet in Aix Roads in 1809 by his invention of the fire-bomb ship. Although his derring-do earned him the title 'the Sea Wolf', his attacks on Admiralty incompetence and corruption in the House of Commons were less popular. Removed from the navy by a conspiracy against him, Cochrane offered his services to the revolutionary movement in Chile, sweeping the Spanish from the Pacific coast of South America. In 1821, summoned to his assistance, his *Rising Star* was the first steamboat to cross the Atlantic from east to west.

Having freed Chile and Peru, Cochrane went on liberate Brazil from the Portuguese before leading the Greek Navy in their struggle against the Turks. He inherited his father Archibald's inventive streak, advocating the adoption of the fire tube boiler and fitting four of his own design in HMS *Janus* in 1844. He became involved with the American geologist, Dr Abraham Gesner, in a project to produce gas and related by-products from the Great Pitch Lake of Trinidad. He named the resulting clarified pitch, kerosene, from the Greek word for wax, Gesner later re-using the word to describe paraffin. In the end, Cochrane's exploits forced the British Government to reinstate him, retiring as an Admiral of the Fleet and probably providing the novelist C.S. Forrester with the model for *Hornblower*.

★ **Leader of the world's first Labour Government:** Anderson Dawson (1863–1910), born in Queensland, Australia, the son of an unemployed Scottish seaman. Orphaned at the age of six, he became a miner, entering politics by way of the Union movement. In December 1899, he headed the world's first Labour Government, although he was defeated after only four hours on the floor of the Queensland Parliament. Eventually he fell out with his party and died in poverty from alcoholism. Another Scot, Andrew Fisher (1862–1928), from Crosshouse in Ayrshire, who entered the mines aged ten, was more successful. He became Australia's first effective Labour Prime Minister, in charge of a majority government and serving three terms between 1908 and 1915.

★ **Founder of Manitoba, Canada:** Thomas Douglas, Fifth Earl of Selkirk (1771–1820). A philanthropist with a mission, he believed that the undeveloped lands of Canada offered a future for the poor of the Highlands. He devoted his fortune to achieving this while also hoping to frustrate the fledgling United States who had their eye on expansion into Canada. In 1803, he bought land on Prince Edward Island and settled over a hundred immigrants from the island of Colonsay. He purchased a substantial interest in the Hudson Bay Company to secure a grant of land on the Red River near Winnipeg and endeavoured to found a colony there. His efforts were bitterly resented by the North West Company who, until the arrival of this man with big plans, had managed to co-exist with their trading rivals. The first group of emigrants in 1812 were persuaded or threatened into deserting, but when a second group arrived in 1815 the North West Company men took stronger action, attacking the colony and killing 22 settlers. Selkirk retaliated by seizing one of their stations. After the North West Company successfully took him to court, Selkirk returned to Scotland, ill and financially broken.

★ **The man who introduced technology to Japan:** Henry Dyer (1848–1918), the son of a Bellshill foundry worker. After serving as an apprentice engineer he won a scholarship to the Andersonian Institution in Glasgow where he met Yozo Yamao, one of the Japanese samurai whom the Scots trader in Japan, Thomas Glover, had arranged to study in Glasgow. Dyer continued his studies at Glasgow University where he won a scholarship to work in Lord Kelvin's laboratory, becoming one of the first students to graduate with a

BSc in 1873. Before he had even graduated he was offered the post of principal of the newly founded Imperial College of Engineering in Tokyo, aged only 24. The fact that the acting Minister of Public Works responsible for the college was none other than Yozo Yamao could have had something to do with the decision.

The six-year engineering courses, taught entirely in English, that Dyer established were revolutionary and demanding. Hands-on experience was a major element of the degree, the last two years being entirely practical with students working on major live projects. Success was judged largely on continual assessment with examinations only at the end of the second and fourth years. Dyer's approach and teaching had an enormous impact on shaping modern industrial Japan. On resigning in 1882, having established the college on a firm footing, he was awarded the Order of the Rising Sun (Third Class), the highest honour awarded to a foreign employee. Dyer spent his retirement travelling between Glasgow and Japan, entertaining visiting students and promoting an interest in Japanese culture.

★ The first US store Santa Claus: James Edgar from Edinburgh. As owner of the Boston Store in Brockton, Massachusetts, from 1890 he encouraged Yuletide custom by strolling round the store talking to children dressed as Santa Claus. Soon every store in America had its Santa.

★ Founder of Pittsburgh, USA: General John Forbes (1710–59) from Fife. Forbes studied medicine in Edinburgh before leaving to join the army. When fighting against the French and their Indian allies on the American frontier, Forbes, nicknamed 'the Head of Iron' for his obstinacy, captured Fort Duquesne, a strategic trading post at the junction of the Ohio, Monongahela and Allegheny rivers. Among his company commanders was a young George Washington, leading a Virginian contingent. Forbes renamed the settlement, Pittsburgh, in honour of the Prime Minister, William Pitt.

★ The man who sold guns to Russia: Charles Gascoigne (1737–1806), the son of a London merchant and the daughter of the Earl of Elphinstone, from outside Stirling. When appointed manager of the Carron Iron Works in 1769, he turned the company round, improving quality control and developing the product which proved a bestseller, the carronade. Through the agency of fellow-Scot Admiral Samuel Greig, an order came from the Imperial Navy of Russia, who were anxious to set up their own iron foundry to make naval guns. Gascoigne ignored the wrath of the Royal Navy and the order to stop supplying the Russians. In 1779, feeling that he was not being given credit for his contribution and lured by the fabulous salary of £4,500 offered by Catherine the Great, Gascoigne moved to Russia to reform her Ordnance Department, taking a number of key workers with him. After founding the iron works and town of Lugansk in the Ukraine, he went native and became a member of the government as State Councillor Karl Karlovich Gaskoin. He was buried in St Petersburg.

★ **The first Scottish samurai:** Thomas Blake Glover (1838–1911), born in Fraserburgh. Glover was an agent of the Jardine Matheson trading company first in Shanghai and then in Nagasaki in Japan, where he helped the samurai to topple their military leader, the Shogun, and restore the Emperor to his throne. He commissioned the first three warships for the Japanese Navy from Aberdeen shipyards, going on to establish his own shipbuilding company, the forerunner of the industrial giant, Mitsubishi. Glover introduced the first railway locomotive into Japan and set up the country's first mechanised coal mine. He helped to smuggle Japanese students abroad to gain a better education and improve their technical skills. He was the first non-Japanese national to be awarded the Order of the Rising Sun for his services to Japanese industry. Built in 1863, Glover's house in Nagasaki is the oldest western-style building in Japan, now the centrepiece of 'Glover Garden', western Japan's top tourist attraction with almost two million visitors each year. Glover's wife, Tsura, the daughter of a samurai, was the inspiration for Puccini's opera, *Madame Butterfly*, since she regularly wore the emblem of a butterfly on her clothes.

★ **The first Roman Catholic church in Russia:** built by General Patrick Gordon of Auchleuchries (1635–99), the laird of a small Aberdeenshire estate. Finding life in a Jesuit college in Prussia uncongenial, he embarked on a military career, serving as a mercenary in the Polish and Swedish Armies before, in 1661, joining the Russian service. Rising rapidly through the ranks, his intervention as commander of the Moscow troops decided the Civil War of 1689 in favour of

Tsar Peter the Great. Peter regarded Gordon as his right-hand man, employing him to reorganise the Russian Army and leaving him in command of the capital in his absence. Peter awarded his friend the greatest honour of all, by personally closing Gordon's eyes when he died in 1699.

★ **Father of the Russian Navy:** a title shared by Peter the Great and Admiral Samuel Greig (1735–88), son of an Inverkeithing shipmaster. After a spell in the merchant navy, he joined the Royal Navy, seeing action during the Seven Years War. Finding little prospect of promotion when peace was declared, he joined the Russian Navy which Catherine the Great was rebuilding. After decisively defeating the Turkish fleet off Chios in the Mediterranean in 1770, he reorganised the Russian Navy on modern lines, rising to the rank of Admiral in command of Russia's Baltic Fleet.

★ **Refrigerated meat:** James Harrison (c. 1816–93) from Dunbartonshire. Harrison emigrated to Australia as a young man where he became the first editor of the *Geelong Advertiser*. Convinced that the country's future lay in exporting meat to Europe, in 1855 he patented an ether liquid-vapour compression fridge. Nearly 20 years later, the *Norfolk* set out for London with a consignment of 20 tons of beef and mutton in Harrison's cooling chamber. Unfortunately, owing to technical problems, the meat had to be thrown overboard and Harrison was bankrupt. But all was not lost. In 1879, Ayr-born entrepreneur and later Premier of Queensland, Sir Thomas McIlwraith, backed an experiment based on Harrison's ideas, fitting the Atlantic steamer SS *Strathleven* with refrigeration equipment. It came from the Glasgow engineers, Bell & Coleman, who had already supplied the machinery for the first successful shipment of chilled beef from America. Loaded with beef, sheep and kegs of butter, the *Strathleven* arrived in London from Melbourne with the first consignment of frozen meat from Australia.

★ **The Scots Taipan:** William Jardine (1784–1843), born in Lochmaben, Dumfriesshire. He joined the East India Company as a surgeon then diversified into shipping and trading on his own account. In 1832, he moved to Canton in China where he went into partnership with James Matheson (1796–1898) from Lairg in Sutherland to form Jardine Matheson and Co. Taking advantage of the ending of the East India Company's trade monopoly they exported tea and silk to Britain in return for Indian opium, one of the few commodities for which there was a profitable market in China. One of their ships, the *Sarah*, carried the first 'free' cargo of tea to London in 1834, but others were not far behind. Fierce competition to be the first to deliver the new season's crop to London led to the famous tea clipper races. When the Chinese Emperor tried to ban the import of opium in 1840, Jardine Matheson persuaded the British Government to launch the Opium Wars, in which a small British expedition decimated the primitive Chinese forces. In the resulting settlement, the Emperor was forced to hand over Hong Kong and trading stations in China from which Jardine Matheson was among the first to benefit.

Jardine returned to the UK in 1839 as a government adviser, Matheson followed him three years later. Matheson purchased the Island of Lewis, building the imposing Lews Castle that dominates the port of Stornoway. At first he gained the gratitude of the local people when his donations of meal saved their lives during the potato famine but, thereafter, he earned their undying hatred when, despairing of the island's ability to support its population, he introduced a scheme of forced emigration. Remaining in family hands, Jardine Matheson grew to dominate Far East Trade. It was the first company to establish a base in Japan when it opened to trade with the West in 1859, and in 1876 built the first railway in China, a 12-mile line from Shanghai to its port Woosong. Today Jardine Matheson, one of the largest and most influential companies in South-east Asia, is still controlled by the descendants of the founders.

★ The first Governor-General of Australia: John Hope, 7th Earl of Hopetoun. In 1901, he proclaimed the Commonwealth of Australia in a ceremony in Sydney attended by 250,000 people. His son was Viceroy and Governor-General of India from 1936–43.

★ Tutor to the Last Emperor of China: Reginald Johnston, born in Edinburgh. He became a district officer in China in the British Colonial Service where he went 'native': becoming fluent in three Chinese dialects, immersing himself in the culture and converting to Buddhism. In 1919, he met the 13-year-old Emperor Pu Yi. The child Emperor had a troubled life. In order to place him on the throne, aged only three, his mother arranged for his father to be poisoned. She herself committed suicide, her plans in tatters after the Revolution and facing increasing pressure from the West. Forced to abdicate in 1912, the Emperor was kept a virtual prisoner in the palace while surrounded by servants who attended to his every whim. When the authorities wished that the Emperor learn some English, Johnston volunteered, providing a useful channel between the British and the Chinese.

The Emperor and Johnston became close friends. Johnston gave Pu Yi a fascination for all things Western, helping the Emperor to choose the name Henry from a list of English kings and diagnosing his short sight. In 1924, when the Communists surrounded the Forbidden City, Johnston helped his protégé to escape to the compound of the Japanese legation, in line with British policy to stir up trouble between Japan and Manchuria. Ten years later, British ambitions were partly realised when the Japanese made Pu Yi Emperor of their new country in Manchuria called Manchukuo. The Second World War saw the defeat of Japan and the return of Manchuria to Chinese rule, and the child Emperor ended his days as a gardener for the Chinese Government.

★ **Father of the American Navy:** John Paul Jones (1747–92), born plain John Paul, the son of a gardener, near Kirkcudbright, Jones went to sea aged 12 and worked on slave ships trading with the West Indies. After killing one of his crew, supposedly in self-defence, in a dispute over pay, Jones fled to America where through his Masonic connections he made contact with the revolutionaries. In 1775, under the name of Jones, he was the first officer to enlist in the infant American Navy. By 1776, in command of the *Alfred* and the *Provident* he captured nine British ships and in the following year, as captain of the *Ranger*, the first United States ship recognised by a foreign power, he sailed for France with a free hand to attack any British shipping that he encountered. He harried the British coast in the summer of 1778 and captured HMS *Drake*, shipping 100 prisoners to France to the embarrassment of the British Navy. The following year he sensationally captured HMS *Serapis* escorting the British Baltic fleet. When his mast was shot and he was asked whether he had struck his colours in surrender, he replied, 'Struck, Sir? I have not yet begun to fight!'

Although his reputation stood very high, Jones felt that he had been insufficiently recompensed by his adopted country. In 1787, he joined the Russian Navy to find the ships in poor repair and the sailors untrained serfs. When his attempts at reform were blocked and the rank of Rear Admiral failed to materialise, he resigned in 1790 and moved to Paris where he was buried, poor health having forced him to reject the offer of a command made personally by George Washington. In 1905, his body was returned to the USA escorted by four cruisers.

★ **The man with statues in Berlin and Peterhead:** James Francis Edward Keith (1696–1758). Born near Peterhead, the son of the Earl Marischal of Scotland, Keith, named James after the Old Pretender, remained a staunch Jacobite. Exiled and dispossessed after the 1715 rebellion, he embarked on a military career on the Continent. In Russia, he attracted the patronage of the Empress Anne, rising to be Governor of Ukraine. On her death her successor, Empress Elizabeth, earmarked Keith as a potential lover. As he was deeply in love with his lifelong mistress, a girl he had found among captured prisoners, Keith fled to Prussia where he became a friend of, and Field Marshal to, Frederick the Great. He won many battles in the Seven Years War before being killed at the Battle of Hochkirk. In 1868, William I of Prussia presented a statue of Keith to his home town and erected one in Berlin.

★ **Chicago's first resident:** John Kinzie (1763–1828), the son of a Scottish immigrant to Quebec. Kinzie trained as a jeweller before setting up in business as a trader with the Indians on the site of the future city of Chicago where his gravestone can still be seen. As the first permanent resident he is considered the 'Founder of Chicago'.

★ **Lee of the Lee Enfield rifle:** James Paris Lee (1831–1904) was born in Hawick. From the age of seven he worked in his father's jeweller's shop in a Canadian frontier town where guns were a major part of the family business. In 1850, Lee opened his own shop at Wallaceburg, a community founded in 1804 by Scottish settlers under the Earl of Selkirk's assisted passage scheme and named by the first postmaster after the patriot, William Wallace. By 1862, Lee had patented his first rifle, a single shot breech loader. The cancellation of an order from the US War Department due to a misunderstanding about the rifle's calibre forced Lee to close his shop. Nothing daunted, he continued to work on his rifles. In 1878, he invented a rifle with a box magazine capable of firing 30 shots per minute – the legendary Lee Enfield. This time orders poured in from the US military and the rifle became standard issue for the British Army for over 60 years. From 1888, the rifle was produced in Enfield outside London, adding its suffix to the name of an inventive Scot.

★ **The first railroad in the United States:** built by Thomas Leiper (1745–1825) from Strathaven. After studying at Glasgow and Edinburgh Universities, he emigrated to Philadelphia and made his fortune in tobacco. After fighting with distinction in the Revolution, he became a member and later President of the Common Council of Philadelphia and was one of the founders of the Franklin Institute. In 1809, he built America's first commercial railroad, a three-quarter-mile horse-drawn tramway connecting a quarry to the docks. It ran until 1829, when it was replaced by a canal.

★ **The boss of the world's largest railroad:** Daniel Craig McCallum (1815–78) from Johnstone in Renfrewshire. McCallum emigrated to New York with his family as a child, where he became a bridge designer and patented an inflexible arched truss bridge in 1851. In 1855, he became general superintendent of the Erie Railroad, seven years later being placed in charge of all the railroads in the USA during the Civil War. His management of the world's largest railroad network played a crucial part in the victory of the Union.

★ **The man who was Mickey Mouse:** James Macdonald (1906–91), who emigrated to the USA from Dundee when only a month old. He spent most of his career with the Disney Studios, taking over the voice of Mickey Mouse from Walt Disney himself in 1946 until 1974. As well as creating many of the classic Disney sound effects, he was the voice of the mice in *Cinderella* and of the chipmunks Chip and Dale, the bark of Mickey's faithful dog Pluto and the howl of the dogs in the pound in *Lady and the Tramp*. For *Snow White* he yodelled when the Dwarfs sang their silly song.

★ **The first person to munch on a McIntosh Red:** John McIntosh, the son of an Inverness emigrant to New York. McIntosh found his red apple growing in his Ontario orchard in 1870. From this tree was derived one of the most widely grown types of apple, which had the further distinction of having a bestselling computer, the Apple Macintosh, named after it.

★ **The first European to cross America:** Alexander Mackenzie (1764–1820). Born in Stornoway on Lewis, Mackenzie emigrated to New York with his family, being sent to school in Montreal for safety on the outbreak of the American Revolution. He rose rapidly in the fur trade to a partnership in the North West Company, founded by Scots settlers and French trappers to challenge the monopoly of the Hudson Bay Company. Being in charge of the western territories gave Mackenzie the opportunity to realise his long-held ambition to open up a route to the Pacific. In 1789, he set off to follow a river flowing west out of the Great Slave Lake hoping it would lead to the Pacific. For 40 days his party drifted down until they reached saltwater, but found it full of ice: this was the Arctic not the Pacific Ocean. Mackenzie named it Disappointment River: today it is the Mackenzie River. By 1793, he was ready for a second attempt, having honed his navigational skills in Britain and purchased better equipment. After a journey over the Rockies, with the help of local Indians whom Mackenzie befriended, the party reached an arm of the Pacific.

Mackenzie wrote on a rock in red paint 'Alexander Mackenzie, from Canada, by land the twenty-second of July, one thousand seven hundred and ninety-three'. His party were the first Europeans to cross the Continent north of Mexico, although they had by no means found an easy route. Unable to persuade the North West Company to back a further expedition, Mackenzie resigned and returned to Britain to raise support. When this failed, despite a knighthood from George III, he went back, serving two terms in the Parliament of Lower Canada before marrying in 1812 and retiring to Scotland. His travels, however, did not go entirely unnoticed. Thomas Jefferson avidly read Mackenzie's book of his exploits, commending it to Lewis and Clerk as they prepared, at his behest, for their more southerly crossing of the continent that opened the way for the American West.

★ **Leader of the team that isolated insulin:** John Macleod (1876–1935). A minister's son from Cluny near Dunkeld, Macleod became a researcher in physiology after graduating in medicine from Aberdeen. At McGill University, he led the team of researchers who, in 1921, first extracted insulin. Fifteen million diabetics in the world today owe their lives to the achievement for which Banting and Macleod shared the Nobel Prize in 1923. Macleod was perhaps lucky to win the prize as he was initially unenthusiastic about the line of research and only Banting's badgering made him relent sufficiently to assign a lab, ten dogs and a student assistant to the insulin research. He ended his career back at Aberdeen University.

★ The first geological map of the USA: William Maclure (1763–1840) from Ayr. Maclure's fortune, amassed while a partner in a London import/export business, permitted him to devote the rest of his life to scientific and philanthropic pursuits. He returned to America, where he had lived in his teens, becoming a US citizen in 1803. For 23 years he was President of, and benefactor to, the Academy of Sciences in Philadelphia. He funded Robert Owen's creation of a utopian community of New Harmony, based on Owen's radical and idealistic management of the mills at New Lanark on the Clyde. Maclure's greatest achievement was the publication in 1809 of the first geological map of North America east of the Mississippi, a work that earned him the title of 'Father of American geology'.

★ The first humane penal colony: Alexander Maconochie (1787–1860). Born in Leith, Edinburgh, he joined the navy against his family's wishes and after being captured by the Dutch had five years' first-hand experience of prison life, an experience which he never forgot. By 1830, he had settled in London, becoming the first secretary of the Royal Geographical Society and Professor of Geography at the new University of London. In 1836, he resigned to accompany Sir John Franklin, the new Governor of the penal colony of Tasmania, as his private secretary. Appalled by the brutal treatment of the convicts, manacled, flogged and savaged by dogs, Maconochie campaigned for reform, upsetting the colonists who relied on prisoners for labour and embarrassing Franklin by his impassioned letters home.

Franklin dismissed him, but reluctantly agreed to put him in charge of Norfolk Island instead. On this beautiful and remote island, where convicts who had offended during their term of imprisonment were sent for punishment, Maconochie instituted a very different regime. A firm believer in the potential for rehabilitation, he stopped the punishments, improved conditions in the cells and allowed prisoners small privileges or the chance to shorten their sentence by earning marks for good behaviour. His policy was vindicated when he gave the prisoners a day's freedom on the Queen's birthday with fireworks, rum and swimming: not one abused his trust. Undertaken without sanction from above, however, his reforms led to his recall in 1844. 'My experience leads me to say that there is no man utterly incorrigible. You cannot recover a man except by doing justice to the manly qualities which he may have – and giving him an interest in developing them.'

★ **The father of Australia:** Lachlan MacQuarie (1761–1824) was born on the island of Ulva, off Mull. After a successful military career in America and India, in 1809 he was appointed Governor of New South Wales replacing Captain Bligh, of *Bounty* fame, who provoked his second mutiny by challenging the monopoly of the sale of rum by the resident troops. MacQuarie was the first governor to treat Australia as a colony with a future, rather than a dumping ground for convicts. He used the funds from the rum monopoly to build a hospital and with prisoners on 'ticket of leave' as labour improved public services. He treated convicts more humanely and encouraged the free settlers to treat them as equals on their release.

The settlers, however, were hostile and conspired to bring about an inquiry into his governorship which criticised his leniency and extravagance. He resigned in 1822 and returned to Britain to clear his name. MacQuarie wrote of his experience that he 'found New South Wales a gaol and left it a colony, found Sydney a village and left it a city'. MacQuarie's example was not lost. As Governor, General Sir Thomas Macdougall Brisbane (1773–1860) from Largs encouraged trade, introducing the growing of vines, sugar cane and tobacco, promoted free emigration and brought in a free press and legislative council. He nevertheless found time to gaze at the little known constellations of the southern night skies, discovering over 7,000 stars. The city and river, Brisbane, are named after him.

★ **Russia's first department store:** founded by enterprising Scots, Archibald Merrilees and Andrew Muir. After setting up a trading company in St Petersburg, they opened an outlet in Moscow in the 1880s, which quickly developed into Russia's first department store and a Moscow institution. Their emphasis on quality goods and service attracted many notable customers including the playwright Chekhov, who called his dogs 'Muir' and 'Merrilees'. A mail order catalogue carried their name and fame from Rostov to Omsk. When the shop burned down in 1900, it was rebuilt in the latest style, its electric lifts causing a sensation. After the Revolution it was nationalised and renamed TsUM, the Central Department Store, although older customers continued to refer to it as 'Muir and Merrilees'. Today TsUM is being transformed again, with the aim of becoming Russia's Harrods.

★ **The first man to play basketball:** James Naismith (1861–1939) was the Ontario-born son of Scottish immigrants who died of typhoid when James was only nine. After completing a theology degree he trained as a physical education instructor, during which time in 1891 he was given a project: to come up with an indoor game to keep unruly, bored students at the Springfield YMCA in Massachusetts amused in winter. Sticking at the task with the persistence he attributed to 'Scottish stubbornness', Naismith dreamed up the rules of basketball. The first game was played with a football and two baskets provided by the janitor, attached to a ten-foot-high running track. Basketball fever swept the country, although Naismith failed to make any money from his game. For most of his career he taught physical education at the University of Kansas, coaching a notably unsuccessful basketball team.

★ **The 'plough that broke the plains':** invented in 1857 by James Oliver (1823–1908), who was born in Liddesdale in the Scottish Borders. Emigrating with his family, he settled in South Bend, Indiana, where in 1857 he patented a process that dramatically improved chill hardening to make lightweight steel. His 'chilled' ploughs were revolutionary: light, easy to repair with their replacement parts, but powerful enough to turn the prairie soils. His company grew to become the world's largest producer of ploughs.

★ **The first European to draw a kangaroo:** Sydney Parkinson (1745–71), a young Edinburgh artist recruited by Sir Joseph Banks to go on Captain Cook's South Seas expedition. When the other artist employed died on the voyage, Parkinson was responsible for recording all the new plants and animals observed. He was the first European to draw a kangaroo, which he spelt as 'Kanguru', when these strange animals were first sighted at Botany Bay in 1770. Sadly, Parkinson died on the way home, from a fever caught in Java.

★ **The model for the FBI:** Allan Pinkerton (1819–84). The Glaswegian cooper had to emigrate with his wife in 1842 to avoid arrest for his radical politics. While running a barrel-making business in Chicago, by chance he was involved in catching a gang of counterfeiters. Finding he liked the work, he became a deputy sheriff in Chicago, but unhappy with the pay, he decided to go into business for himself in 1850 as Pinkerton's National Detective Agency. Pinkerton's became a legend in its founder's lifetime. Pinkerton insisted on the highest standards in his operatives – no bribes, no rewards and no divorce work. His high success rate and flair for publicity – Pinkerton's prided themselves on always getting their man – ensured that the business rapidly went nationwide. The word 'private-eye' came from his logo of the ever-open eye accompanied by the slogan 'We never sleep'. After foiling a plot to assassinate the newly elected President in 1861, Pinkerton was employed by Lincoln to run a secret service of spies behind Confederate lines, the first such unit in the USA. Pinkerton's agency provided the model for the FBI and the 'op' of the American detective novel.

★ **The Fresno scraper:** the father of the modern earthmover was invented in 1883 by James Porteous (1848–1922), a Scottish millwright who emigrated in 1873. There is a story that he picked Santa Barbara, California, as his destination simply by following the people in front of him in the ticket queue. By being able to scrape and move a load of soil and discharge it at a controlled depth, the Fresno scraper quadrupled productivity in moving the earth required to lay roads, railways and drainage.

★ **The first person to explore much of Canada's north coast:** Dr John Rae's (1813–93) boyhood on the exposed northern islands of Orkney proved an excellent training ground for the Canadian Arctic. After qualifying in Edinburgh, he joined the Hudson's Bay Company as a ship's surgeon, Orkney being a favourite recruiting ground. His undemanding job at a remote trapping station gave Rae time to learn the techniques of hunting, snow-shoe walking and dog-sledge driving, needed for survival in the Arctic wastes. A true stoic, after wading waist deep in water with a covering of snow in sub-zero temperatures without a change of clothes, he described himself as 'not quite comfortable'. Set on mapping its vast territory, the company identified Rae as the man for the job. On his first expedition up the west side of Hudson's Bay he mapped 625 miles of unknown coast.

On reporting to his English superiors in 1847, he heard of concerns over the fate of Sir John Franklin's expedition to find the Northwest Passage. Rae agreed to join the search, travelling with only two companions around the largely unexplored coasts of Victoria Island – 1,000 miles over difficult terrain in 39 days. Of Franklin there was no trace. During his next expedition to fill in gaps in the map from his first exploration, Rae heard from the local Inuit of white men who three years before had trekked south and died some way to the west. They had objects that had come from the ill-fated expedition and revealed that in desperation the starving men had resorted to cannibalism. Rae's report had a mixed reception. The British public could not accept that any officer of the Royal Navy could become a cannibal. Although he eventually received the reward on offer, almost alone of those who searched for Franklin, Rae was not knighted. The contrast between the lean, efficient man on foot and Franklin, whose only achievements were to lead an expensively equipped expedition to total disaster and cause equally expensive expeditions to be mounted in vain, was too painful to contemplate. Rae continued to travel, thinking nothing of walking 40 miles to dinner.

★ **The patron saint of the golf course:** Donald Ross (1872–1948). Brought up in Dornoch, with its magnificent links course, Ross happened to be the golf professional at the Royal Dornoch Golf Club when a Harvard professor played a round. He suggested that Ross should think of emigrating, in view of America's awakening enthusiasm for the game. Taking the professor's advice, Ross became America's first great golf course designer, turning it from an engineering job into an art form. A year after his arrival in 1899, he created America's first indoor golf school, going on to design over 400 courses as well as finishing in the top ten in four US Opens as a player.

★ **The first European to set foot on American soil:** Henry Sinclair, Earl of Orkney (1345–1400). Although a debatable claim, there is increasing evidence that Sinclair beat Christopher Columbus by a century, setting foot on American soil on 2 June 1398, having sailed round Newfoundland to Nova Scotia. The next year it is likely that he explored the coastline of Massachusetts and Rhode Island. Supporters point to archaeological evidence and the presence of Gaelic words in the dialect of the Micmac Indian tribe. Detractors argue that Sinclair's voyage originates from a manuscript written more than a century later by Nicolo Zeno, a Venetian, either to honour two of his ancestors who may have sailed with Sinclair or as an elaborate practical joke. Whatever Scotland's specific claim, it is now generally accepted that traders from Europe's Atlantic seaboard from Portugal to Norway reached North America before Columbus.

★ **America's first architect:** Robert Smith (1722–77) was the son of a Dalkeith baker. He trained as a builder and carpenter before emigrating in 1749 to Philadelphia, possibly recruited by the Governor, James Hamilton, who was an early patron. After remodelling Hamilton's house and building the Second Presbyterian Church, he soon built up an extensive practice throughout the colonies. As designer of many early public buildings, Smith can claim to be America's first architect.

★ **America's first seed catalogue:** Grant Thorburn (1773–1863). Born in Dalkeith, he emigrated to New York at the age of 21, jumping bail on the charge of treason for his political beliefs. He set up a hardware store and, finding that one of his bestselling items was potted plants, he moved into selling seeds; the first to do so on a large scale in America. In 1822, he produced the first seed catalogue in pamphlet form and the first with illustrations.

★ **The father of US ornithology:** Alexander Wilson (1766–1813). The son of a penniless Paisley whisky distiller, Wilson was the first person to study and draw the birds of America, identifying 39 previously unknown species. His *American Ornithology* was the first significant book with colour plates published in the US. The author of an even more famous book of birds appeared on the streets of

Edinburgh in 1826 dressed like a backwoodsman. Hoping to attract subscribers for his *Birds of America*, John James Audubon took rooms in George Street. Although the university agreed to subscribe, Audubon's paintings attracted little attention until he was visited by the Edinburgh engraver W.H. Lizars. Lizars not only printed the first plates, but commissioned the portrait of Audubon which now hangs in the White House.

★ Signatories to the US Declaration of Independence: John Witherspoon (1722–94), the son of the minister of Yester in East Lothian, who traced his ancestry back to John Knox. Witherspoon followed the family tradition, rising through the Church to become leader of its Evangelical wing. In 1766, he was invited to take up the Presidency of Princeton College, an invitation which, after some hesitation, he accepted two years later. He transformed what was essentially a theological college into a full university. He identified closely with his adopted country, his strong support of the revolutionary cause resulting in his election as a delegate to the Continental Congress. The other native Scot to sign the Declaration of Independence was the colonial lawyer James Wilson (1742–98) from St Andrews.

10

A Scots Hotch Potch

LARGEST, OLDEST, TALLEST

★ The largest opencast mine in Europe: Dalquhandy in Lanarkshire. The same county also claims one of Europe's largest waste landfill sites.

★ The UK's tallest palm house: the Temperate Palm House in the Edinburgh Botanic Garden built in 1858.

★ The world's largest arts festival: Edinburgh Festival Fringe which has launched the careers of many actors and comedians including Jonathan Miller, Alan Bennett, Peter Cooke, Dudley Moore, John Cleese and most of the Monty Python team, Billy Connolly and Rowan Atkinson.

★ The longest suspension bridge in Europe: the Forth Road Bridge when opened by HM Queen Elizabeth II in 1964.

★ The oldest living thing in Europe: the Fortingall yew tree estimated to be between 3,000 and 5,000 years old. Its once vast trunk measured an amazing 56 ft in girth, by far the largest ever recorded for the species. There is a legend that Pontius Pilate, who tried Jesus Christ, played under the tree as a child: his father was supposed to be a visiting Roman official and his mother a local girl.

★ The largest public reference library in Western Europe: the Mitchell Library, Glasgow. It was founded in 1877 from the bequest of Stephen Mitchell, a Glasgow tobacco merchant whose company, Stephen Mitchell & Co., later became one of the founding members of the Imperial Tobacco Group.

★ The largest public housing system per head of population of any post-war non-Communist country: developed in Scotland over the three decades after the Second World War to cope with a long legacy of poor housing. It included the UK's most concentrated programme of multi-storey flat building undertaken by Glasgow Corporation. In the 1960s it built over 250 high-rise blocks, including Red Road, Europe's highest tower block.

★ **The largest water-wheel in the world:** when built around 1830 to power a cotton mill on Shaws Water near Greenock, the 120 hp wheel was 70 ft in diameter.

★ **The tallest hedge in the world:** Meikleour beech hedge, Perthshire. The 100 ft hedge was planted in 1745 and it is clipped every ten years, the job taking ten men six weeks to complete.

★ **Europe's largest ballroom:** a claim put forward in the 1930s by the Marine Gardens, Portobello. Opened in 1910 in 'Edinburgh by the sea', the Marine Gardens also boasted a zoo, a funfair and a Somali village complete with inhabitants.

★ **The longest bridge in the world:** a record held by the Tay Bridge at just under two miles when opened in 1878. Eighteen months later, it collapsed while a train was crossing the High Girders, killing all 75 passengers and crew. Its sister, the Tay Road Bridge, briefly held the same record on opening in 1965.

★ **The world's largest game of Pooh sticks:** involving 2,313 Pooh sticks floating down the Tweed from the Chain Bridge in July 2000, to celebrate the world's most famous bear and to raise money for charity.

A SCOTS AIR

★ **'Abide with Me':** composed by Henry Francis Lyte (1793–1847), born in Ednam outside Kelso. A vicar in Brixham, Devon, he was a prolific composer of hymns including 'Praise, my soul, the King of Heaven'.

★ **'Advance Australia Fair', the Australian national anthem:** written by Port Glasgow-born Peter Dodds McCormick (1835–1916). On emigrating to Australia aged 20, he taught in Sydney, while taking an active part in church choirs and Scottish societies. The anthem was first sung in public in 1878 by a Mr Andrew Fairfax at the St Andrew's Day concert of the Sydney Highland Society. McCormick made a few amendments before it was given full honours by a 10,000 strong choir at the inauguration of the Australian Commonwealth in 1901.

SCOTTISH FIRSTS

★ 'Ellen's Song to the Virgin': written by Sir Walter Scott as part of his poem *The Lady of the Lake*. It is better known today as Schubert's 'Ave Maria'. Several other composers including Sibelius and Arthur Sullivan set Scott's ballads and poems to music.

★ 'The Maple Leaf Forever': composed by Alexander Muir (1830–1906). Born in Lesmahagow, Muir emigrated to Canada as a child, becoming a Toronto schoolmaster. He wrote it as Canada's confederation song in 1867 and it influenced the adoption of the maple leaf as Canada's national symbol.

★ 'O Canada': the English lyrics of Canada's national anthem were written by Justice Robert Stanley Weir (1856–1926), whose parents had emigrated from Scotland.

★ 'O Susannah': composed by Stephen Foster (1826–64), of Scots descent on both sides of his family. America's and possibly the world's first commercial songwriter, he died in poverty despite writing such classics as 'Swanee River', 'Jeanie with the Light Brown Hair' and Beautiful Dreamer'.

★ 'Waltzing Matilda': written by Andrew Barton 'Banjo' Paterson (1864–1941). Paterson's father was an East India captain descended from a long line of Lanarkshire farmers. The song was written in memory of a travelling shearer or 'jolly swagman' involved in a bitter strike of sheep-shearers and implicated in the burning of a shearing shed. Shortly afterwards he was found drowned in a nearby waterhole. Although the official story was that he had committed suicide fearing capture, rumours were rife that he had been murdered by the sheep ranchers. The tune is 'Thou Bonnie Wood of Craigielea', written by the Scot James Barr in 1805 and played to Paterson by Christina McPherson, a friend of his fiancée.

★ 'Ye Mariners of England': the quintessentially English song was composed by a Glaswegian, Thomas Campbell (1774–1844), after seeing the British fleet lying off Copenhagen. When he moved to London in 1803, he stayed with his friend, the Scottish civil engineer Thomas Telford. His later career as a poet was less successful although his *Gertrude of Wyoming*, a tale of settlers and Indians in Pennsylvania, is the first long poem with an American setting composed by a British author.

SCOTS IN GOOD COMPANY

★ **Bell Telephone Company:** the US telephone corporation, known affectionately as Ma Bell, was founded in 1877 by Alexander Graham Bell, later becoming A.T. & T. Its research arm, Bell Labs, produced 11 Nobel Prize winners and gave the world the transistor, the laser and packet switching.

★ **The world's oldest independent biotechnology company:** Biogen, co-founded by Edinburgh Professor Sir Kenneth Murray in 1978.

★ **A. & C. Black:** publishers of *Who's Who*, were founded in 1807 when 23-year-old Adam Black opened his bookshop in Edinburgh. He secured the rights to both the *Encyclopaedia Britannica* and the novels of Sir Walter Scott.

★ **The Burmah Oil Company:** Britain's first oil multinational was founded by Scots entrepreneur David Sime Cargill in 1886.

★ **The Castle Line:** founded by Donald Currie from Greenock in 1862. Sailing between Britain, India and South Africa, 'Currie's Calcutta Castles' were named after Scottish fortresses. Currie's ships ran to timetable whether full or not, an unprecedented innovation. In 1900, the line merged with South Africa's Union Steamship Co. to form the world-famous Union-Castle shipping line with Donald Currie at the helm.

★ **Cunard:** three of its four founders in 1840 were Scots: George Burns, Robert Napier and David McIver.

★ **Forte Group:** born in Italy in 1908, Charles Forte started work in his father's café in Alloa. From small beginnings he created the multinational hotel and catering group, taking on Britain's first airport catering contract at Heathrow and its first motorway service station at Newport Pagnell on the M1.

★ **ICI (Imperial Chemical Industries):** one of the world's largest chemical companies was formed in 1926, by merging the UK's four major chemical companies. The architects of the deal were Glaswegian Sir Harry McGowan, chairman of Nobel Industries, and Sir Alfred Mond, who planned the merger while crossing the Atlantic on Cunard's Clyde-built *Aquitania*.

★ **Macmillans:** the publishers was founded in 1843 by the brothers Daniel and Alexander Macmillan from the Isle of Arran.

★ **Saxone:** the shoe shop retailer traces its roots to A.L. Clark & Co. established in Kilmarnock in 1820 to make handmade shoes.

★ The Shore Porters Society of Aberdeen: established in 1498, the Shore Porters is the world's oldest documented company still trading, the world's oldest transport contractor and one of the oldest co-operatives in existence.

SOCIETY FIRSTS

★ The Astronomical Institution of Edinburgh: founded in 1811, was the first British society devoted to astronomy.

★ British Association for the Advancement of Science: Sir David Brewster played a key role in the setting up of the association in 1831 in reaction to the 'academic establishment' of the Royal Society, and was a founder member.

★ The Calotype Club: the world's first photographic society founded in 1843 by a group of enthusiastic Edinburgh lawyers after a visit to Sir David Brewster to see the calotype process of photography. They produced what may be the world's oldest surviving photograph album, a collection of the club's photographs produced in 1848.

★ The Chartered Institute of Bankers in Scotland: the world's first banking professional body. It was founded in 1875, 'to improve the qualifications of those engaged in Banking and to raise their status and influence'. Since 2000, Scottish bankers who undertake annual professional development courses have the unique distinction of calling themselves 'Chartered Bankers'.

★ The Commonwealth Association of Architects: founded in 1965 by Sir Robert Matthew the architect who was also its first President. Today the association represents over 45,000 architects throughout the Commonwealth.

★ The Edinburgh Music Society: the first music society in the UK was founded in 1728.

★ The Honourable Society of Improvers of the Knowledge of Agriculture in Scotland: the first agricultural society in the UK, which operated from 1723–45.

★ The Institute of Chartered Accountants of Scotland: the world's oldest accountancy body. Its roots go back to the Society of Accountants of Edinburgh, which received its Royal Charter in 1854 and the Institute of Accountants of Glasgow founded earlier in the same year. The Scots invented the term 'chartered accountant' and the use of the initials CA after members' names.

★ **The Institution of Civil Engineers**: founded in 1818 by a group of engineers including Thomas Telford who was chosen to be its first President.

★ **The Institution of Fire Engineers**: founded by Edinburgh Firemaster, Arthur Pordage, in 1918, to put the study of fire on a scientific footing.

★ **The Royal Institution of Naval Architects**: established in 1860 with John Scott Russell as a founder member.

★ **The Society for the Improvement of Medical Knowledge**: the first medical society in the UK founded in 1737 with William Cullen as one of its founder members. It still flourishes in the capital as the Royal Medical Society.

★ **The Society of Chemistry**: the world's first chemical society, established in 1841, with the distinguished Glaswegian Thomas Graham in the Chair.

FIRST IN POLITICS

★ **Britain's first woman trade union leader**: Margaret Fenwick, General Secretary of the Jute, Flax & Kindred Textile Operatives' Union.

★ **First Leader of the Labour Party in Parliament**: James Keir Hardie (1856–1915).

★ **One of the first two working-class MPs in Britain**: Alexander Macdonald (1821–81), Lanarkshire miner, leading trade unionist and, from 1874, MP for Stafford.

★ **First Soviet Consul in Britain**: John MacLean (1879–1923). The Glasgow school teacher, pacifist and revolutionary was appointed in recognition of his support of the Bolshevik Revolution.

★ **Britain's first and last Prohibitionist MP**: Edwin Scrimgeour who in 1922 defeated Winston Churchill in Dundee.

★ **The first female Conservative Minister and the first woman to hold a Scottish seat**: Katherine Stewart-Murray, Duchess of Atholl (1874–1960).

★ **The first Communist MP in Parliament**: J.T. Walton Newbold returned for Motherwell in 1922.

SCOTS AS PRIME MINISTER

★ **The Earl of Aberdeen** (1784–1860): he was forced to resign over mismanagement of the Crimean War.

★ **A.J. Balfour** (1848–1930): East Lothian-born, he succeeded his uncle Lord Salisbury in 1902 and is remembered for his support of Palestine as a home for the Jews.

★ **The Earl of Bute** (1713–92): he was tutor to George III who appointed him Prime Minister.

★ **William Ewart Gladstone** (1809–98): his father was born in Leith, Edinburgh, into a flour and barley merchant's family.

★ **Sir Henry Campbell-Bannerman** (1836–1908): the son of a Glasgow Lord Provost, he was Prime Minister during the Boer War although personally opposed to it.

★ **Andrew Bonar Law** (1858–1923): born in Nova Scotia, but brought up in Glasgow, he came out of retirement to be Conservative Prime Minister in 1922.

★ **James Ramsay MacDonald** (1866–1937): illegitimate son of a Lossiemouth maidservant, he became the first Labour Prime Minister, returning to lead a National Government during the Depression.

★ **Harold Macmillan** (1894–1986): the 'You've never had it so good' Tory Prime Minister was descended from the Scottish publishing family.

★ **Sir Alec Douglas Home** (1903–95): he resigned his title of Earl of Home to become Prime Minister.

★ **Tony Blair** (1953–): first Labour Prime Minister of the third millennium, he was educated in Edinburgh and his grandmother was a Glasgow Communist.

SCOTS CENTRE STAGE

★ **The most celebrated medium of all time:** Edinburgh-born Daniel Dunglas Home (1833–86). Thrown out by his family who believed that he was possessed by demons, by the 1850s Home was an international celebrity, performing his feats of furniture levitation, hot-coal handling and musical instruments played by unseen hands, before European royalty.

★ **The most nominations for Best Actress without ever winning an Oscar:** Deborah Kerr (1921–). The Helensburgh-born star played opposite Burt

Lancaster in one of Hollywood's greatest love scenes in *From Here to Eternity*. She was awarded an honorary Oscar in 1994.

★ The highest paid entertainer of his day: Harry Lauder (1870–1950), the Portobello lad who became friend of royalty, film stars and four American Presidents – Teddy Roosevelt, Woodrow Wilson, Warren Harding and Calvin Coolidge.

★ The sexiest man of the century: Sean Connery (1930–), the Edinburgh milkman, 007 regularly tops the polls for the world's most attractive man with the world's sexiest voice.

SCOTS ON THE SHELF

★ The First English language Bible in America: printed by Scots-born Robert Aitken in 1782. His daughter Jane produced the world's first Bible to be printed by a woman in 1808.

★ The text which established pathology as a subject: *The Morbid Anatomy of the Human Body* written by Matthew Baillie (1761–1823) in 1799. Born in Shotts, he studied anatomy under his uncles, the Hunter brothers. Joanna Baillie, the poet, was his sister.

★ The first firemen's manual in English: written by Edinburgh's first 'Master of the Fire Engines', James Braidwood (1800–61). Apart from topics affected by subsequent changes in technology, much of Braidwood's guidance contained in his *The Training of Firemen and Method of Proceeding in Case of Fire* in 1830 is still used today.

★ The most comprehensive single volume dictionary of the English language: compiled by the Edinburgh publishing firm of W. & R. Chambers from 1872. In 1901, it was renamed *Chambers's Twentieth Century Dictionary* to reflect the new century. Now simply *The Chambers Dictionary*, it is the official dictionary of Scrabble®.

★ The first book on poisons in the English language: *Treatise on Poisons*, written in 1829 by Professor Robert Christison (1797–1882) of Edinburgh University.

★ The first full Concordance to the Bible: Alexander Cruden (1700–70). Despite suffering frequent bouts of insanity, Aberdonian Cruden compiled single-handed this massive reference work to the Bible, still published in updated editions as *Cruden's Concordance*.

★ The first textbook of surgery written in English: *The Whole Course of Chirgurie* written by Peter Lowe (1550–1610) in 1597. Born possibly in

Errol, Lowe became Court Surgeon to Henri IV of France before returning to a similar position in the court of James VI. In 1599, he obtained from James the charter which founded the Royal College of Physicians and Surgeons of Glasgow. He also published a treatise on syphilis which identified it as a venereal disease.

★ The first edition of the *Oxford English Dictionary*: James Murray (1837–1915). Born in Denholm near Hawick, as the *OED*'s first editor, Murray was in charge of the mammoth task for 28 years and established the dictionary's authoritative standards.

★ The first ever comprehensive history of American literature: written by Professor John Nichol of Glasgow University in 1885.

★ The first edition of the *Encyclopaedia Britannica*: compiled, edited and printed in Edinburgh from 1768–71. The initiative came from printers Andrew Bell and Colin Macfarquhar, the first editor being antiquarian William Smellie.

★ The original self-help manual: *Self-help* was written by Haddington doctor Samuel Smiles (1812–1904) in 1859. Immensely influential, especially in the USA because of Smiles' belief that anyone could reach the top, the book extolled the Victorian virtues in statements like, 'No laws, however stringent, can make the idle industrious, the thriftless provident, or the drunken sober.'

★ The first chemistry treatise based on atomic theory: compiled by Thomas Thomson, (1773–1852) first Professor of Chemistry at Glasgow University.

THE SCOTS AT WAR

★ The optical range finder: patented by Paisley-born Archibald Barr (1855–1931) and William Stroud within a month of entering a War Office competition in 1888 for a new infantry single observer rangefinder with an accuracy of 4 per cent at 1,000 yards. Their design allowed guns to be fired more accurately. By 1898, Barr & Stroud's Patents of Glasgow had sold 150 rangefinders worldwide and were negotiating orders from the Japanese Navy. Their company now designs the latest generation of military opto-electronics.

★ The RAF: William Douglas Weir (1877–1959), the head of the Glasgow engineering family when Secretary of State for Air in

Lloyd George's cabinet during the First World War. He was responsible for combining the naval and army air services into the RAF. In so doing he coerced a reluctant Hugh Trenchard into heading the new force in 1918, giving rise to the saying: 'If Trenchard was the father of the Royal Air Force, as is generally accepted, it was Weir who held the shotgun at the wedding.'

★ **The SAS (Special Air Service):** founded by David Stirling (1915–90). While serving in the North African desert in 1941, he came up with the idea of a highly trained special force to wreak havoc on enemy supply lines, bases and morale.

★ **The first hydrographer to the Royal Navy:** Alexander Dalrymple (1737–1808). Son of Sir James Dalrymple of New Hailes near Edinburgh, after a career in the East India Company he took on the task of sorting the navy's charts in 1795. From the start of the Napoleonic Wars, for every ship lost to enemy action, eight had been lost through running aground due to the lack of accurate charts. Dalrymple arranged and catalogued the Admiralty's collection of charts and surveys, and helped to save the fleet.

★ **The oldest regiment in the regular British Army:** hotly disputed between the Royal Scots, first raised in 1633, and the Coldstream Guards, who joined the British Army three weeks later. The Coldstreams claim to be the oldest regiment in continuous existence and the sole representative by direct descent of Cromwell's New Model Army, the first regular army in Britain.

★ **The breech loading rifle:** Lieutenant Colonel Patrick Ferguson (1744–80) born in Pitfour, Aberdeenshire. Demonstrated in front of King George III and army chiefs, his weapon could fire four or five shots a minute at a target 200 yards away and still fire even after water had been poured down the barrel. It could be loaded and fired from a prone position, impossible with other weapons of the time. Ferguson's invention proved too radical for conservative military minds.

★ **Ballistics as an exact science:** Sir Andrew Noble (1832–75). Born in Greenock, he invented a chronoscope to measure very small intervals of time in order to measure the speed of bullets and shells.

★ **Shrapnel shells:** first manufactured at the Carron Iron Works in 1784.

★ **Cordite, the explosive:** Sir James Dewar (1842–1923) who invented it jointly with Sir Frederick Abel.

★ **The percussion lock:** Alexander Forsyth (1768–1843). Though minister of Belhelvie in Aberdeenshire like his father before him, Forsyth was also an amateur blacksmith with a smithy in the manse grounds. He invented the percussion lock to ignite explosive charges in guns in 1806. Lord Moira, the Master of the Ordnance, was interested in the invention, providing Forsyth with rooms to develop it. Although the conservative army took their time in approving it, the lock was widely adopted.

★ **The Anderson Shelter:** called after Sir John Anderson (1882–1958) who was born in Dalkeith. As Home Secretary he was in charge of air raid precautions. In 1938, he commissioned engineer Sir William Patterson (1874–1956) to design a small and cheap shelter that could be erected in people's gardens to provide protection against bombing. When presented with a prototype he immediately tested it by jumping on it with both feet, before appointing a committee of experts to make a more detailed evaluation. Within a few months nearly one and a half million families' second home was their Anderson shelter. In 1943, Anderson became Chancellor of the Exchequer, introducing PAYE for paying income tax.

★ **The gas mask:** John Stenhouse (1809–90). The Glasgow chemist developed the first mask containing porous charcoal in 1854.

★ **Fighter Command:** established by Hugh, Lord Dowding (1882–1970) with Dowding as the first Leader. The son of a Moffat schoolmaster, he established Fighter Command in 1936 as part of a complete reorganisation and expansion of the Royal Air Force in preparation for war. With its nerve centre at Bentley Priory to the north of London, Fighter Command was the apex of a command and control network which brought together fighter aircraft, radar and ground defences into the formidable striking power that proved the key to Britain winning the battle of the air in the Second World War.

SCOTS IN FICTION

★ **007:** created by Scots author Ian Fleming. Fellow Scot Sean Connery was cast as the first screen James Bond in *Dr No* in 1962.

★ *The Belles of St Trinian's*: St Trinnean's School for Girls in Edinburgh was the inspiration for Englishman Ronald Searle to write the St Trinian's novels. In 1941, while a Sapper in the Royal Engineers. he visited Kirkcudbright where he met an Edinburgh evacuee family with two daughters at St Trinnean's. He drew a cartoon based on their description of the school. While in a Japanese prison of war camp, he created his St Trinian's characters on scraps of paper, publishing them at the end of the war in the magazine *Lilliput*. Edinburgh actor Alastair Sim played the school's formidable headmistress in the St Trinian's films.

★ Big Brother: George Orwell wrote *1984* while living in the most northerly house on the island of Jura, having been unsuccessfully treated for TB in a hospital outside Glasgow.

★ Miss Jean Brodie: Muriel Spark (1918–) modelled Brodie, who enjoyed her prime, on her Edinburgh headmistress and Marcia Blane's school on her own, James Gillespie's.

★ Professor Challenger: The hero of Arthur Conan Doyle's *Lost World* was based on Professor William Rutherford, who taught Conan Doyle as a medical student in Edinburgh in the late 1870s.

★ *Robinson Crusoe*: Daniel Defoe took as his model the true story of Alexander Selkirk, who was born in Lower Largo in 1676. On a privateering expedition off the coast of South America, he fell out with the Captain and, believing the ship was no longer seaworthy, demanded to be put ashore at the first opportunity. He was duly abandoned on the uninhabited island of Juan Fernandez. His ship sank shortly afterwards, the few survivors spending the next seven years in Spanish jails. Selkirk survived on the desert island for four years before being rescued by another British ship. Returning home, he could not settle, dying of a fever back at sea.

★ Desperate Dan: the cartoon character which first appeared in the *Dandy* comic on 4 December 1937. A threat to retire him in 1997, when he sailed off with the Spice Girls, had to be abandoned after a storm of protest including a 'Bring Dan Back' hotline.

★ *Don Juan*: A bit of a Don Juan himself, George Gordon, Lord Byron (1788–1824) was half-Scottish by birth and spent much of his childhood in Aberdeenshire.

★ *Dracula*: Bram Stoker (1847–1912) is said to have been inspired by the ruins of Slains Castle near Cruden Bay, where he was a regular visitor.

★ **Flashman**: The nineteenth-century adventurer and womaniser was created from a character in *Tom Brown's Schooldays* by George MacDonald Fraser, who although born to Scots parents just over the Border in Carlisle was brought up in Glasgow. When the first of the Flashman series was published in 1969, he gave up his job as deputy editor of the *Glasgow Herald* to pursue Flashman's exploits.

★ **Frankenstein**: The first lines of the novel *Frankenstein* were written by English authoress Mary Godwin at a villa in Dundee where she lived for two years before marrying the poet, Percy Bysshe Shelley. After eloping they spent their honeymoon in Edinburgh.

★ **Sherlock Holmes**: Arthur Conan Doyle modelled Holmes on Dr Joseph Bell, his tutor when studying medicine at Edinburgh University in the late 1870s.

★ *Dr Jekyll and Mr Hyde*: modelled by Robert Louis Stevenson on the eighteenth-century Edinburgh character, Deacon Brodie; upright city politician by day and reckless burglar by night.

★ **Peter Pan and Wendy**: Scots playwright J.M. Barrie (1860–1937) invented the name Wendy. His inspiration came from Margaret Henley, the daughter of Edinburgh poet and journalist, W.E. Henley, who doted on Barrie and called him 'my friendy'. Because she couldn't pronounce her 'r's, the words came out as 'my fwendy' or 'fwendy-wendy'. Sadly, Margaret died aged only six, some years before her namesake appeared on stage in 1904: thereafter thousands of fond parents christened their daughters Wendy, and Barrie donated the royalties on his bestseller to London's Great Ormond Street Hospital for Children.

★ *Lucia di Lammermoor*: Donizetti's opera is based on Sir Walter Scott's *The Bride of Lammermoor*.

★ **Harry Potter**: J.K. Rowling created the magic in an Edinburgh café in 1997. She has since adopted Edinburgh as her home.

★ *Little Black Sambo*: Helen Bannerman (1862–1946) was the author of this once hugely popular story for young children, which is now largely banned as 'non-PC'. She lived in Edinburgh.

★ **Long John Silver**: Shiver my timbers, it's the villain of Robert Louis Stevenson's *Treasure Island*.

★ *Toad of Toad Hall*: created by Kenneth Grahame (1859–1932). Born in

Edinburgh he became Secretary to the Bank of England, as well as the author of the classic *Wind in the Willows*.

★ *Wee Willie Winkie*: Although William Miller (1810–72), woodworker and poet, died poor, the citizens of Glasgow erected a monument to the 'Laureate of the Nursery' in the Necropolis.

SCOTS ON FILM

★ **The first photograph of a native American**: taken by David Octavius Hill (1802–70) and Robert Adamson (1820–60), pioneers of photography as an art form. The American missionary was in Edinburgh in the mid-1840s.

★ **The ABC chain of cinemas**: founded in 1928 by canny Glaswegian lawyer John Maxwell. With a portfolio of over 300 cinemas throughout the UK by the time of his death in 1940, ABC (Associated British Cinemas) claimed to be the world's second largest cinema circuit.

★ **The first colour photograph**: appropriately of a tartan ribbon, was prepared by James Clerk Maxwell (1831–79).

★ **The first documentary**: directed by John Grierson (1898–1972), the founding father of the documentary film movement. He coined the word 'documentary', defining it as the imaginative creation of reality. He made *Drifters*, the first British documentary, and scripted Scotland's only Oscar winner, *Seaward the Great Ships*. He founded the Film Board of Canada, possibly the country's greatest cultural institution of the twentieth century.

★ **The longest continually running film festival**: not Venice, not Cannes, but Edinburgh. The Edinburgh International Film Festival was founded in 1947 as a documentary festival.

★ **The first inflight movie**: Shown in a converted Handley Page bomber in 1925, the film was based on Sir Arthur Conan Doyle's *The Lost World*.

★ **The world's first Panorama, forerunner of the cinema**: created by Irishman Robert Barker in Edinburgh in 1784. It showed the view of Edinburgh from Calton Hill.

★ **The first special effect on film**: The famous camera trick of the substitution shot was first used in the film *The Execution of Mary, Queen of Scots*, shot by Thomas Edison in 1895. It also used actors for the first time. The actors froze while a dummy was substituted for the actress playing Mary just as the axe was poised to fall: the camera was then restarted to capture the 'beheading'.

SCOTTISH SPORTING FIRSTS

★ **The Queensberry rules in boxing:** sponsored by John Sholto Douglas, the 8th Marquis of Queensbury, although the actual rules were drafted by Welshman John Graham Chambers in 1867.

★ **The modern rules of bowling:** developed in Scotland and codified by William Mitchell, a Glasgow solicitor in 1848.

★ **The world's first recorded curling club:** Kinross, although there is evidence that the game has been played in Scotland since at least the early sixteenth century. It is not surprising that the peculiarly Scottish 'roaring game' should clock up so many firsts including: the first national organising body, the Grand Caledonian Curling Club founded in 1838 and receiving royal recognition five years later; the first club in Canada, the Montreal Curling Club, founded by Scottish immigrants in 1807; the first curling club in the USA, the Orchard Lake Curling Club of Detroit, set up in 1832 by a group of Scottish farmers at the home of one Robert Burns.

★ **The Soccer World Cup:** kicked off by Glaswegian retail magnate Sir Thomas Lipton (1850–1931). On being granted the Grand Order of the Crown of Italy, where he had business interests, he responded by presenting a trophy – the Lipton Crown of Italy World Cup – for a world football competition to celebrate the rapidly growing sport. The first competition was held in 1909 in Turin with teams from Italy, Germany, Switzerland and Great Britain. Britain was nearly not represented but Lipton refused to be put off when the English Football Association declined to nominate a team. Probably through a Lipton employee and former referee for the Northern League, an amateur colliery team from West Auckland, County Durham, was selected to represent Britain. They beat FC Winterhour of Switzerland 2–0 in the final, not conceding a goal throughout the entire competition. Two years later they defeated Italy's Juventus 6–1 in the final. The modern World Cup had to wait until Uruguay in 1930.

★ **First working football manager to be knighted:** Sir Alex Ferguson, born in Glasgow in 1942. He also led the first British football team to win the triple honour of the Football League, the FA Cup and the European Cup in the same season.

★ The world's first football international: held in Glasgow in 1872. The teams were England and Scotland: the result was a 0–0 draw.

★ First team to bring the European Cup to Britain: Celtic, after beating Inter Milan 2–1 in Lisbon in 1967. This ended a triumphant season under the 'Big Man', Jock Stein, when Celtic also won the Scottish League, Cup and League Cup.

★ The world's first golf club: the Honourable Society of Edinburgh Golfers founded in 1744. Originally called the Gentlemen Golfers of Leith, they drew up the first recorded rules of the game and persuaded the City Council to provide a trophy to be played for annually.

★ The world's first 18-hole golf course: 1764, St Andrews. Produced by reducing the Old Course from 22 holes to 18, which then became the standard.

★ First women's golf tournament: held in Musselburgh in 1810 with a prize donated by the Golf Club for 'the best female golfer who plays on the annual occasion'.

★ The world's first women's golf club: the Ladies' Golf Club founded at St Andrews in 1867.

★ First British Open Golf Tournament: 1860 at Prestwick on the Clyde coast. This was also the first professional golfing tournament, early pros making the most of their income by playing for bets.

★ The first ever supersonic land speed record: achieved in 1997 by *Thrust* SSC designed and managed by Edinburgh-born Richard Noble, who himself had broken the land speed record in 1983 reaching 633 mph. In 1997, Noble's *Thrust* SSC, with a young RAF pilot Andy Green at the controls, travelled across the desert at 766.109 mph, faster than the speed of sound.

★ First rugby international: held in Raeburn Place, Edinburgh, in 1871. Scotland won. There was in fact an 'international' the previous year in England, but very few of the 'Scottish' players were actually Scottish.

★ First seven-a-side rugby tournament: held in Melrose in 1883. The idea came from a player, Ned Haig, as a way of raising funds for the club. Sevens are now played all over the world. Every year on the second Saturday of April the World's Premier Club Sevens takes place at Melrose.

★ The world's youngest snooker champion: Stephen Hendry on 29 April 1990, aged 21 years 106 days.

★ One of the first people to swim the English Channel both ways and, at 55, the oldest person to swim the Channel, a record he held for the next 28 years: Portobello's Ned Barnie.

★ The world's oldest tennis court still in use: built within the royal palace of Falkland in Fife in 1539. It still hosts a real tennis court, the word 'real' being used to distinguish the game of kings from its upstart relation, lawn tennis.

A FEW INFAMOUS CLAIMS TO FAME

★ The world's worst cannibal: believed to be Sawney Bean. In the early seventeenth century, Bean and his extended family of 45 lived for 25 years in a cave near Ballantrae, Ayrshire, feeding off up to 1,000 travellers and other victims whom they waylaid on the road.

★ The word 'dunce': meaning an obstinate, stupid person, comes from the insult levelled by sixteenth-century Protestant Reformers at followers of the teachings of Duns Scotus (*c.* 1266–1308) one of Europe's greatest medieval philosophers. Most noted for his defence of the doctrine of the Immaculate Conception, his following among early modern Catholic theologians rivalled that of Thomas Aquinas and he was beatified by Pope John Paul II in 1993.

★ The first printed use of the 'f' word: in a poem of 1503 penned by the great East Lothian-born poet William Dunbar entitled 'Ane Brash of Wowing' or 'In Secreit Place'. The other early recorded uses of the word are also from Scotland which ironically was among the first countries to try to ban swearing in public:

> He clappit fast, he kist, he chukkit
> As with the glaikkis he were ourgane—
> Yit be his feiris he wald haif fukkit:
> Ye brek my hairt, my bony ane.

★ The last person to be publicly hanged in Britain: Michael Barrett, an Irishman living in and arrested in Glasgow. In 1868, he swung outside Newgate Prison in London for his alleged part in the Clerkenwell prison terrorist bombing which killed 13 people.

★ **Hollow earth:** proposed by the Scottish physicist Sir John Leslie (1766–1832). Although otherwise respected, he was the last major name in science to believe that the earth was hollow. Jules Verne based his classic tale *Journey to the Centre of the Earth* on Leslie's idea that two small stars might be orbiting around each other inside the earth.

★ **The worst case of homesickness:** suffered by exiled Scot Sandy Macfarlane from Embo in Sutherland which drove him to inflict his misery on others by writing 'Grannie's Hielan' Hame'.

★ **The world's most sent-up hotel:** the Gleneagles Hotel, Torbay, Devon: run by Donald Sinclair (1909–81) and his Scottish wife, the models for Basil and Sybil in *Fawlty Towers*.

★ **Loo, the universal slang for lavatory:** one explanation of its origin is the quaint custom of Edinburgh citizens of emptying their full chamber pots out of the windows of their high tenements with the helpful shout to unsuspecting passers-by below of *'regardez l'eau!'* – 'watch out for the water!'

★ **The world's best loser:** Sir Thomas Lipton (1850–1931), retail millionaire and keen yachtsman, who with his five Shamrocks tried for 31 years from 1899 to win the coveted Americas Cup. Having won people's hearts by being the 'the world's best loser' he was presented with a gold cup by the Americans for his good sportsmanship.

★ **One of America's greatest outlaws:** Butch Cassidy alias Robert LeRoy Parker. Folk hero and leader of the Wild Bunch, Parker's mother's family came from the Stirling area.

★ **The Poll Tax:** conceived by Douglas Mason, Fife Councillor and member of the Adam Smith Institute, as a substitute for local authority rates. Prime Minister Margaret Thatcher loved the idea. The Poll Tax or Community Charge, as it was officially known, was introduced in Scotland on April Fool's Day in 1989 and south of the border a year later. It led to a mass non-payment campaign in Scotland and riots in London before finally being abolished in 1993.

★ **One of the world's most famous pirates, 'Captain' William Kidd:** born in Greenock around 1645, he took to the seas on the right side of the law fighting for Great Britain against the French in the West Indies. He became a wealthy man, owning ships and property in

New York including 56 Wall Street. Two years after William III asked Kidd to apprehend 'freebooters, pirates and robbers' off the east coast of North America, Kidd decided that the life of a pirate was better and jumped ship. After many adventures, he met his fate at the end of a hangman's noose.

★ The world's worst poet: William McGonagall (1830–1902), whose verse is so awful that he is regarded with great affection. His poems have been translated into Russian, Chinese, Japanese and Thai.

★ Not proven: awarded most famously to Glaswegian Madelaine Smith on trial for poisoning her ex-lover in 1857, by feeding him mugs of cocoa laced with arsenic. Scotland is the only country in the world to offer juries the option of a 'not proven' verdict, which means that they believe the accused likely to be guilty, but are unconvinced by the prosecution's evidence. Madeleine Smith ended her days in New York, having turned down several approaches to star in a silent movie of her life.

Index